MW01121491

Introduction To
Hinduism

Jayaram V

Published by
Pure Life Vision LLC
New Albany, Ohio

Introduction to Hinduism

Publisher Cataloging-in-Publication Data

V, Jayaram, (Vemulapalli)
Introduction to Hinduism
       p. cm
       Includes bibliographical references
       ISBN- 13: 978-1-935760-11-5
       ISBN -10: 1-935760-114
       1. Hinduism. 2. Hinduism--Customs and practices. 3. Hinduism--Religious life.
       I. Title.

       BL1212.72.V15 2012
       294.5— dc22   2012937986

Printed in the United States of America
10 9 8 7 6 5 4 3 2 1
First Edition

Introduction to
Hinduism

Jayaram V

ALSO BY JAYARAM V

Think Success: A Collection of Writings on Success and Achievement through Positive Thinking, Volume I

Think Success: A Collection of Writings on Success and Achievement through Positive Thinking, Volume II

Think Success: A Collection of Writings on Success and Achievement through Positive Thinking, Combined Volume

The Awakened Life: A Collection of Writings on Spiritual Life

Brahman

The Bhagavadgita Complete Translation

The Bhagavadgita Simple Translation

Essays on the Bhagavadgita

FORTHCOMING

Selected Upanishads

Perspectives on Hinduism

The Yogasutras – Translation and Commentary

Selected Thoughts and Quotations

Contents

For all the masters who keep the wheels of dharma moving forward with their knowledge and wisdom – Jayaram V

Author's Note

After a study of some forty years and more of the great religions of the world, I find none so perfect, none so scientific, none so philosophical and none so spiritual than the great religion known by the name of Hinduism." -Annie Wood Besant

"That which we call the Hindu religion is really the eternal religion because it embraces all others." - Sri Aurobindo

Hinduism is a very ancient and complex religion. Writing about it is a challenge. Hinduism has been an integral part of my life from an early age. In presenting this book, I am guided by the belief that to be born as a Hindu is a blessing and to come to this religion and know about it in detail is even a greater blessing.

Hinduism is one of the most sublime religions of the world. The world is slow to recognize its importance in the development of human thought and acknowledge its contribution in the progress of our civilization. Only in recent times, it has been gaining the attention of intellectuals and educated people in various parts of the world. The popularity of yoga, migration of educated middleclass Indians, the teachings of many spiritual teachers who travel the world and the growth of internet are largely responsible for this.

It is my conviction that to write about Hinduism or speak about it, you do not have to study it academically. I have been asked numerous times what my academic credentials on Hinduism are. People want to quote me, but they also want to know whether I have academic credentials to back up my knowledge. It is my conviction that our knowledge of religion does not necessarily come from university degrees in Hinduism. It comes by faith and practice. To write about a religion you do not practice is not a convincing proposition for me.

Religion as a subject has been taught in India for over 4000 years. It is still taught in many traditional schools and universities in

India on a limited scale. However, if you look at the history of Hinduism, many who contributed to its knowledge base were self-taught individuals. Self-study (*svadhyaya*) has been an important part of religious education and awareness in Hinduism. Those who are familiar with it know its importance and value in one's spiritual development. The tradition never discounted those who studied and practiced *dharma* on their own. Religious education may make one a good priest or a religious person, but not necessarily a good scholar or a spiritual person.

My knowledge of Hinduism is derived from self-study (*svadhyaya*) only. Some of the knowledge I presented here is intuitive, which helps me to write about it with understanding and awareness. It is my conviction that you arrive at religious knowledge by virtue of your past *karma* and study of the scriptures with an open mind.

This book presents the essential features of Hinduism for both lay practitioners and those who want to know more about it. It clarifies a few misunderstandings and misconceptions about its tenets and includes some important facts of its history. It also contains my views and opinions about its doctrines and beliefs. In presenting the information, I tried to maintain balance, clarity and objectivity. Where information was lacking, I used circumstantial evidence, inference, imagination and intuition to provide clarity. In the book, you will also find hidden symbolism and mysteries associated with the beliefs and practices of Hinduism.

This book is the first in a series of books I will be writing on Hinduism in the coming months and years. I hope this book will improve our understanding of Hinduism, the most ancient living religion of the world.

Jayaram V

Antiquity of Hinduism

Hinduism is an eternal tradition (*sanatana dharma*). Its knowledge and wisdom said to exist eternally in the highest heaven in the form of the *Vedas*.

The scriptures affirm that Hinduism is practiced not only by humans but also gods, by beings of the other worlds and God Himself. From time to time, He descends upon earth as an incarnation or an emanation to increases our understanding of the eternal tradition as part of His duty and as the upholder of *dharma*.

In fact, from the *Bhagavadgita*, the epics and the *Puranas* we learn that God, the Supreme Self, practices Hindu *Dharma* as His duty, apart from upholding it and enforcing it, even though He is not interested particularly in anything.

He teaches it to gods, demons and humans, according to their knowledge and intelligence, through *Brahma*, the creator god, because such knowledge is necessary for ensuring the order and regularity of the worlds and keeping them in their respective spheres, without which there would be chaos and darkness.

Hinduism envisages God in many roles. One of them is that of a teacher or revealer. He is the World Teacher, who opens our minds to transcendental truths that cannot be easily grasped without purity and inner awakening.

The Vedas are just a tip of the iceberg

The *Vedas* constitute the core teachings of Hinduism. They are considered eternal. It is said that in each cycle of creation, God reveals them to the humanity for their welfare.

Why they are important? It is because they contain knowledge of various types of sacrifices that are central to creation and preservation of the worlds and beings. Sacrifices here denote not only ceremonial sacrifices but also all actions we perform internally and externally with an attitude of sacrifice and service.

To live for your own desires and interests is animal nature; to live for others or God with a sacrificial attitude is human and divine. The Vedas point to this ideal. With the help of sacrifices, we can sustain the worlds and ensure our welfare.

It is possible that the *Vedas* we have today are remnants of a vast body of divine knowledge made available to us in the beginning of creation. We might have lost portions of it as the world progressed and suffered from many catastrophes and upheavals. Some knowledge may still be hidden and revealed in course of time. Men of wisdom may be able to tap into this vast reservoir of knowledge and reveal it to us when the time is due.

Veda means knowledge. The revelations of God are part of this vast body of eternal knowledge stored in the heaven. Knowledge that liberates purifies and uplifts the humanity comes to us from this source only.

We may quarrel about which aspect of it is right because of our desires, attachment or limited knowledge, but in truth, all knowledge whose source is God is divine. In the course of our existence we are introduced to only that part of it that is essential for our spiritual advancement upon earth.

Scholars of Hinduism regard the wisdom enshrined in the *Vedas* as absolute, while the philosophies derived from it as perspectives (*darshanas*). They are justified in this regard since human mind cannot comprehend absolute truths except relatively.

The *Vedas* are important because they allow us to gaze into the secret and the subtle universe of God, which is ordinarily beyond our reach, and see it with the vision of a mystic to understand the truth concerning creation and our very existence.

They are the windows to God's eternal secrets that cannot be known objectively in a state of duality. They reveal to you the mysteries of His creation, knowledge of the Self and the hidden universe of worlds, beings and forces, which you cannot easily grasp with your mind or senses.

You will also learn from them the meaning and significance of sacrifices and the way to perform them both ritually and spiritually or externally and internally so that you can play your dutiful role in His creation and be part of that hidden universe of God, which only few can envision.

Since the *Vedas* are central to Hinduism and exist eternally in the supreme heaven of God as verbal sound currents, Hinduism is considered an eternal religion (*sanatana dharma*). Its source is eternal, but the knowledge and philosophies derived from it may change from time to time, just as a tree with its roots firmly planted in the same soil keeps growing and changing from time to time and season to season.

While it has core values and essential practices, which distinguish it from other religions, it is not a religion in the strictest sense of the word. Its teachings, beliefs and practices are too diverse, complex, and difficult to categorize it as a monolithic religion.

Not a religion or a dogma

Historically, Hinduism was practiced by diverse groups of people under different names and traditions. Its growth was uneven and depended mostly upon the benevolence and the patronage of the kings and emperors who ruled the subcontinent, like the *Sungas*, the *Guptas* and the *Barasivas* in the north and the *Satavahanas*, the *Cholas*, the *Chalukyas* and the *Rayas* in the south.

In the early days, it met with stiff opposition from Buddhism and Jainism and later from Islam and Christianity. Yet, it survived and flourished. Despite deep conflicts among Hindu rulers, divisions within the community and differences among various sects who hardly agreed upon its doctrines and fundamentals, it grew overtime, accumulating mass and momentum, and gained wider acceptance.

As time went by and as people became increasingly aware of its relevance and significance in their lives and liberation, it gained acceptance as the single most dominant religion of India, a status it continues to hold despite missionary activities, atheistic and materialistic ideologies and irreverent political groups that are keen on replacing an ancient faith with an economic agenda.

Unlike Buddhism, Christianity or Islam, Hinduism is not guided by a rigid dogma. It has no specific origins. Perhaps it is apt to say that it evolved rather than was founded. It is even more difficult to say in which part of the Indian subcontinent it originated and who its earliest practitioners were. While we do not know its exact origins, we know for sure that India, the land of the *Vedas* (*vedabhumi*) has been its home and sanctuary since the earliest time where it thrived through difficulties, despite political and social upheavals, natural calamities, invasions and occupations by people who practiced different religions and dogmas.

Although Hinduism is not a religion in the strictest sense of the word, we have to consider it a religion for comparative study, to understand its importance and relevance in the body of world religions and to differentiate it from them.

We follow a similar approach in this book. We will consider Hinduism a religion, without compromising its complexity and uniqueness or the scope of its teachings and philosophy.

In this chapter, we will examine the antiquity of Hinduism to know how the historians of the colonial era failed to grasp its true significance and undermined its importance in the development of human thought and the progress of human civilization.

The western bias

Even today, in the western world, there is a noticeable bias against Hinduism, its beliefs and practices. When it comes to any discussion on Hinduism, you will find three types of people in general: those who like it, those who have no opinion about it and those who dislike it simply because their faith does not approve it.

The bias is evident even among the scholars in western countries, in their writings as well as treatment, who tend to conclude that civilized thought began with the Greek and Roman civilizations and everything else was either a poor adaptation or a mere accident.

They continue to do it even now, although we have strong evidence to believe that there was a healthy exchange of ideas and practices between Greece and the Indian subcontinent through Persia, and probably the one who benefited most from the interaction was the former. Accustomed, as they are, to equate European history with the world history, they are nurtured by the belief that the history of the world is the history of a few tribes who began their adventure in Mesopotamia, moved on to Europe, parts of central Asia and then to the Americas.

For them the world below and beyond the Mediterranean in ancient times was mostly barbaric and where it was civilized was but a poor imitation of the Greek or Roman civilizations. While ancient people believed that the earth was flat and lived in little worlds of their own, many educated people in the western world presently think and speak as if the world begins in Europe and ends in America! It is as if the world has just two continents and two oceans.

Their thinking and vision have rubbed off on the education system also. Ask people who are living in these regions what they know about Asia or Africa or their cultures, and you will be surprised to know the answers. This prejudice, which is racial and religious, is extended into many areas of human knowledge.

Western universities, even the UNO funded organizations, seldom recognize the contribution made by Hindu scholars to various branches of knowledge. They recognize the western professors who study Hinduism the American or European way and continue to hold on to the colonial interpretation of Indian history and prejudiced notions about Hinduism as a religion that is neither Christianity nor Islam, but somewhat Pagan.

Take yoga for example. People in the 18th and 19th century America and Europe characterized yoga as a decadent and evil system and considered those who practiced it either eccentric or insane. In fact, during this period many attempts were made to discredit the pioneers who introduced yoga to the western world with court cases, wild allegations and accusations. When Walt Whitman wrote a poem on *Brahma*, he was ridiculed for dabbling with the *"pagan"* ideas of the Orient.

The European historians of early 20th century grudgingly placed the beginning of Indian history around 2500 BCE and the emergence of the Vedic religion around 1500 BCE with the composition of the *Rigveda*, the earliest of the *Vedas* around that time. However, this is not true.

In fixing the antiquity of Hinduism, they were guided by their own biblical views of how the world was created by God in just seven days a few thousand years ago. They were averse to make any suggestion that seemed to stretch the biblical timeframe or contradict the essential beliefs of Christianity regarding creation and the origins of human civilization.

Whatever research they did with regard to the antiquity of Indian civilization had to agree with the timeline they proposed for the world in general under premise that no human settlements would have existed prior to the probable date of Genesis or the advent of Judaism.

This unfortunate pandering on their part distorted the history of Hinduism very significantly and resulted in the readjustment of its earliest origins by at least three or four millenniums. It undermined its value and contribution in the awakening of religious knowledge and spiritual wisdom among the early agricultural and cattle rearing communities.

Hinduism is at least 10000 years old

Hinduism is a much older religion, whose antiquity is difficult to fathom. It evolved out of the synthesis of numerous cultures and practices, of which the Vedic tradition was the most important. Just as we cannot trace the origins of the human civilization, we cannot measure the antiquity of Hinduism with certainty, partly because there were no written scripts of that period and partly because the ancient Indians had poor sense of history. They hardly maintained historical data and whatever information they preserved was lost or destroyed during the many invasions. They also relied mostly upon retentive memory to store and retrieve knowledge, and pass it on orally from one generation to another.

The antiquity of Hinduism can be better estimated from the astronomical evidence available in the Hindu Scriptures, the folk-traditions and anthropological studies peculiar to the Indian sub-continent, and some geographical and etymological references mentioned in the sacred texts.

These sources suggest that what we understand as Hinduism today has a long and unbroken history of at least 10000 years or more with its roots well established in the *Sindhu-Sarasvathi* civilization, which existed as early as 8000 BCE.

While many dates have been suggested for this civilization, in their book, "In Search of the Cradle of Civilization," the authors, George Feuerstein, Subhash Kak and David Frawley, presented the following chronology of Indian history.

Rock Art Period	40000 BCE to 8000 BCE
Indus – Sarasvathi Tradition	8000 BCE to 1300 BCE
Early Harappan Period	3300 BCE to 2600 BCE
Mature Harappan Period	2600 BCE to 1900 BCE
Late Harappan Period	1900 BCE to 1300 BCE
Regionalization Period	1300 BCE to 800 BCE
Northern Black Polish Ware	800 BCE to 500 BCE

According to the authors, the Aryan invasion into India is a "little more than a scholarly myth, a myth that has proven incredibly hypnotic." There is no evidence to suggest that the Vedic people invaded the Indus cities and established a new civilization. Indian population, as the biological evidence suggests, has lived for over 50000 years in the Indian subcontinent. Genetic evidence suggests that the splitting up of the Indic and European branches took place about 9000 years ago. In these 9000 years while many civilizations came and gone and many religions disappeared into the dark tunnel of time, India managed to remain as "the oldest continuous civilization on earth."

The authors proposed that the migration of the Indo-Europeans into India took place in the beginning of *Indus-Sarasvathi* civilization, around 8000 B.C. or so rather than around 1500 BCE as speculated by the European historians of the British era. According to them, the Vedic civilization was essentially Indian in character and the Vedic people might have been responsible for the Indus valley civilization as well.

Based on the available archeological evidence they arrived at the conclusion that the Indus valley civilization was a pluralistic society and people probably practiced Vedic rituals and shared many Vedic beliefs.

According to them, The *Indus-Sarasvathi* civilization comprised of a large area of about 300,000 square miles, with over 2400 urban and rural settlements, from the Himalayas in the north to *Karnataka* in the South, with a large concentration of them in the western region, most of which is currently desert.

The history of the civilization did not begin with *Harappa* or *Mohenjo-Daro*, which rather seem to represent its peak period. It began much earlier, during the Neolithic times with settlements such as *Mehrgarh*, which was discovered in excavations.

 The *Indus-Sarasvathi* civilization represented sizeable population and an area that far exceeded "in size the combined area occupied by the Sumerian and Egyptian civilizations." It was also "twice the size" of the ancient Mayan civilization. They traded with faraway lands both by sea and by land, and excelled in town planning, civic sense, agriculture and metallurgy.

The civilization flourished along the ancient river *Sarasvathi*, then a major river with many tributaries, which is extolled in the *Rigveda* as the most sacred river, before it was swallowed by the desert sands.

According to the authors, some catastrophic and geological events and climatic changes around 1900 BCE resulted in the drying up of the *Sarasvathi* River and forced the people in the region to migrate eastwards into the Gangetic valley and further. The authors also contend that the composition of the *Rigveda*, which has brief references to these events, was probably completed around this time.

It was followed by a second phase of urbanization in ancient India starting around 1000 BCE mostly on the banks of the river Ganges and its tributaries. During this period, there were further advances in science and mathematics and the development of new religious beliefs, doctrines and practices, which led to the "rise of the modern Hindu civilization." According to the authors, India has the longest cultural and religious history in the world, a fact that should inspire the people of India and instill confidence in them to work for nation building.

The Vedic tradition was uniquely Indian

Whatever may be the truth, the Rig Vedic people who emerged out of the *Indus-Sarasvathi* civilization did not start a new religion in the sub-continent when they moved eastwards and established their settlements in northern India.

They were practicing a religion that was the most ancient, in many ways prehistoric, and uniquely Indian. Many of the hymns and rituals of the *Rigveda* stand testimony to this fact. Hinduism or much of what we know today as Hindu tradition originated in India in response to local conditions.

The idea of Brahman as the universal power hidden in sacred sound, the concept of sacrifice as the source of creation, the hierarchy of divinities, the techniques and the terminology of the sacrifices, and internalization of the rituals as the means to liberation and self-realization, these ideas are uniquely Indian.

Sacrifices were performed in most ancient cultures, but the Vedic Indians gave a new meaning and theological interpretation to the idea of sacrifices. They internalized the sacrifices and with the human personality as the framework started a new enquiry into the nature of human existence and its relevance to the very existence of the universe itself. Through the practice of yoga, they empowered themselves to extend themselves beyond their minds and bodies and feel oneness with the rest of the creation.

These thoughts sprouted in the Indian soil and were uniquely Indian. They stemmed from intellectual churning as well as spiritual yearning and from analytical enquiry and inner experience.

While we do not know clearly who or from where the ancestors of the Vedic Indians originally came, it is certain that the Vedic religion developed on the Indian soil as a distinct and unique native tradition.

Except for a few broad based similarities with Zoroastrianism and some ancient traditions such as the one practiced by the people of *Mitanni*, it was uniquely Indian in both content and character. It created a distinct Indianness (*bharatiyata*) and unique personality traits among the people who practiced it, whose traces are still discernible in the present-day Indians, even among those who have shifted their allegiance to other religions and ideologies or migrated to other countries.

Scholars may find it difficult to acknowledge it for intellectual or political reasons; but the truth is the history of India has been essentially the history of Hinduism until the birth of modern and secular India and the emergence of progressive ideologies. Its influence extended into various aspects of Indian life and polity. It consumed the attention of Indians and occupied their minds and thoughts, even those who invaded the country from outside.

Whether people practiced it or not, it loomed large in their consciousness as either the religion of the faithful or the religion of the non-believers. If it was not the subject, it was the object. If it was not practiced, it was opposed, criticized, suppressed or even distorted. Even in secular matters, one can discern its undeniable influence in the form of the values it promoted and the spirit of tolerance it inculcated.

The myth of racial discard and divisions

The Vedic Indians were heterogeneous people who represented various mixed racial, ethnic and cultural types, as the modern Indians are today. There is no evidence to suggest that there was strife and discord among them based on race.

People accepted their lot because of their belief in karma, attributing to themselves the causes of their suffering and misfortune.

The castes and *varnas* divided the society into groups and communities; yet they did not cause social strife, since people accepted the caste distinctions as divine dispensation, arising from their previous actions.

The caste system did not prevent powerful warrior kings born in lower castes to rise to power by merit and rule their subjects with the approval of the priestly class.

In matters of polity and governance, the rulers showed exemplary tolerance and allowed people to practice their faith, while keeping their own beliefs and practices to themselves.

Even the word *Arya* was not used to denote race, but a person of wealth, influence, certain linguistic ability and noble character.

Social divisions existed in the early Vedic society, as they exist today and as they exist in any pluralistic society. However, it did not cause social strife or racial disharmony. Color was a criterion aesthetically but caste was mostly about the family professions people practiced.

We have archaeological evidence to believe that the ancient Vedic society was heterogeneous with social distinctions; but overall people accepted their lot and lived in peace and amity. The masses were better off than those who suffered from serfdom, religious persecutions and racial tensions in Rome or medieval and modern Europe during the two world wars.

Race was not a divisive factor in ancient India. People were not bought and sold based on racial basis. Character and morality defined a person's stature. We find ample evidence of this in both the epics, the *Ramayana* and the *Mahabharata*.

In both cases, we find diverse groups of people playing active role in society as well as polity. *Rama* was helped by diverse ethnic and linguistic groups. Both the *Pandavas* and the *Kauravas* were supported by people from different social, political and racial backgrounds.

In fact, if history is any indication, the Indians of ancient and medieval period had reservations against the foreigners who invaded the country from the adjoining territories and left behind them a trail of destruction and plunder.

They destroyed their temples, carried away their men and women as slaves, terrorized people into submission by raising mountains of human corpses in public places and often proudly proclaimed themselves as the servants of God or men of valor.

For the native Indians, they represented the lowest of the human race, whom they called *mlecchas* (the unclean), and treated them with both disgust and distrust.

It is a matter of convenience for people to migrate to other places in search of livelihood or to escape from the hands of an oppressive ruler. India, a super power of the ancient world, witnessed several waves of migration in its long history.

While the invaders who came from outside often left a trail of destruction and returned to their homelands after gathering their plunder, the people who migrated to the subcontinent following such aggressions or otherwise, lived in harmony and amity with the native people, often adapting their ways and their social and religious beliefs.

As a result, Indian society grew increasingly complex and heterogeneous in the very early phases of its long history. People belonging to different racial and ethnic backgrounds coexisted peacefully, sharing common values and religious beliefs. They fitted well into the system, in the larger interests of their families and their survival. The ancient Vedic society was characterized by diversity based on certain beliefs and practices, but not based on race.

The idea of an ancient society based on racial divisions was born in the minds of the European historians, for whom race was an important factor in their personal and social lives. They believed in the racial superiority of Europeans and in the superiority of the religion, which they practiced.

At the same time, they entertained deep distrust and racial and religious prejudices against the native Indians. Most of them studied Hinduism and Hindu scriptures, to highlight the superiority of Christianity rather than to understand or appreciate the native traditions. They did their best to undermine the native religions and find fault with their beliefs and practices to help the missionaries in their effort to Christianize the natives whom they considered ignorant and uncivilized.

It was difficult for them to accept the idea that India was the cradle of civilization or that it represented an ancient body of religious knowledge and philosophy that was far superior to that of either Greece or Rome. The images of ancient India, which they held in their ignorant and prejudiced minds and which they projected outwardly in their speeches and writings, distorted Indian history and presented India as an extension of Europe and a remnant of an ancient Aryan civilization.

It created an impression that the British and the Europeans were reenacting an ancient drama and had some legitimacy in their occupation of the country to complete a task that was left unfinished by their ancestors in remote past. It justified the imperial arrogance of the British authorities who were vested with the governance of the colonial empire that India had been a white man's burden all along and needed another round of sacred schooling in the virtues and values of western wisdom.

It also contributed to the misunderstanding and confusion in our understanding of the nature and character of ancient India and its history. The myth of Aryan invasion gave credence to the British power in colonial India and helped them divide the country and people on racial and geographical basis.

Hinduism is not just about Vedic religion

The history of Hinduism cannot be determined solely based on the history of Vedic tradition because Hinduism is not a monolithic religion, but a collection of several religious traditions, both theistic and atheistic, that thrived in ancient India and acquired a substantial following of their own. Some of them were complete religions in themselves, with their antiquity stretching farther than that of even the Vedic religion.

Broadly speaking, apart from the Vedic religion, the following sectarian movements contributed richly to the development of Hinduism.

1. **Saivism:** It is one of the oldest and the popular Hindu sects, which regards Lord *Siva* as the Supreme Being, with its antiquity stretching far back into prehistoric times and perhaps beyond the Indian subcontinent. In the ancient world of remote antiquity, Lord *Siva* was worshipped by various groups and communities both within and outside the subcontinent. Lord *Siva* was propitiated by the Vedic priests; but He was more popular outside the pale of Vedic society where He was worshipped with different names. By the time the Vedic people migrated to the Gangetic valley, Saivism was

already a popular religion in various parts of India, including Kashmir and the Himalayas. The *Pasupata* Saivism was one of its earliest sub sects, whose followers worshipped Lord *Siva* as an embodiment of consciousness and energy. Later, Saivism was popularized in the south by *Nayanars* between fifth and eighth century CE.

2. **Vaishnavism**: Originally known as *Bhagavatism*, which regards Lord *Vishnu* as the Supreme Being, it emerged as a major religious movement during the epic Period with the recognition and elevation of many solar deities, such as *Rama*, *Krishna*, *Parasurama* and *Balarama*, as the incarnations of Lord *Vishnu* and their inclusion in the *Vaishnava* pantheon. It gained strength during the *Gupta* period, following the decline of the Vedic gods such as *Indra* and *Varuna*. It was popularized in the south by the *Alvars* around eighth century CE.

3. **Shaktism**: Rooted in the fertility cults of the prehistoric world and worship of the Mother Goddess dating back to Paleolithic period (20000 BCE), Shaktism may be even older than Saivism. Followers of the sect regard *Shakti*, the Mother Goddess, as the Supreme Being and worship her in various forms and with various names such as *Uma*, *Lakshmi*, *Radha*, *Durga*, *Parvathi* or *Chandi*. If Saivism and Vaishnavism are the two eyes of Hinduism, Shaktism is the connecting bridge between the two.

4. **Tantrism**: Although it is also rooted in the ancient fertility cults and Vedic sacrificial rituals, Tantrism developed as a separate movement in both Buddhism and Hinduism during the Gupta and post Gupta periods (300CE-600CE). Followers of *Tantra* try to gain control over their bodies by manipulating their sexual energy and the various *chakras* or energy centers present in them. They also use the impurities of the mind and body in self-transformation to stabilize them in the contemplation of God as universal consciousness and transcend the limitations of the mortal existence.

5. **Smartaism**: Rooted in the sacrificial worship of the Vedic deities, Smartaism accepts the polytheistic worldview that God has many forms and one may worship Him in different ways. It was popularized by *Shankaracharya* during the eighth

century CE with his assertion that people might worship various divinities without compromising their loyalties to their personal gods. The tradition approves the ritual and systematic worship of the five principal deities (*pancopasana*), namely *Vishnu, Surya, Ganesha, Durga* and *Siva. Smartaism* is a ritual tradition centered on the worship of various deities in both temples and homes. It is the most visible and popular aspect of Hinduism widely practiced by the whole community despite their allegiance to their personal gods and teacher traditions. Present day Hinduism is greatly influenced by it.

6. **Ascetic movements**: Ascetic movements have been part of Indian religious scene since the earliest times. Most of them arose as a reaction against the populist practices of Hinduism that failed to address the most fundamental problems of human existence such as removal of sorrow and bondage. They emphasized the importance of freeing the mind and body from the shackles of Nature and society practicing various techniques to suppress the modifications and achieve liberation. Hinduism had no problem assimilating them since they also aimed for liberation, which was one of the goals of human life, and similar practices were approved in the tradition and recommended for those who had entered the phase of renunciation (*sanyasashrama*). Ascetic movements and the teacher traditions played an important role in the preservation and continuation of Hinduism since the earliest times. Even today they play an important role in preserving the core teachings of Hinduism and in bringing to light many experiential aspects of the religion that are not well known to the general public. In the absence of a centralized authority, these movements compensated for the leadership vacuum and preserved its ancient traditions.

7. **Rural and tribal traditions**: Hinduism is not a religion of the elite priests or higher castes alone, as some critics of Hinduism attempt to project it. It has been a religion of the masses ever since it spread into the Gangetic valley, long before the birth of the Buddha. There was neither oppression nor coercion in the expansion of Hinduism across the Indian subcontinent. Slowly

and peacefully, it gained acceptance among the masses, who were mostly ignorant, illiterate and had no direct access to the knowledge of the scriptures. Yet, they adapted themselves well to the ideals of Hinduism. In the process, they also brought with them some of their own beliefs and practices into the religion and made it earthly, vibrant and colorful. In its long history, many rural and tribal traditions centered on the worship of Nature, animals, spirits, ancestral deities and village gods found their way into Hinduism and became part of it. Although these traditions were relatively unknown and practiced on a limited scale, they contributed to the richness and diversity of Hinduism and made it singularly complex.

Hinduism is as old as the primitive man is!

Hinduism has its roots in the prehistoric religions of the world. Since it is one of the oldest surviving religions, by studying it, we can understand how human beings developed their religious beliefs, looked beyond their selfish concerns and accepted the idea of Godhead to make peace with themselves and the powers that created them. We can understand how religious beliefs and practices influenced human behavior and how they viewed themselves in the vast creation of God, seeking solutions to the problems they could not resolve humanly with their limited abilities and faculties.

Remnants of prehistoric past are embedded in the beliefs and practices of Hinduism. We can trace some of the Vedic and non-Vedic principles and practices of Hinduism to the ancient religions of the Neolithic and Paleolithic periods, when the aboriginal men were slowly stretching their minds to understand the mysteries of their own existence and of the world and resolve the dread of disease and death!

Recent excavations at *Mehrgarh* and other Indus cities prove beyond doubt that the antiquity of Hinduism goes beyond the traditional dates ascribed to it by the early historians. Similarly, its early history provides a glimpse into the beginnings of human civilization.

One of the astounding features of Hinduism is that it is the oldest living religion that has retained its mass appeal as well as the breadth and depth of its universal vision. In its long and checkered history, it absorbed many traditions and beliefs, without compromising its core beliefs and losing its vitality. As a result, Hinduism continues to remain today as one of the most popular religions of the world, defying the traditional definitions of religion and withstanding severe competition from organized religions and materialistic ideologies.

The Definition of Hinduism

Although Hinduism is a very ancient tradition dating back to prehistoric times, the word "Hinduism," by which it is known to the world and which defines it and distinguishes it from other religions, is of much later origin.

Interestingly, Hinduism is a foreign word used originally to define an unfamiliar tradition by those who did not practice it and who were not familiar with it. Those who coined the word and used it had initially no idea what it represented and embodied. For them it meant the faith of a people whom they called Hindus, who were culturally, racially and ethnically different from them.

In ancient India you had either a yogi, a *bhakta*, a tantric, a *sanyasi*, a *sankhya vadin*, a *vedantin*, a *lokayata*, a *rishi*, a *muni*, a *pandit*, a *prajna*, a *yogini*, a *devi*, a *swami*, a *jina*, a worshipper of *Siva* or *Vishnu*, a *siddha* or *Buddha*, but never a Hindu.

The origin of Hindu, the Persian connection

Neither the word "Hindu" nor "Hinduism" is a Sanskrit word. Both were used initially by people who were not Hindus and who never practiced the faith. The Indians were not aware of the words until much later. Neither those who mastered the *Vedas* nor those who visited temples and worshipped their gods ever used them until Islam arrived in the country and the invaders began calling them Hindus.

The word is now a part of Indian lexicon, but at one time, it was hardly known to anyone except to a few Persians who had to write contracts, deal with Indians or write the wording for the inscriptions issued by their rulers who employed Indians or extended their authority over Indian provinces.

Since the earliest times India had trade contacts with foreign lands and the Indians were probably called by different names by different people in their own languages. The Persians coined the word Hindu to refer to those who lived in the land beyond the Indus River.

In the *Avesta*, the Zoroastrian scripture, it is mentioned that *Hapta-Hindu (Sapta-Sindhu)* was the fifteenth of the sixteen lands created by the Zoroastrian God, *Ahura*. The scripture also refers to a mountain in the region called *Us-Hindava*, which may be probably either in the Himalayas or in the *Hindukush*.

India had close relations with Persia and the lands beyond since ancient times. The Indus merchants (7000-2500 BCE) traded with Sumer and Mesopotamia and even as far as West Asia and Egypt. The Persian rulers employed Indians and the Indian rulers employed Persians in their armies and administration.

There were also similarities between the Vedic religion practiced by the ancient Indians and Zoroastrianism practiced by the Persians. Like the *Rigveda*, the Zoroastrian scripture *Zend Avesta* was composed in a Sanskrit dialect bearing close resemblance to the Vedic. Both the scriptures contained names of common gods such as *Indra, Vayu, Yama, Mitra* and *Varuna*. Both worshipped fire (*Agni*) and moon and performed sacrifices known to the Indians as *yajnas* and to the Zoroastrians as *yasnas*.

There were also some fundamental differences between the two. For example, the Vedic Indians referred to their gods as *devas* and to the demons as *asuras* while the Persians did the opposite. They called their demons *devas* and their gods *ahuras*, a modified version of *asuras*. While we do not know the exact reason for this development, it might be probably due to some rivalry between the two faiths in their formative stages.

The relationship between the two extended into other areas. Punjab was part of the Persian Empire during the reigns of Darius and Xerxes. Both employed an Indian contingent of infantry, cavalry and chariots and engaged them in wars with Greece. Persian coins were circulated in the Indian provinces adjoining the Persian Empire, where Persian influence was noticeable. Indian merchants traded with Persia both by land and by sea, while Indian scholars maintained close relations with both Persians and Greeks. Indians also adapted with some changes the *Kharosti* script, which was derived originally from the Aramic script of the Persians.

While the Persians referred to the Indians as Hindus, denoting their geographic ethnicity rather than their religion, the Greeks called them *Indos*, which was also derived from the same root word, *Sindhu*. Just as the Persians, the Greeks also maintained trade and cultural contacts with India since the earliest times, mostly through Persia.

Some Greek philosophers even visited India and learned from Indian teachers about Indian philosophy, astronomy, mathematics and related subjects. When they returned to Greece, they used the knowledge they learned in their debates and discussions. The earliest reference to the word is found in the works of Herodotus.

When Alexander invaded India, the Macedonian army referred to the land east of the river as India. The Greek historians who wrote about the exploits of Alexander preferred to use the same name.

Thus, we can see that the word, "Hindu" was originally a geographical terms used to identify people who lived in the Indian subcontinent. The reference was not to their faith but to their ethnicity or geographical identity.

The word came to be associated with their faith later, when the Muslims began to settle in the Indus region, following the eastward expansion of Islam, and started using the word "Hindus" to refer to the people of India, which they called Hindustan or the land of the Hindus. For them the Hindus represented a nation of people who did not practice Islam.

The British who followed a few centuries later called the land India or Hindustan according to their convenience. From this perspective, the words *Hindu* and *Indian* were originally used synonymously and so were *Hindustan* and India. Fundamentally, they were used to denote a nation of people, their ethnicity or cultural identity rather than their religion.

All the four words are derived in one form or the other from the root word "*Sindhu*" meaning river in general and the Indus River in particular. Whether it was *Hindus, Indos, Hindoos,* or Indians the reference was obviously to the people who lived in the Indian subcontinent and shared among themselves a unique identity, history, culture and probably ancestry.

The Indians however did not use them until long after the British settled in India. It is said that the earliest reference to Hindu is found in the *Gaudiya Vaishnava* texts of the 16th century A.D. It was only a few centuries later, with the consolidation of the British Empire and with the emergence of English educated middle class that the words came to stay in the Indian minds and became part of their cultural and religious identity.

For the educated Hindus of the British era the word was a very convenient way to establish their identity against the British as well as the native Muslims. The British used the same identity to divide the nation into Hindus and Muslims and preclude any possibility of joint effort on their part for freedom. They also used many words to refer to them as natives, *baniyans*, heathens, pagans, gentoos and Indians.

Sanatana Dharma

Hinduism is traditionally known as the eternal religion (*sanatana dharma*), a name, which many Hindus still prefer to use instead of Hinduism because the name Hinduism reminds many of the abuses their ancestors and their religion suffered in the hands of the past invaders like the Delhi Sultans, the Moguls and the British. Besides, as we have seen, the word Hindu was used originally in a secular sense rather than religious.

Sanatana means eternal and *dharma* means duty or obligatory duty. The expression has twin meanings. According to our tradition, duty is not only for humans, but also for everyone, including gods, celestial beings, demons and even God Himself.

The duty of each is eternal, in the sense that creation after creation, beings have to perform their duties to keep the world and the world order going. So is the case with God. His duty never ends. He has to wake up at the beginning of each creation and do His duty before He dissolves the worlds and goes into sleep for billions of years.

So is the case with us. We have to wake up every day and do our respective daily duties, before we go to sleep. When we die, we return to the earth to complete our unfinished tasks. Our duties are thus eternal and obligatory. If we do not perform them, the worlds will fall into disorder.

Since our religion speaks about them and insists that we perform them without fail, it is aptly called eternal religion or a religion that speaks about eternal duties.

Secondly, the basis of the religion is the *Vedas*, which are believed to be eternal. Hence, our religion, which is derived from them, is also known as eternal religion. Creation after creation and in the beginning of each *manvantara*, or the reign of a Manu, the progenitor of human race, God reintroduces the *Vedas* to the human beings for their welfare so that they know what their duties are and how they should perform them.

Hinduism is thus a religion of continuity, a religion that appears in each creation and does its duty as the Voice of God to impart knowledge and liberate people.

Bharat

Since ancient times the native scholars referred to the land of their birth as *Bharata*, after the famous King *Bharata*, who is considered the progenitor of the entire *Bharata* clan or all the people whose origins could be traced to the subcontinent.

Literally translated, "*Bharata*" means lover of knowledge. The name is well justified considering that since ancient times, India witnessed the birth of exceptional wisdom, great philosophies, scientific discoveries and world religions. India is still officially known as Bharat.

The faithful know their faith

Thus, we have seen that the word *Hindu* did not originate in India and it was not originally meant to refer to a person of a particular faith. It was not used by the Indians until the 17th century. If we go by the original definition of the word Hindu, all the people who live in India qualify as Hindus irrespective of the religion they practice.

Today, the word Hindu is misunderstood mostly than understood. Many people, even Hindus, have no idea how the word originated and what it actually means. Those who are aware would not like to talk about it because of the sensitive nature of the subject.

The Indus River, which witnessed the birth of Hinduism and the rise of a great ancient civilization that stretched all the way from northwest to the shores of Arabian Sea, now flows mostly in Pakistan. It has no religious significance in Hinduism and it is hardly ever seen by many Indians. For the new generation, Indus means a bank or a music company.

The river *Sarasvathi* that once flowed in Vedic India now dried up and disappeared. It is also almost forgotten and its place is now taken over by the Ganges.

The words Hindu and Hinduism are now understood and interpreted in a very narrow sense. The word "*Hindutva*" is now used increasingly to denote the religious pride, exclusivity or exceptionalism of a rather intolerant and aggressive group of Hindus who feel wronged by the prejudices and the imperialism of the western world and academia that views the world and the humanity in terms of the modern and the orient.

In their hearts, reverent Hindus know what their faith means to them and represents to them. They do not require a name or a clear definition to recognize it or understand it. For them their faith is eternal and representative of life and creation itself. It encompasses every aspect of their lives and reminds them of their duties and obligations as beings of the earth, children of Nature, and aspects of God.

The definition is for the scholars, and the difficulty of understanding it is for those who do not practice it or those who follow other religions that do not recognize it or accept it as an alternative approach to worship God.

While intellectuals and scholars may debate in their drawing rooms and academic circles as to what constitutes Hinduism, the Hindus of today know exactly what their faith means and what it stands for.

Their understanding and definition of Hinduism may vary from one to another, but it does not deter them from practicing their faith or holding it in esteem. They may not define clearly who the Hindu are or what their religion represents, but in their heart, they know what it means and what it means to them.

Even if they are ignorant and have not studied religious scriptures or met teachers of wisdom, they can instantly recognize and accept fellow Hindus, irrespective of whether they worship the same gods, live in the same region, speak the same language, wear the same dresses and religious marks or hold similar beliefs about life and liberation.

The present-day Hindus come from different regions and countries. They speak different languages belong to different backgrounds, hold diverse political opinions, may even differ from other Hindus on political, ideological, social, ethical or ethnic grounds, but at a deeper level a common thread of unity, cultural identity and sense of brotherhood runs through them held in its place by a very ancient tradition that is uniquely theirs.

They know clearly that their tradition embodies the highest ideals of the humanity, having the ability to withstand the scrutiny of centuries and satisfy the religious, moral and spiritual needs of the people who want to live in the contemplation of God or realize the primary aims of human life. They know that as it existed in the past, it would continue to exist even after they pass away handing over their duties to their descendents.

Hinduism is not a religion in the narrow sense of the word. It represents a faith that encompasses a wide range of beliefs and practices, which originated in the Indian subcontinent with its roots in prehistoric times and transformed over a long period of six or seven millenniums into a dynamic world religion followed by a vast number of people of diverse backgrounds. It is a living tradition, which lives in the hearts and minds of its adherents. The word "Hindu" might be secular in its origin, but Hinduism is a distinct religious tradition having its own identity, spiritual value and importance in the progress of human civilization.

Its ideals and practices may be found in other religions, but it has its own set of beliefs and practices that are uniquely its own. A typical Hindu is not dogmatic about his or her religion, but takes pride in its uniqueness and its highest ideals.

Hindus of today are known for their tolerance towards other religions. Their tolerance stems from the very ideals, knowledge and wisdom, which Hinduism upholds.

Today if some Hindus are becoming increasingly defensive about their religion, it is because they have to cope with the pressures from dogmatic religions, which are uncompromising in their attitude towards other religions and refuse to acknowledge them as their equal. We have to wait and see how things would shape up for Hinduism in the modern world where it has been now spreading out into various parts of the world through migrating Hindu families and their effort to adhere to their ancient faith even in distant lands.

The Distinction of Hinduism

Truly speaking, when we talk of Hinduism, we do not know what Hinduism actually means. We also do not know which Hinduism we refer to, whether the ritual kind or the spiritual kind.

We may have a vague idea of what it is, but we do not know for sure whether we are talking about a religion, a group of religions, or an assortment of diverse beliefs and traditions, which do not necessarily agree on everything and which may be even opposed to one another in certain vital aspects. Sometimes this leads to the argument that Hinduism cannot be considered a religion in the strictest sense of the word, but an assortment of many religious views, beliefs and philosophies that share a common history and geography.

The popular impression of Hinduism among many is that it is a body of religious knowledge practiced in India, and Hindus elsewhere, as an eternal tradition since ancient times and in many respects is comparable in its complexity to none of the major world religions we know.

Such definition may satisfy a legal mind, or an organization interested in classifying people or implementing laws, but certainly not scholars or students who want to capture its essence and essential philosophy.

Hinduism offers many alternatives

For those who are born and brought up as Hindus, Hinduism means the faith their parents and ancestors believed and practiced and they practice now. It does not matter whether their beliefs agree with those of their family members or their fellow Hindus. It does not matter whether they even practice it with the sincerity and conviction expected of them.

Many Hindus do not read their scriptures or perform their religious duties. They may not know what their religion represents and what they are supposed to do as dutiful Hindus. Some of them may even bear Christian, Muslim or Buddhist names, wear symbols of other religions out of vanity or visit their religious shrines and yet in their hearts may consider themselves Hindus. They may also practice a New Age religion and consider it an aspect or offshoot of Hinduism.

Those who do not practice Hinduism, who have not been taught the virtue of tolerance but see the humanity in terms of believers and nonbelievers or those who go to heaven and who go to hell, may find it hard to understand and appreciate the complexity, diversity and depth of Hinduism. They may also fail to grasp the essential unity and the common themes underlying the diverse beliefs and practices of Hinduism.

In Hinduism, when microscopically examined from ground up, its beliefs and practices may look overwhelming and contradictory, but if viewed from a higher ground with the wisdom of a yogi they may represent a unified vision of the same universal truth manifesting variously to meet the diverse spiritual needs and aspirations of people in various stages of spiritual progress.

In Hinduism, believers learn through experience that truth is relative to the point of view and the source of our differences and quarrels about eternal wisdom is essentially about the way we look at it and understand it.

Hinduism is different and distinct

Hinduism differs from other organized religions in the following aspects:

- **It is not based upon the teachings of a particular founder.** In fact, Hinduism has no founder. It grew out of many traditions, philosophies, sectarian movements and the teachings of countless seers, sages, saints and teachers. Most of the teachings are however rooted in the Vedas.
- **It is not based upon a particular scripture** or specific code of conduct. Hindus respect the *Vedas* as revelatory

scriptures, the Agamas as sacred, the Sutra literature worth studying, and the Hindu law books as an authority on virtuous living and social propriety. However, Hinduism is not based upon them alone.

- **It is not controlled by a central institution** or religious authority such as a church or a *sangha* or association. The temples and pilgrim centers enable the Hindus to come together and participate in public ceremonies and religious festivals; but visiting temples or performing rituals is not obligatory. Hindus are not organized, but the feeling of unity and fellowship runs through the community.

- **It is not opposed to freedom of enquiry** and integrating diverse thoughts and beliefs into a complex worldview that acknowledges human limitations in understanding eternal and absolute truths. Hinduism derives its core knowledge and philosophy from diverse religious sects and six schools of philosophy, which are considered standpoints or perspectives (*darasanas*). Some of them are atheistic and some theistic. Together they give Hinduism its distinct character as a complex religion of multiple doctrines.

- **Hinduism strongly believes in the possibility of reaching God through multiple paths.** It accepts the assertion of the *Bhagavadgita* that God can be realized in numerous ways and spiritual knowledge should be imparted only to those who qualify. Therefore, it accepts other religions as various paths to salvation and does not favor organized attempts to proselytize people.

- **Hinduism is neither rigid nor dogmatic.** It is not bound to any temporal or spiritual authority. It is enriched by the past and revitalized by the present, with a vast repository of knowledge drawn from different sources, which gives it flexibility as an open-ended religion to accommodate diverse ideas and respond to changes and challenges of the modern times. It has been enriched and revitalized in the past by numerous spiritual teachers, scholars and ascetic traditions. It continues to attract new followers and grow in strength and importance because of the ongoing efforts of many teachers and scholars.

- **It believes in Creator God and individual souls**. It believes in the bondage of the souls and their rebirth until they are liberated. It prefers liberation and eternal life to a place in the heaven of gods. It emphasizes unity in diversity and the plurality of worlds as part of a grand illusion created by God. The same God appears in numerous forms in a hierarchy of worlds He creates and populates with diverse groups of beings and gods, each entrusted with specific roles and duties that are essential to maintain the order and regularity of the worlds.

- **It believes in a permanent heaven**, the Abode of Supreme Brahman, but not in a permanent hell. Beings who fall into darkest hells can redeem themselves by good actions and devotion to God. In this *karma* (actions) plays an important role. Beings reap rewards and punishments according to their actions. If they want to escape from this permanently, they have to perform them without desires and as a sacrifice.

- **It regards the world as unreal or an illusion** (*maya*) created by God to delude the beings and keep them bound to Nature. Therefore, one should not get involved with its attractions or aversions. To discern the truth hidden in creation and overcome delusion and ignorance one has to cultivate knowledge and intelligence by practicing various yogas and disciplining the mind and body. With knowledge, one knows the truth about the Self and the causes of bondage; and with intelligence, one learns to stabilize the mind in the contemplation of God and free it from both attraction and aversion to the pairs of opposites.

Hinduism is a continuation of traditions

That Hinduism is not a religion in the strictest sense of the word, but an ancient tradition in continuity and perpetual evolution is an unquestionable fact. The complexity and diversity of Hinduism cannot be reduced into a few defining words. To define Hinduism is like trying to force the waters of an unfathomable ocean into a small vessel, or to capture the essence of human life in a few words.

Hinduism is a continuing tradition. It evolves, transforms and advances in response to the needs and aspirations of its followers, almost on the lines of natural selection, assimilating the best of the ideas and discarding those that have either served their purpose or lost their value and significance.

In the course of its long history, Hinduism assimilated many past traditions, at times leaving them intact in its vast repository of knowledge. At the same time, it adheres to the core values derived from the *Vedas*.

Hinduism is like an Asvaththa Tree

With a structured definition, we may be able to capture the essential elements of Hinduism and satisfy our intellectual curiosity. However, it is highly doubtful if that would justify the significance of a tradition that began in the prehistoric times and eventually grew into a complex set of principles and practices, which we recognize today under the generic name of "Hinduism."

Interestingly, it is still in its assimilating and transformative phase!

Hinduism can be truly compared to an *Asvaththa* tree whose roots are in heaven and whose branches are spread throughout below. The roots are the *Vedas* whose source is the highest heaven. The branches are the various schools of philosophy and practices that became part of it during it subsequent development in the Indian subcontinent in response to external threats or challenges from within.

The scriptures that are based on revelations (*srutis*) have their source in heaven. Those that are based on human knowledge and wisdom (*smritis*) or this worldly. The trunk is the Divine Law (*dharma*) that supports all this and ensures the order and regularity of creation. The tree may grow and spread in various directions but its roots remain rooted to the same soil and it draws nourishment from the same source.

Hinduism is a way of life

Those who are familiar with Hinduism know that it is not a religion but a way of life. If educated Hindus know one truth about their faith clearly, it is this only. They know that religious practice does not have to be confined to a few superficial or ritual aspects of human life, but can be integrated into the very process of living whereby every action one performs becomes an act of worship and sacrifice.

Hinduism is about how you may live your life dutifully, morally, sincerely, religiously and spiritually so that it becomes a means to a higher purpose, which is liberation or enlightenment. In a way, this is the central purpose of any religion. It is meant to bring you closer to God and return you to your original nature.

In Hinduism, life and religion are inseparable. Religion is present everywhere, like the omnipresent Brahman, dominating and regulating every aspect of human life, infusing it with divine presence and making life more meaningful and purposeful to its followers. It virtually controls every aspect of a devotee's life.

Though its followers have immense freedom to choose their own methods of worship and religious practice out of diverse alternatives presented in the scriptures, the invisible hands of religion mould their thinking at every step and make them dutiful towards their gods and their own actions and obligations.

Beneath their conditioned minds religion looms, like a subterranean fire or the undercurrent of a flowing river, influencing their decisions and actions.

Hinduism views mortal life as both a trap and an opportunity. It is a trap if you ignore your spiritual nature and if you live selfishly or irresponsibly, ignoring your duties, accumulating things and strengthening demonic qualities.

It is an opportunity if you work for your liberation and lead a divine centered life cultivating purity and divine qualities. If you are wise, you will make use of the circumstances arising in your life and the very actions that ordinarily bind you to free yourself from the cycle of births and deaths.

If you are deluded or if you lack wisdom, you will let evil forces control your life and lead you into dark and demonic worlds from where redemption is very difficult.

Hinduism was shaped by time and history

To understand Hinduism, it is essential to examine its antecedents and historical processes, which contributed to its emergence as a major world religion of such depth and diversity. We have to know what shaped its philosophy and made it more relevant and useful to the spiritual needs and aspirations of diverse groups of people with varied backgrounds.

The vitality of Hinduism stems from its flexibility to adapt itself to the demands of an ever-changing world, its willingness to accommodate diverse views and freedom of enquiry and its readiness to revitalize itself through change and internal reform.

Since it lacks central authority, anyone who can capture the imagination of the masses can potentially influence its course and create necessary conditions to ensure its continuity and survival. This happened several times in its long history.

Over the ages, Hinduism has been enriched by the selfless contribution of extraordinary men and women, countless scholars, seers, sages, institutions, kings and emperors. By criticizing, correcting and improving the prevailing traditions and customs using the ancient wisdom of the scriptures as the standard to suit the requirements of their times, they kept the tradition alive and relevant, providing knowledge and guidance to a multitude of beings, at a time when barbarism and savagery still ruled many parts of the world.

Throughout its history, with the help of enlightened and selfless masters, Hinduism remained sensitive and alive to the spiritual and temporal needs of the people who reposed their faith in it and looked to it for solace and comfort.

It survived discrimination, persecution, misinformation and religious oppression. It absorbed apathy and animosity. It also never stopped growing and progressing, while its central teachings and essential scriptures remained the same.

What changed was not the belief system, but its understanding by the people who studied it without the weight of conformity. They reinterpreted the scriptures according to their knowledge and intelligence, threw light upon the hitherto unexamined aspects of its ancient secrets and practices, kept its knowledge current and relevant and in the process kept people's interest and curiosity in their religion alive and strong.

As a result, Hinduism flourished despite the absence of centralized authority, political support and serious challenges it faced from opposing traditions.

Hinduism is a multifaceted religion

Hinduism gained strength by assimilating many traditions, retaining their best beliefs and practices that were in harmony with those enshrined in the *Vedas*.

It also benefited richly by the contributions of countless people who worked for it out of duty, devotion, and love or under divine inspiration.

They explored its scriptures, spread its message among the masses, clarified its intriguing aspects and helped people in sustaining their faith and practicing its ideals.

By unearthing its hidden secrets and presenting them in newer and more meaningful ways, they attracted the masses and brought them under its influence, elevating it in the process to a world religion and making it the most popular religion of the

Indian subcontinent. Because of them Hinduism grew into a complex religion of oceanic proportions, assimilating diverse traditions and philosophies, without losing its vitality and originality and without sacrificing its basic ideals and core values or shying away from the growing competition it faced from other religions.

In a very peaceful and harmonious way, it integrated both the old and the new and attracted both the religiously devoted and the spiritually inclined to practice its tenets and test their validity.

As a result, in Hinduism today you will find diverse methods of worship, philosophies, beliefs and practices ranging from the most complex to the simplest.

Hinduism is incomprehensible to many

Hinduism not only maintained its hold upon its adherents but also managed to survive against the onslaught of newer and more organized religions and the invasion of foreign ideas that stood in stark contrast with its own.

In this great confrontation, it managed to hold its ground by virtue of its own diversity and the depth of its philosophies. Confronted with the challenges thrown by these religions, scholars were able to look anew at the age-old scriptures and draw new interpretations, which helped them strengthen the religion and protect it from possible disintegration.

However in this regard it was also shielded by its complexity and uniqueness that were incomprehensible to those who were not conversant with its scriptures and essential practices.

The incongruity and the inconsistencies inherent in Hinduism make it one of the most difficult religions to understand for those who do not practice it.

Many people outside the pale of Hinduism do not know what it represents or stands for. They do not know why it permits the worship of many deities, while acknowledging the universal

Supreme Self as the creator, preserver and the destroyer of the worlds and beings. They do not understand the significance of sacrifices or their importance in human life. They do not know why Hindus cremate their dead rather than burying them or why they perform daily sacrifices and obligatory duties.

Until recently, Hinduism was not well known outside India because the religion was explicitly averse to teaching or revealing its knowledge and wisdom to those who were unqualified, undeserving, uninitiated, insincere and non-believers.

The European scholars, who tried to understand the Hindu scriptures or translate them, had great difficulty in convincing the native scholars to share their knowledge with them.

Even now, some aspects of the religion are largely unknown to the public. It is also difficult to unearth the symbolism hidden in the scriptures.

Hindu scriptures declare that religious knowledge and wisdom are not meant for propaganda or religious conversions, but meant for the faithful and the discerning people who have the discretion to use them rightly for their liberation.

Since the knowledge contained in them was secret and likely misused or misinterpreted if fallen into wrong hands, they insisted that it should be shared only among qualified people with defining aspiration and not to be disseminated freely.

In Hinduism, this tradition has been in practice since earliest times and some sects follow rigorous selection procedure to induct new members into their fold and even then, the initiates are not revealed everything. They are kept under watchful observation until they make satisfactory progress and prove their merit.

In the past, the practice worked both ways.

It ensured its purity and continuity in the midst of social and political upheavals. At the same time, it made the religion rather secretive and difficult to grasp unless one was born with certain caste privileges. It also led to many myths and misunderstandings about its beliefs and practices among those who were not conversant with it and who had little access to its hidden and secretive knowledge. The foreigners who came to India as either travelers or conquerors had no knowledge of the deeper aspects of the religion or its esoteric practices. Therefore, they drew their own conclusions based upon their superficial observation and wrote whatever they thought was justified

The secrecy associated with the religion increased further with increasing invasions as people became apprehensive of those who came from outside with an intent to plunder and destroy the country's wealth and culture. They held them in contempt and avoided them as far as possible, keeping themselves aloof and not sharing with them any information.

In ancient India, many invaders were converted to native faiths; but after the advent of Islam, that possibility was ruled out since the Muslim rulers were notorious for their bigotry and religious persecutions and spared no effort to promulgate their religious policies.

As a result, Hinduism remained inside a cocoon, largely unknown and unappreciated, or misunderstood and misinterpreted, while Buddhism, born in the same soil, spread in many countries and became a world religion in a very short time.

Hinduism has undergone many reforms

The strength of Hinduism comes from its core philosophy enshrined in the *Vedas*. While many people think that Hinduism undergoes constant reforms and acquires new knowledge, the truth is with each reform it sheds the superfluity it gathers from the world around and returns to its pristine source, which is the knowledge enshrined in the *Vedas* and other ancient texts.

In its long history, Hinduism went through this cleansing process several times, undergoing many internal reforms and revivals in response to the criticism it faced and the weaknesses it developed. Whenever it was overshadowed by worldly influences, deluded beliefs and unhealthy practices, it was reformed and improved by people from within its ranks who rose to the occasion with exceptional clarity and wisdom. They revitalized it and prepared it for future challenges. It made Hinduism responsive and resilient.

One of the earliest internal reforms happened during the later Vedic period when the Vedic rituals were internalized and the model of sacrifice was used to evolve specific methods of yoga to achieve peace and liberation.

With this, the tradition recognized not only sacrificial rituals performed outwardly with elaborate procedures but also all desireless actions performed selflessly by people with a sacrificial attitude as part of their obligatory duties or as an offering to gods or God.

The dissolution with superficial rituals is well evident in the *Katha Upanishad* where *Svetaketu* feels disappointed by his father's insincerity in offering worthless gifts.

One can see a similar shift in emphasis from the ritual aspects of the religion to the spiritual in the early *Upanishads* such as the *Chandogya, Brihadaranyaka* and *Svetasvatara Upanishads.*

In many ways, the *Upanishads* were products of reformatory reaction against the excessive reliance upon gods, material comforts and sacrificial ceremonies and the neglect of the inner spirit and the Supreme Self.

They proposed an alternative way to perform sacrificial rituals internally without compromising their basic duties and obligations and attain the higher ends, namely peace, purity and liberation.

The Upanishads played an important role in this development. They contrasted the ritual knowledge (*karmakanda*) with spiritual knowledge (*jnanakanda*) and the perils of performing sacrifices solely for material and selfish gains. They urged people to live selflessly for the sake of God, performing internal rituals, and aim for liberation rather than a place in the ancestral world where their stay was temporary and from where they would return to the earth to take another birth.

The spirit of reform and revival continued in the epic period. The *Buddha* was not the first reformer of ancient India. He was one in a series of many great souls who were born in India. He is remembered well because his teachings gained widest acceptance and they were well preserved.

There were others from various ascetic sects and teacher traditions who also played a significant role in improving and reforming native faiths and suggesting alternative approaches and philosophies to resolve the problem of human suffering.

The most prominent among them was Lord Krishna. He reformed the Vedic tradition in no small measure and sowed the seeds of its greatness.

In a way, He gave a definite scope and purpose to Hinduism by integrating its numerous traditions and philosophies around the central theme of achieving liberation.

He revived many ancient and forgotten practices of the Vedic religion, reformed and reinterpreted them and presented them to the people in practical and simple terms as a comprehensive and coherent philosophy of life, duty and liberation.

His teachings are available to us in the form of the *Bhagavadgita*. The scripture itself may not be His direct rendition, but it is certainly based upon His teachings and the knowledge He shared with His followers and close relations.

To a careful reader of the scripture it becomes self-evident that the scripture cautions people against demonic nature and its ramifications in the practice of the religion and achieving liberation. Lord Krishna discarded meaningless and superficial practices that crept into the Vedic religion and represented the ancient wisdom of the *Vedas* to resolve the problem of human suffering. He synthesized the various approaches to liberation, resolving their contradictions and presented them as complimentary paths leading to the same goal.

His teachings are based on the *Vedas*, but His presentation is uniquely His own. Through the wisdom of the *Bhagavadgita* He reminded people of the knowledge they had forgotten.

Despite the reforms initiated by Lord Krishna, Hinduism declined during the post epic period, when the power and influence of the warrior caste declined and rituals once again took precedence over the deeper philosophical aspects of the *Upanishads*. These developments exposed the weaknesses of Hinduism and contributed to the birth of many new movements and philosophies.

Some of them challenged the authority of the *Vedas* and the usefulness of the Vedic rituals. Some even questioned the very existence of God and the possibility of life after death and urged people to live happily without worrying about their after lives.

With each new movement and organized reaction, the Vedic religion suffered a little blow. By sixth century BCE, Hinduism was riddled with caste inequalities and empty ritualism. Vedic sacrifices lost their value as priests practiced them out of personal greed rather than the obligation to nourish the gods.

It alienated people as well as kings and emperors from the mainstream Hinduism and prompted them to look for alternatives.

The six *darsanas* or the six schools of Hindu philosophy, the emergence of *carvakas* or *lokayatas*, *parivrajakas*, *ajivakas* and *nirgaranthas*, apart from Buddhism and Jainism, were products of this churning only.

These movements opposed the monopoly of the Vedic priests and the injustices they promoted and perpetrated in the name of castes and Vedic ceremonies.

Reaction against these developments within Hinduism led to the rise of devotional (*bhakti*) movements that emphasized social equality, the popularity of Vaishnavism and Saivism and the assimilation of many native traditions, with the *Vedas* still holding their ground as the source of all knowledge.

The *bhakti* movement was reformatory in its character and intent. It aimed to bring the excluded sections of Hindu society into the religious fold by helping them worship their favorite gods without the need for scriptural knowledge or the privileges of the upper castes.

It allowed them to practice their religion in the confines of their own homes without the need to seek priestly mediation or spend money beyond their means on sacrificial rituals.

It culminated in the decline of the ceremonial aspects of the religion and the rise of popular movements such as Saivism, Shaktism and Vaishnavism.

Tantrism was another offshoot of the same reformative temperament that seized the Indian minds. Its rise and popularity, at a time when Buddhism and Jainism were on the ascendance, added complexity and depth to Hinduism and provided it with the much needed vitality and diversity to forge ahead in difficult times.

The schools of Monism (*advaita*), Dualism (*dvaita*) and Qualified Dualism (*vishishtadvaita*) were also products of such internal churning only that strengthened Hinduism and prepared it well for the coming confrontation from Islam and Christianity.

The new philosophies proposed in Hinduism were rooted in the ancient wisdom of the *Upanishads*. They attracted the attention of the enlightened minds and encouraged them to explore the essential truths of our existence and our relationship with God and the world in which we lived. They suggested alternative ways in which human beings could relate themselves to God or know themselves through inner transformation. These divergent theories of creation and existence competed aggressively against one another to defend their views and appeal to the masses. Competition among them was so intense that sometimes it led to intolerance, debates, discussions and even quarrels.

Thus, in its long and checkered history Hinduism underwent many internal reforms. It survived because with each reform it shed the weight of its excesses and returned to its roots, drawing inspiration afresh from its ancient wisdom enshrined in the *Vedas*.

Out of the tumult and the flux it suffered from divisive elements, eventually it emerged as a strong and stable religion, with a comprehensive philosophy and set of principles that could appeal to people of all backgrounds.

Despite the troubles and challenges, and although battered and bruised at times from incessant attacks, it survived in spirit and dignity, gaining both depth and complexity.

Like a banyan tree, it remained rooted to the same soil, while growing in vigor and strength and spreading its branches in all directions.

This diversity and complexity of the religion so acquired during the post Vedic and pre-medieval periods saved it subsequently from the destructive onslaught of modern and organized religions like Islam and Christianity. When these two religions made their way into the country, they had immense political influence and vast resources at their disposal. They had the ability and the strength of organization to overwhelm and win over people of any faith to their fold.

However, they did not succeed much in their effort to convert the people, since they could neither comprehend their beliefs and practices nor shake their faith in their gods and ancestors.

The complexity of Hinduism and the faith of its followers, made mass conversions an impossible dream

They were able to destroy their temples and places of worship, but not their conviction and tenacity. They were able to suppress them and oppress them through persecutions and bigotry, but not shake their beliefs and faith.

They managed to convert a few under the fear of persecution or with the lure of wealth and power, but in the end, they left a large section of society untouched and intact.

Although the religion was bruised and battered in parts by their violent and brutal methods, it survived the onslaught and escaped total annihilation.

It is an undeniable fact of history that inspite of persistent attacks by Muslim theologians and Christian missionaries, Hindus largely remained loyal to their ancient gods and traditions. The internal reforms played a key role during this period also and helped them to sustain their faith.

Hinduism has assimilated many folk traditions

Hinduism assimilated many folk traditions, when village communities and tribal people joined mainstream Hinduism, bringing with them their ancient beliefs and practices, and began worshipping their local deities using the ceremonial procedures of the Vedic ritualism.

The process began during the early Vedic period and continued for long. Unknown to the Vedic scholars who frequented the urban settlements in search of fame and recognition and even to the kings who remained busy with wars, the assimilation of these groups of people happened quietly under the supervision of many seers and sages who travelled extensively into remote areas preaching *dharma* and looking for patrons and followers. They brought into its fold entire communities, tribes and forest dwellers who practiced their own traditions and spoke innumerable languages and dialects.

The same happened in rural areas, when proponents of *bhakti* (devotion) went to villages and preached devotion as the highest virtue. While people accepted Hinduism, they continued to practice their own methods of worshiping spirits, gods, demigods, plants, trees, animals, snakes, lakes and rivers as an expression of devotion.

It added a new layer of complexity to Hinduism, but at the same time contributed to its richness, variety and diversity and to its popularity in various parts of India.

Thus, we can see that what we today understand as Hinduism originally started as small streams and in course of time became a great ocean of traditions, beliefs, practices and approaches that Hindus today acknowledge as the many facets of one vast truth.

The Scriptures of Hinduism

We have discussed before that unlike other major religions, Hinduism is not derived solely from a particular scripture or a revelation of God. Its beliefs and practices are drawn from various sources. It suggests various paths to liberation and provides many alternatives to people to practice their faith according to their knowledge and inherent nature.

If you want to worship God in the form of images and symbols, in Hinduism you have the permission. If you want to practice yoga, restrain your senses and contemplate upon Him, you can do it too. How you worship God and practice your faith is essentially your choice, as long as it is consistent with the ideals of *dharma* or your obligations as a responsible human being and a member of your family and society.

Underlying this freedom given to individuals is the fundamental belief that beings differ in their spiritual progress, inner purification, knowledge and intelligence according to their predominant *gunas*, dominant desires, past life impressions, and their individual *karmas* and therefore need different solutions according to their individual needs to overcome their imperfections and achieve liberation.

In this article, we will examine how Hinduism derives its knowledge and wisdom from diverse sources and how they shaped its doctrines and practices over the millenniums into its current form.

The main sources

It is difficult to say when exactly Hinduism originated because it originated not from one source, but many and each has a history of its own stretching over a very long time, some dating back to even prehistoric times. If Indus Valley people also practiced some form of Vedic religion, an opinion which is gaining ground, we can trace its origins to as far back as 7000 BCE.

However, we do not know exactly what scriptures they followed or what religion they practiced. Recent research in Indian history indicates that both civilizations were indigenous and probably related and the Vedic tradition that we know might have emerged from the Sindhu-Sarasvathi civilization that preceded it, imbibing some of its traditions and practices.

Based upon the scriptural and archeological evidence, we can draw the inference that the tradition underwent many changes and drew inspiration from many sources in the course of its long and checkered history. The chief literary sources from which it derived it knowledge and philosophy are listed below.

- the *Vedas*
- the *Upanishads* (which are actually the end portions of the *Vedas*)
- the *Vedangas*, which are works related to the study of the Vedas
- the *Puranas* which contain historic accounts of gods, sages, various kings and their lineages
- the *Bhagavadgita*
- the treatises associated with various philosophical schools known as the *Darshanas*
- the Sutra literature containing the knowledge of the rites and rituals and ancillary subjects such as yoga.
- Two major epics known as the *Mahabharata* and the *Ramayana*
- *Agamas* and other literature of Saivism
- Vaishnava literature
- Tantric texts
- Ancient law books known as *Dharma shastras*
- Compilations known as *karakas*
- Commentaries known as *Bhashyas*
- Secular literature, such as the works of *Kalidasa*, *Kalhana* and others
- Regional literature especially the Tamil literature of the *Sangam* era

- Inscriptions and archaeological sources

Great saints, devotees, scholars and men of knowledge and wisdom like the *Alvars, Nayanars, Shankaracarya, Ramanujacarya, Madhavacarya, Nimbarka, Vallabhacharya, Tukaram, Caitnya, Tulasidas* and many others also contributed greatly to Hinduism through their works. Most of their compositions are still available.

Through their works, they not only brought to light its hidden wisdom and philosophical depth but also contributed greatly to its continuity and popularity during difficult times by sustaining people's hopes and aspirations in the faith of their ancestors.

The following discussion reviews the importance of some chief sources of Hinduism and their contribution to its treasure of wisdom.

The Vedas

The *Vedas* are called *nigamas*, in contrast to the *agamas* of Saivism. In Hinduism, they are considered divine in origin, composed by neither humans nor gods, but said to exist in the highest heaven as eternal wisdom and revealed to human beings for their welfare in each cycle of creation.

Since they are not created but only heard in meditative states, they are considered revelatory scriptures called "*srutis*" (the heard ones) in contrast to the memorial works known as "*smritis*" (the remembered ones) created by human beings based on their knowledge, memory and intelligence.

The Vedic people regarded the *Vedas* as timeless (*sanatana*), revealed by the Supreme Self for the welfare of the beings upon earth.

They are also considered eternal since they are present in the consciousness of God eternally, while we may receive them as per His divine plan. They would remain in the mortal world until the end of each creation, when they are withdrawn and reintroduced dutifully at the beginning of the following creation.

The *Vedas* are the heart and soul of Hinduism. They form the basis of the Vedic religion and in many ways of Hinduism, since its core principles and practices are derived from them only. They give us direction in a universe without maps, reveal to us how God and the divinities uphold dharma, deal with evil, live virtuously and contribute to the order and regularity of the world.

By providing us with righteous knowledge, they help us to live as the dutiful servants of God. By providing us with the knowledge of various sacrifices, they teach us the virtue of renunciation and sacrificial actions.

The *Vedas* were composed by a select group of seers (*rishis*) created by *Brahma* in the beginning of creation specially for revealing them to the human beings by drawing them from the highest heaven.

It is difficult to date them since no records have been maintained about their compositions, except vaguely. They are also very large compositions with thousands of hymns composed at different times and probably in different geographic locations.

Some scholars believe that the early composures came from the family of the *Angirasas* (angels). The Rigvedic hymns were ascribed chiefly to seven seers whose names vary. According to one list, they are *Atri, Kanwa* or *Kashyapa, Vashistha, Viswammitra, Jamadagni, Gotama*, and *Bharadwaja*.

The word "*Veda*" is derived from the word "*vid*" which means to know. The *Vedas* are books of knowledge, both spiritual and temporal, about this world and other worlds, and about God and His creation.

Devout Hindus regard them as inviolable and sacred and revere them as the ultimate source of all knowledge.

It is said that we can find answer to every human problem in the *Vedas* and whatever knowledge yet to be known is hidden in them in seed form. As a result, some scholars tend to trace everything to the Vedas, including modern inventions and scientific theories such as quantum physics, gravity, airplanes, locomotives, spaceships, space travel and automobiles. While we cannot be sure of some claims, we can say that the *Vedas* contains many secrets and spiritual truths about gods, creation, Nature, God, souls and the means to liberation.

As books of knowledge and wisdom, they serve us well in performing our duties and fulfilling the four aims of human life, namely duty, wealth, happiness and liberation. They also help us to reach out to gods and seek their help in achieving peace and prosperity.

For a long time the *Vedas* were passed down from generation to generation through oral tradition. Considering that they were large texts with thousands of hymns, it was a stupendous task for anyone to master all the *Vedas* and remember them by heart.

Maintaining the purity and integrity of the texts was of utmost importance to the priests since their livelihood depended upon the efficacy of the rituals, which it in turn depended upon the purity and sanctity of the verses in the Vedas.

Therefore, the teachers and the priests alike followed a strict code of conduct and very tedious methods to ensure that the texts were not compromised during their transmission from one person to another or from one generation to another.

The Vedas are books of sounds. Their efficacy depends largely upon the quality of the chanting and the sounds emitted during a sacrifice. The experience of the priests in this department is vital.

This is based on the long held belief that each syllable in the *Vedas* is sacred and eternal and represents a form or aspect of Brahman, which has to be pronounced correctly and exactly as specified in the rules of pronunciation to avoid unintended consequences, evil influences and negative results in the performance of the sacrifices.

Therefore, the Vedic priests put great emphasis on the correct pronunciation of the *Vedas* and made sure that the students and apprentices did not complete their education until they mastered this particular aspect of their learning and became adept in chanting. They also made it customary to perform expiatory rituals at the end each ritual or sacrifice to ward off negative consequences arising from unintended lapses and errors.

Parts of the Vedas

The *Vedas* are four, namely the *Rigveda* (also spelled as *Rgveda* or *Rkveda*), *Yajurveda*, *Samaveda* and *Atharvaveda*. Of them, the *Rigveda* is clearly the oldest, followed by *Yajurveda* and *Samaveda*.

Based on the references available in ancient scriptures, Indologists believe that originally there were only three *Vedas*. The fourth one, the *Atharvaveda* appeared later as the Vedic people learned to use ritual magic to ward off evil, cure diseases and influence others. Each *Veda* has its own distinction and religious significance. However, they also contain many verses that are common to all, an arrangement necessitated in part probably due to the loss of some original hymns or the use of same hymns by different types of priests for different rituals.

Each *Veda* is divided into the following four divisions.

- The *Samhitas*, also known as the *mantra* section, containing the collection of the original hymns in praise of various gods and goddesses
- The Brahmanas or guidebooks dealing mainly with the procedural aspects connected to the performance of the sacrificial rituals
- The *Aranyakas* or the forest-books containing information on the procedural and philosophical aspects of certain special sacrifices that are kept mostly secret
- The *Upanishads* forming the end portions of the *Vedas* and constituting a separate school of Hindu Philosophy known as the *Vedanta*

The four divisions are meant to serve the human beings during the four stages (*ashramas*) of their existence upon earth, namely the phase of celibacy (*brahmacharya*), the phase of a householder (*grihastha*), the phase of retirement (*vanaprastha*) and the final phase of renunciation (*sanyasa*). They also correspond to childhood, youth, adulthood and old age respectively.

The four divisions are also reclassified into two parts. The first two constitute the ritual part (*karmakanda*) which deals with duty and sacrificial actions and the remaining two constitute the spiritual part (*jnanakanda*) which deals with internal sacrifices that lead to wisdom and liberation. The former is helpful to those who practice the yoga of action (karmayoga) and the latter to those who pursue the yoga of knowledge (*jnanayoga*)

The Rigveda

Among the four *Vedas*, the *Rigveda* is the oldest, the most original in terms of content and importance. *Rigveda* means knowledge of the verses (*riks*). It contains 1017 (according to some 1072 or even 1028) hymns or *suktas*, divided into ten *mandalas* or books of varying lengths, each named according to the subject matter or after the seer who revealed them. They are composed mainly as invocations to various deities.

Scholars believe that they were probably composed during different periods and a few may have been even later day inclusions. We do not know when the composition of the Rigvedic hymns began and when it was completed. It is presumed that the work might have reached its mature form by 2000 BCE.

The gods and goddesses of the *Rigveda* are immortal light beings of supreme intelligence, having the power to bestow boons and special favors upon their worshippers who invoke them through sacrifices and offer them sacrificial food as nourishment.

The gods, who belong to the subtle world, depend upon humans, who belong to the gross material or food world, for nourishment, while humans depend upon them for realizing their subtle desires and protecting them from afflictions such as physical or mental harm, enmity, sickness, disease, poison, injury, pestilence, floods, drought and other natural calamities.

The sacrifices enable them to communicate with gods and benefit from their association and magical powers. The *Vedas* are meant to facilitate this sacred bond between both so that the divine order is maintained and regulated in the three worlds as ordained by God.

The Vedic deities

The Rigveda contains invocations to various gods and goddesses. Chief among them are *Agni* (fire), *Indra* (the lord of the heavens), *Soma* (the moon), *Surya* (the sun) who is also referred to as *Savitr* and *Vivasat*, *Dyaus* (sky), *Maruts* (storm winds), *Prithvi* (earth), *Vayu* (wind), *Apa* (water) and *Ushas* (dawn), *Varuna, Mitra, Aditya, Vishnu, Pushan*, the two *Asvins, Rudra* and *Parjanya*. In addition to them, we find references to celestial beings such as *Rbhus, Apsaras* (nymphs), and *gandharvas* (celestial musicians). They inhabit the higher worlds of light while the *Asuras* (demons) inhabit the lower darker worlds.

Indra is one of the most popular gods of the *Rigveda*. He is extolled in the hymns as the lord of the heavens and credited with the slaying of the snake demon *Vrata* to separate the earth from heaven and release the waters from the imprisoned clouds.

By releasing the rainwater from the skies, he brought life to the earth and helped the human beings to harvest food, which is essential for sacrifices and for the nourishment of all beings. As per the *Kena Upanishad*, he also went nearest to Brahman during one encounter and tried to know about Him. Hence, that alone qualified him to become the leader of gods.

In the *Rigveda*, we do not find much reference to gods such as *Brahma, Vishnu* or *Siva* who rose to prominence later as the triple gods (*Trimurtis*) of creation, preservation and destruction.

One of the most important hymns of the *Rigveda* is the Creation hymn, which describes how the worlds and the beings were manifested in the beginning by That One (tad ekam).

Another important hymn is the hymn of the Cosmic Person (*Purusha Sukta*), which describes how the Universal Person (*Purusha*) created the worlds, beings and the four castes, namely the priests, the warriors, the merchants and the workers in a sacrifice from parts of His own cosmic body.

The *Rigveda* also contains hymns extolling *Aditi* (the mother of gods), *Brahmanaspati* (the teacher of gods), *Usha* (the goddess of dawn), *Saraswathi* (the goddess of learning), *Aswins*, (the gods of healing), *Rudras* and *Maruts* (the gods of wind and storms).

Many hymns refer to the virtues of *Soma* juice, derived from some unknown plant containing intoxicating properties and used in the rituals for mind-altering experiences.

The other Vedas

The *Yajurveda* contains knowledge of *Yaj* or sacrifices. Here, the emphasis is more on the mechanics of performing the rituals for the invocation of gods, such as the implements to be used and the offerings to be made by the priests who perform them.

It is divided into two sections, the White and Black *Yajurvedas*. The former contains only hymns; while the latter contains both hymns and some prose.

The White *Yajurveda* has only one *Samhita*, the *Vajasaneyi Samhita*, which contains hymns chanted during important ceremonies such as the *Rajasuya*, *Asvamedha* and *Purushamedha* sacrifices. *Satapatha Brahmana* is its associated *Brahmana* text.

The Black *Yajurveda* contains four *Samhitas* including the well-known *Taittiriya Samhita*, each associated with a *Brahmana*. The *Samhita* is also popular because of the hymns addressed to *Siva* or *Rudra*, which are used in His ritual worship.

The *Samaveda* is more lyrical in nature. Historically, it is the second *Veda*. It is considered the book of chants since it relies upon not only magical sounds but melody also, which indicates that the early Vedic people had some knowledge of the earliest musical forms and notes, the precursors to Hindu classical music.

It contains 1810 hymns (according to some 1549). Nothing is original about this *Veda*, except for the emphasis upon rhythm and melody. All but 75 hymns are taken from the *Rigveda* only. They are chanted by a special class of priests known as *Udgatri* priests, according to a particular rhythm, usually during *soma* sacrifices performed in honor of the moon. In the *Bhagavadgita* Lord Krishna declares that among the Vedas He is the *Samaveda*.

As stated earlier, the *Atharvaveda* was originally not part of the *Vedas*. It was included later. It contains 730 hymns, divided into 20 books, most of which deal with magical spells for healing, long life, good health, protection from evil, charms and so on. It also includes several hymns of the *Rigveda*.

According to some scholars in the *Atharvaveda*, we see a blend of Vedic beliefs with certain animist practices of the time. *Atharvaveda* not only deals with gods and goddesses but also with "dark and demonical powers" that need to be supplicated and won over.

However, such opinions may allude to the presence of human motivation in the composition of the *Vedas* and depict the *Vedas* as mere literary or scholastic works, which is contrary to the traditional belief that the *Vedas* are not manmade.

The mantra tradition

An important aspect of Hinduism is its *mantra* tradition. A *mantra* is a sacred sound or a combination of sounds from sacred texts uttered by worshippers mentally or verbally and released into the universe with a certain state of mind, aspiration and intensity to communicate with gods, and prompt them to reciprocate with their benevolence and power of manifestation.

The *mantras* are the heart of sacrificial ceremonies. They bring magic into worship. They are available in the *Vedas* as the sounds hidden in the sacred hymns. Each of the Vedic hymns is divided into one or more stanzas or *mantras*.

It is said that the *mantras* carry within themselves the power of Brahman, which can be unlocked if they are properly recited using correct pronunciation and with a particular vibration. To increase their efficacy, it is customary to prefix each *mantra* with *Aum*, the *mantra* of *mantras*, before it is recited.

It is also said that hidden within each *mantra* is a presiding deity, which gives it latent or manifesting power. It is awakened when the *mantra* is uttered by the worshippers in a proper manner as specified in the *Vedas*. Once activated, it accompanies the sounds and reaches the gods who then visit the sacrificial place to accept the offerings. In ritual practices, several deities are awakened in this manner with the help of Vedic chants.

Purity is an essential aspect of the *mantra* tradition. The worshippers must keep their minds and bodies pure. Their intentions must be pure, pronunciation must be pure and the sacrificial place must be kept thoroughly clean and sacred. Unless these conditions are met, the *mantras* may not yield auspicious results. Sometimes they may even prove counterproductive and lead to unintended results.

Hence, the Vedic tradition places a great emphasis upon not only learning and memorizing the Vedas correctly by heart but also mastering the pronunciation and understanding the subtle nuances of various sounds associated with the Sanskrit alphabet. A priest is not allowed to participate in sacrificial ceremonies directly upon graduating in Vedic studies. First, he has to spend several years learning the *Vedas* under an adept master. Then he has to work for several years as an apprentice under experienced priests, before he earns the right to lead the ceremonies as a senior priest or head priest. The priestly families follow this practice even today to maintain the purity and sanctity of the scriptures as well as the sacrifices.

The Vedic hymns contain an apparent meaning and a hidden symbolism. This is so because the sacrificial ceremonies can be performed both externally and internally. It is also because according to the *Vedas* each human being upon earth represents the Supreme Brahman in a microscopic way.

Just as the gods are located in the universe, they are also located in the human personality as hidden deities or energies. Through austerities, specific prayers and spiritual practices, they can be invoked and awakened and their help can be taken to fulfill our desires or attain the four aims of human life. The hidden symbolism of the *Vedas* was brought to light in the last century by Sri Aurobindo in his work, "the Secret of the Vedas."

Upanishads

Upanishad means sitting near. These texts are introduced to students only in the advanced states of their learning since their knowledge leads to inner awakening and enlightenment. They are taught only in person. Hence the name *Upanishad*. They constitute the end part of the *Vedas*.

The actual number of the *Upanishads* is uncertain. The principal *Upanishads* are thirteen and the important ones are 108. Composed during different times, they belong to different *Vedas*. Some of them are relatively modern, while some very ancient.

The important ones are the *Brihadaranyaka, Chandyoga, Isa, Aitareya, Taittiriya, Katha, Prashna, Kena, Mundaka, Mandukya,* and *Svetavatara Upanishads.*

The philosophy contained in the *Upanishads* goes by the name *Vedanta*, meaning the end of knowing or the end part of the *Vedas*.

The knowledge has the power to liberate us from the cycle of births and deaths and lead us towards eternity.

The *Upanishads* contain profound philosophy about life and liberation. They are essentially spiritual texts. They contain the knowledge of Brahman (the Universal Self), Atman (the individual self), creation, liberation, the Abode of God, heaven and earth, life after death, transcendental knowledge, aspects of Nature, *gunas*, the importance of sacrifices, the superiority of eternal life and so on.

They also dwell deep into human nature, the state of the embodied beings and their relationship with Brahman. Among all the scriptures of Hinduism, the *Upanishads* occupy a unique place. They provide us with an insight into our spiritual nature and the mystical vision of God for which Hinduism is well known.

The Vedangas

Other important texts of the Vedic period include the six *Vedangas* and the *Sutra* literature. *Vedangas* literally means the limbs of the *Vedas*. The six *Vedangas* are *shiksha* (study of phonetics), *chhanda* (meter), *vyakarna* (grammar), *nirukta* (lexicon), *jyotisha* (astrology), and *kalpa* (methodology of rituals). Except for *vyakarna* (grammar) and *nirukta* (lexicon), which are common to all the four, each *Veda* has its own set of the remaining four *Vedangas*.

The *Vedangas* are useful in the study of the *Vedas* and in the performance of the Vedic rituals. They improve their efficacy by training the students to minimize errors and improve the quality of their chants and performance. They serve as ancillary or supplementary texts and provide ground rules for performing the rituals with greater precision. They prepare the students studying the *Vedas* for priesthood by helping them to master correct pronunciation, understand the construction of words and sounds in the hymns and their meaning, and perfect the methodology and mechanics of the rituals so that they can be performed correctly and effectively.

In addition to the *Vedangas*, each *Veda* is also associated with one *upaVeda* as shown below.

- *Rigveda – Ayurveda*
- *Yajurveda – Dhanurveda*
- *Samaveda – Gandharvaveda*
- *Atharvaveda - Arthasashtra*

The Sutra literature

Sutras are books that contain aphorisms or short and vague statements of truths. They are grouped under *Kalpa*, which is one of the six *Vedangas* mentioned before. Thus, technically, the *Sutras* are part of the *Vedangas*. They are mentioned specifically here because of their importance in the Vedic rituals. They establish the ground rules for performing various Vedic sacrifices and ceremonies.

The *Sutras* are divided mainly into four types, *Srauta* (on how to perform rituals), *Sulba* (on how to build altars), *Grihya* (on how to perform domestic rites) and *Dharma* (on how to live life according to ones *dharma*).

The *Grihya* and *Dharma Sutras* are often combined under the generic name *Smarta Sutras*. Under each of these four types, there are further sub-sets of *Sutras*, which are associated with different *Vedas* according to the rituals involved.

The Puranas

The *Puranas* contain historical accounts of people and events based upon racial memory, history, mythology, legends and paranormal experiences. They aim to spread religious knowledge and inculcate faith and devotion among people through stories, myths and legends in a medium and language people understand.

Listening to them is a form of worship and contemplation upon God. Hence, they are used mostly to keep people engaged in the thoughts of God as they listen to the subtle aspects of the religion through stories and anecdotes.

The *Puranas* played a significant role in the development of art and literature in ancient India. They influenced the emergence of various art forms such as the traditional dance dramas and the puppetry by giving them the context and the narrative.

The *Puranas* may not help a historian to reconstruct past events accurately, but they do allude to important historical events and lineages of ancient dynasties, from which one may build a vague picture of historical events and ancient warriors and clans. In some ways, they offer a strange combination of history and mythology freely intermixed. They constitute *smriti* literature, the heard ones, although they contain conversations of gods and celestial beings and some important revelations about creation and other celestial events. They also inculcate feelings of devotion and piety among the faithful.

The *Puranas* and the epics are collectively known as the fifth *Veda* (*Panacamaveda*). They present narrative accounts of various gods, sages and ancient kings of immense repute and their lineages. They also describe the process of creation and the conflict between the good and evil forces of the universe.

While as historical accounts they have limitations, for a student of religion they offer profound information and insight into the nature of Hinduism. They also play an important role in drawing the attention of people of all ages and backgrounds to religious and spiritual subjects, which they may otherwise ignore in pursuit of their worldly goals.

The *Puranas* became popular during the post Mauryan Period (200 CE), but they must have been in existence in some form long before that. Their popularity coincided with the emergence of several sub sects of Hinduism, the decline of Vedic gods and the emergence of *bhakti* movement. The texts contributed in no small measure to the popularity of Hinduism among the masses. While the teaching of the *Vedas* was restricted to higher castes, the knowledge of the *Puranas* was disseminated freely among all.

By presenting complex religious and philosophical truths in a simple manner, they not only enlightened the masses about their gods and religion and increased their awareness and religious fervor but also kept them well entertained with complex and exhaustive storylines.

Of the many *Puranas* available, only 18 are considered prominent, which are classified chiefly into *Brahma, Vishnu and Siva Puranas*. The eighteen great *Puranas* (*mahapuranas*) are *Siva, Vishnu, Agni, Padma, Brahma, Bhagavata, Narada, Skanda, Bhavishya, Vamana, Markandeya, Matysa, Linga, Kurma, Varaha, Garuda, Brahmanda, Brahmavaivarta*. In addition to them, tradition also recognizes 18 ancillary *Puranas* (*Upa Puranas*). Prominent among them are *Devi Bhagavata, Kapila, Narasimha, Ganesha, Samba and Siva-rahasya*.

The Darshana literature

The *Darshanas*, meaning viewpoints or perspectives are schools or systems of Hindu philosophy. There are six such *Darshanas* or schools of Hindu philosophy, namely *Nyaya, Vaisheshika, Samkya, Yoga, Purva Mimansa and Uttara Mimansa*. They are also grouped into three main systems, namely *Nyayavaisheshika, Samkhyayoga and Mimansa*. Of the six schools, the first two are based on the *Vedas* (*Sruti*). The next two are based on *Smrits* such as the *Puranas* and the epics. The last two are based on *Sastras* or scholarly works.

A study of the *Darshanas* provides us with immense insight into the ancient Indian wisdom and the complex body of philosophical thought that prevailed in ancient India. They provide us with different perspectives on reality, the nature of world and existence, God and Nature.

The basis of each school is a principal text, called a *sutra*, usually attributed to its founder or an important person in the lineage. Thus, we have the following six texts supporting the six systems: *Nyayasutras* by *Gautama, Vaisheshikasutras* by *Kanada, Samkhyasutras* by *Kapila, Yogasutras* by *Patanjali, Mimansa Sutrasa* by *Jaimini and Vedanta sutras* by *Badarayana*.

Since the *sutras* are short aphorisms, explicit commentaries (*bhasyas*) have been written in the past to explain them and bring out the truths hidden in them. Some of these schools do not acknowledge God or His role in creation, but they accept the existence of eternal individual souls and analyze reality.

The Bhagavadgita

The *Bhagavadgita* is a divine discourse of immense spiritual value, which teaches people how to perform their duties, live responsibly and avoid the consequences of their actions.

It contains the teachings of Lord Krishna to Arjuna in the middle of the battlefield about the meaning of the true Self, renunciation, the nature of *karma*, the three qualities, the state of God and Nature, the definition of a true devotee and many other truths about life and liberation. In 18 chapters, it covers the essential features and practices of Hinduism, emphasizing the importance of duty, detachment, renunciation and devotion.

The book has profoundly influenced many generations of Hindus. It still plays a significant role in molding their lives and thinking. Although it was composed subsequently, it enjoys a special status in Hindu religious literature on par with the *Upanishads*. Together with the *Upanishads* and the *Brahma Sutras*, it is recognized as the three most important works of Hinduism, known as the three outgoings (*prasthanatraya*) because their study leads to liberating knowledge and wisdom. Over the centuries, many scholars translated the *Bhagavadgita* and wrote their own commentaries interpreting it variously according to their knowledge and understanding. The *Bhagavadgita* continues to enjoy widespread popularity among Hindus. It is referenced and recited frequently for spiritual and religious guidance and inner transformation.

The epic literature

The strength of Hinduism comes not only from its scriptures but also from two major epics, the two of a kind in the literary history of world, namely the *Ramayana* and the *Mahabharata*. In terms of their length and popularity, they are perhaps the longest and the most popular epics in the history of the world with great literary, religious and spiritual value.

Together, they are called the books of history (*Itihasas*) containing the heroic deeds of great warriors and legends of remote past, whose antiquity and historicity are difficult to determine.

Yet, none can deny their importance in our understanding of Hinduism and its spiritual richness as the most popular texts of Hinduism providing valuable insights into the political, social and economic conditions of a very distant past. Apart from the main narrative with their plots, subplots, twists and turns, they also provide us with valuable information on how to live religiously, virtuously and dutifully to fulfill our obligations and work for our liberation. It is likely that they were rendered into their present form over time by a succession of composers, singers and poets.

From a historical perspective, the epics are more reliable than the *Puranas* as sources of history. As popular religious texts, they occupy a place of their own in Hinduism. They played a significant role in preserving and promoting Hinduism among a cross section of Hindus, in strengthening their faith and increasing their religious awareness and commitment to duty and morality.

We may even conclude that the two epics saved Hinduism by spreading the faith among the masses, who were otherwise denied an opportunity to study the scriptures or know about their religion because of rigid caste rules. Even today, their appeal among the people is more profound than that of any *Veda*, *Smriti* or *Sastra*. Any study, discussion or knowledge of Hinduism would be incomplete, without referring to them.

Agamas

The *Agamas* are theological manuals, which provide practical guidelines on religious and spiritual worship. They constitute the *smriti* literature. Each *Agama* consists of four parts: the philosophy (*jnana*) associated with worshipping the principal deity, the spiritual and mental discipline (*yoga*) required to practice the worship, rules for the construction of temples (*carya*), and rules for performing various festivals and ceremonies (*kriya*).

Like the *Upanishads*, the *Agamas* contain knowledge of creation, Nature, Brahman and Atman. Depending upon which deity is the object of discussion, they are broadly divided into *Vaishnava*, *Saiva* and *Shakti Agamas*. According to one classification, there are 108 *Vaishnava Agamas*, 28 *Saiva Agamas* and 77 *Sakta Agamas*. As the name indicates, these *Agamas* recognize *Vishnu*, *Siva* and *Shakti* as the ultimate realities. The most famous *Vaishnava Agamas* are the *Pancaratra Agamas*. The *Agamas* are also often described as *tantras*.

Scholarly works

Many teachers, scholars and religious leaders played a prominent role in the continuity of Hinduism and its popularity as a religion of the masses. Through their devotion and dedication to the cause of *dharma*, they increased our knowledge and understanding of Hinduism, ensured its continuity in the face of opposition and revived it from time to time from certain decline. Except for their contribution and dedicated effort, Hinduism would not have survived the ordeals through which it passed in its long history.

While their list is long, we may mention a few names such as *Gaudapada, Manu, Isvara Krishna, Shankaracharya* who composed works of great value or provided commentaries on the existing texts. Others who deserve a mention in this regard are the *Alvars, Nayanars, Ramanuja, Madhuvu, Ramananda, Vallabhacharya, Nimbarka* and *Tulsidas*. Among the more recent scholars, we may mention *Raja Ram Mohan Roy, Swami Dayanada, Sri Ramakrishna, Swami Vivekanada, Ramana Maharshi, Aurobindo, Bala Gangadhar Tilak,* and *Mahatma Gandhi*.

Through their teachings, compositions, commentaries and religious works, and by serving as role models through their lives and actions, they exemplified the highest ideals and the spiritual values of Hinduism and inspired many Hindus to return to their religion and practice it.

The Contradictions of Hinduism

Hinduism represents a wide range of thoughts, beliefs, opinions, sects, philosophies and practices, which make it a rather complex tradition difficult to understand. The problem is compounded further by its long history stretching over at least seven or eight thousand years, which is shrouded in mystery and controversy.

The *Samhita* portion of the *Vedas*, for example, contains invocations to various gods while the *Upanishads* speak about a universal and eternal Supreme Self who alone should be the object of our contemplation.

If *Vishnu* is the highest supreme Lord in Vaishnavism, *Siva* enjoys the same status in Saivism, whereas in popular Hinduism both are considered as aspects of Brahman and part of Trinity. In fact, if we refer to the *Vedas* we find limited references to both.

Such contradictions provide a good example of how Hinduism progressed over time taking its inspiration from diverse sources and assimilated them without compromising its basic values and fundamental beliefs. While many traditions joined the stream of Hinduism and were lost or forgotten, those that survived and became part of present-day Hinduism continue to retain their identity and attract their own following.

Some of the surviving traditions are so large and well organized that they qualify as religions in their own right. However, they are part of Hinduism because they believe in the *Vedas* ands share many common beliefs and practices.

People follow these diverse traditions according to their inherent nature, beliefs and attitudes, showing respect for those, which they do not follow. In popular Hinduism, you find a fine integration of these diverse traditions. Nowhere is it more visible than in a modern Hindu temple, where you find all the important gods and goddesses of Hinduism installed and receiving their due share of worship and offerings from their devotees.

Hinduism is not dogmatic. It does not suffer from the weight of institutional authority or prophetic injunctions since neither a single group nor a master can claim its exclusive ownership.

People are stifled by neither philosophy nor dogma. They have an option to practice their beliefs according to their knowledge and awareness and make progress on the path of liberation at their own pace. In making their choices, they may make mistakes. If they do, it is part of their *karma* and spiritual evolution.

The contradictions of Hinduism are justified because beings differ in their knowledge and awareness and may require different solutions and pathways to attain liberation. You cannot lump them together and say that everyone should follow one path or practice the same methods of worship.

Religious communism is not its forte. It is as impractical as to suggest one solution for all problems or one cure for all illnesses. The scriptures concur with this view. They suggest that one may worship God in different ways or pursue different paths to achieve liberation and eventually they all lead to Him only.

We find a similar echo in the *Bhagavadgita*, which suggests that the paths to liberation are many and howsoever people may approach Him, God accepts them and liberates them. It also declares that the knowledge of the *Gita* should be imparted only to those who qualify since teaching it to the unqualified may result in its misuse or misinterpretation.

In other words, your liberation and spirituality are directly linked to your past efforts, your awareness and spiritual development.

Nature does not to liberate you. It makes every possible effort to keep you chained to this world. To go against it and achieve liberation one has to withstand a lot of pain and suffering. Since it is a difficult and painful process, people do not willingly practice their faith with required seriousness or work for their liberation. They indulge in the delusion of superficial religiosity and go around it in circles, delaying their liberation.

The inclination to seek liberation comes after many births. Until then people grope in the darkness and pursue different paths, according to their dominant desires or predominant nature. They may believe or disbelieve in God. They may worship Him in different ways and pursue different paths and goals according to their dominant desires and attitudes, holding diverse opinions about God, the world and themselves.

Hinduism caters to their individual needs, by suggesting various ways in which they can worship God or participate in good deeds and improve their chances of liberation and inner purification. It warns you against evil paths, but does not prevent those who prefer to follow them.

It insists clearly that knowledge should be imparted only to those who qualify for it and who are ready for it. Even if you have right knowledge, you should not confuse those who do not have it and they should be given an opportunity to arrive at it incrementally by the merit of their own actions.

Thus, in Hinduism we find a healthy tolerance for a confluence of ideas and contradictory opinions about life and liberation. No one is punished for blasphemy or hearsay. One may believe or disbelieve in God or worship Him in numerous ways, according to their inherent *gunas* or past life impressions (*samskaras*).

On the one extreme, you may find people following perverted methods of worship and on the other, exemplifying the highest ideals of spiritual practice. Both approaches are recognized and accepted in Hinduism.

While puritans may dislike unconventional ideas and practices such as atheism or left-handed tantric methods of worship, the more broadminded Hindus who imbibe the expansive vision of Hinduism, may tolerate them as the illusions of the mind and consider them as distractions on the path of liberation.

In Hinduism, one line of thought holds that people act differently under different circumstances according to their dominant desires, knowledge and wisdom. Since they are deluded, you cannot expect them to act differently even in religious matters.

Differences are bound to exist among people because not all possess right knowledge or the same discernment. Until they reach perfection in their knowledge and discernment, they should be allowed to find their way through ignorance and confusion and arrive at truth through trial and error.

Theism and atheism

One of the interesting aspects of Hinduism is its tolerance towards those who hold unconventional ideas and approaches such as atheism, agnosticism or materialism. Hinduism does not uphold or approve these ideas but acknowledges them as aberrations in one's knowledge and thinking and part of one's ignorance and delusion.

Atheism and materialism challenged the Vedic tradition long before the Buddha, who himself never acknowledged the role of God in creation. The materialists who were also atheists by beliefs were known as *lokayatas* meaning worldly people. They also went by the name *carvakas*, after legendary *Carvaka*, an ancient Indian philosopher and founder of an atheistic school that opposed Vedic sacrifices, the existence of God and the validity the Vedas.

Although they criticized the *Vedas* and Vedic practices rather vehemently, they contributed to the growth of Indian philosophy by suggesting an alternate approach to living and exploring truth that hinged upon empirical and direct experience, elements of which gradually found their way into mainstream Hinduism.

The atheistic traditions of ancient India acknowledged some aspects of Vedic tradition and discarded the rest. They differed from it only in certain aspects, especially with regard to knowledge that could not be validated by direct experience.

For example, they acknowledged four out of five elements (*mahabhutas*) recognized in the *Vedas*, namely fire, earth, water and air, which could be validated through perception. Of the three standards of truth (*pramanas*) upheld by the Vedic scholars, they acknowledged only one, namely direct experience (*pratyaksha*), rejecting the other two, inference and testimony, as unreliable. Of the four aims of human life (*purusharthas*) identified by the Vedic tradition, they acknowledged only two, namely wealth (*artha*) and pleasure (*kama*) rejecting the other two, namely religious duty (*dharma*) and liberation (*moksha*).

From the traditional perspective, the main difference between theism (*asti*) and atheism (*nasti*) was essentially about the existence of eternal Self and life after death. Some traditions, which had elements of both, acknowledged the presence of eternal individual Selves but did not believe in the existence of the Supreme Self.

From a Hindu perspective, atheism is a sign of ignorance and delusion or the inability of the human mind to perceive truth beyond its abilities and faculties. It is caused by the impurities of the mind and body or the delusion enveloping the soul. However, it has a role and a place in our spiritual evolution upon earth. It represents one end of the human knowledge and provides an alternate philosophy against which you can test your own beliefs and practices to arrive at truth.

Atheism is a seemingly convincing philosophy, which relies heavily or rather blindly upon direct human experience and rejects everything else as delusion. While it trusts our experiences in exploring truth, it ignores the inherent limitations of our human faculties and intellectual abilities in ascertaining truths.

The concept of twice born is directly related to this. From the Vedic perspective, a human being who relies exclusively upon his mind and body is equal to an animal. Only when he cultivates spiritual awareness and religious knowledge through study and practice and uses them to discern the truth hidden within him, he enters into the realm of gods and becomes a twice born.

Thus, Hinduism acknowledges atheism as a perspective born out of our ignorance, delusion and impurity. It is an imperfection, which can be overcome only through an inner awakening and direct spiritual experience. Hinduism agrees with the atheists in that it does not want you to believe in anything blindly but go by your own experience and test the transcendental truths through self-effort.

Like the materialists, it concurs with the notion that the purpose of human life is enjoyment, but cautions you against forming attachments through excessive indulgence and reminds you of your other aims, without which your life upon earth would be incomplete.

Like them, it wants you to arrive at spiritual truths through direct experience only, but using different means. Faith is the support, but experience is the sustainer. While no effort is required for direct mental or perceptual experience, spiritual effort in the form of austerities, detachment, discipline and yoga are required to experience transcendental truths. They need effort and sacrifice. Since the atheists do not venture in these areas, their knowledge remains incomplete and they remain deluded.

Thus, from this perspective, atheism is the result of a lazy mind that refuses to look beyond the limits of its convoluted philosophy and give a chance to the spirit to show itself in the silence of the mind. It is born out of ignorance and impatience.

You cannot deny the existence of a place upon earth simply because you have never visited it or do not to visit it because you lack the means and the will. If we have to go by the methods (*pramanas*) of the atheists, we have to deny the existence of everything that we cannot validate directly through our experiences. We know that is an absurd proposition.

It is true that the knowledge we gain through scriptures (*sabda*) or inference or the experience of others is inferior to the knowledge we gain through direct experience (*pratyaksha*). In that, Hinduism is in full agreement with the argument of the atheists. However, since not everything in the world or within us is reachable through ordinary experience in wakeful state, it suggests that we should also rely upon other means, such as inference or testimony of the scriptures to validate transcendental truths that cannot ordinarily be validated with average intelligence or through direct human experience.

Diversity and complexity

Another notable feature of Hinduism is its overwhelming heterogeneity. A complex religion which refuses to fit into a set pattern and a multi-dimensional and multi-faceted tradition founded upon the wisdom of countless generations, it contains within itself beliefs and practices of diverse groups of people who lived in different times and places, but shared some fundamental beliefs and common knowledge. Countless people, scriptures, institutions and schools of thought contributed to its growth. They enriched its knowledge and shaped its principles and practices. Many streams of thought joined it to create a vast pool of knowledge and wisdom.

There are historical reasons why Hinduism developed as such. In its long history, stretching over several millenniums, many factors contributed to its diversity, which are listed below.

1. Vedic religion grew in complexity as it assimilated numerous new traditions that accepted the *Vedas* as the basis of their beliefs and doctrines. The new people who joined Vedic society did not forsake their own beliefs and practices and assimilated them into it.
2. New philosophies and religious movements emerged with the *Vedas* as the focal point. Hinduism assimilated them as perspectives since they enhanced or clarified the wisdom found in the *Vedas* even while debating its validity.
3. Teacher traditions, ascetic movements, saints and devotees of various theistic devotional sects enriched Hinduism

with their scholarly works, interpretations, teachings and devotional services.

4. The traditions that grew independent of Hinduism also became part of it when the British and European scholars ignorantly grouped all native traditions under the banner of Hinduism without acknowledging their distinctions.

The coming together of diverse beliefs, practices and philosophies made Hinduism very complex, difficult to define and even more difficult to understand. That Hinduism has been practiced since its earliest times by a heterogeneous population is well evident in the diversity of present day Hindu population who speaks numerous languages and dialects and belongs to diverse ethnic and linguistic groups, each having a long history, culture and traditions of its own.

In the following discussion, we will examine the contradictions inherent in Hinduism and examine how they were assimilated and integrated into it, resulting in the formation of a very dynamic and complex religion with numerous layers of beliefs and practices built into it.

Good vs. evil

Hinduism views both good and evil as part of the delusion created by God in the manifested worlds. Their source is God. The ideal it promotes is sameness towards both. Both the divine and demonic beings and divine and demonic qualities are part of His creation and constitute His numerous forms. Together they constitute a pair of opposites and give us an opportunity to cultivate virtue and sameness (*samatvam*) through detachment.

The idea inherent in this approach is if you love God, you have to be equal to His creation and love Him universally in every possible way, without being choosy and selective. By nature, we tend to be selective and preferential in our thinking and attitude as we are driven by the *gunas* and the desires they induce, whereas the ideal required for liberation is to remain unconditional and equal in our lives to all the dualities and pairs of opposites.

God's love flows in all directions. He is complete in all respects and shows no partiality or preference. He may respond to the abiding love of His devotees out of duty and for the sake of *dharma* rather than any desire. He loves all beings equally, irrespective of whether they are gods, humans or demons.

In the early stages of your spiritual growth, you have to practice virtues and abide by the rules and restraints, but eventually you have to outgrow your judgmental attitude towards all pairs of opposites and learn to accept them with sameness and stoical indifference. The general attitude one is expected to cultivate in Hinduism towards good and evil becomes self-evident when we realize the significance of the richly engrossing stories of the *Puranas* or the complex philosophies presented in the *Darshanas*.

While the demons are clearly depicted as evil forces and the gods as good, both are also described as the children of *Brahma* and brothers to humans. *Brahma*, the progenitor of beings, shows no partiality in his treatment of them. While he is well aware of their weaknesses and tolerates them, he regards them equally with fatherly love as his children. He even imparts to them knowledge, according to their inherent nature, to help them in their survival.

The other two gods of the Trinity, namely *Siva* and *Vishnu*, also show no partiality in their attitude towards the three worlds. They treat them generously with boons and favors according to their individual merits and tolerate all kinds of excesses committed by them until they go overboard and their actions begin to upset the balance and order of the worlds.

Even when they know that the demons seek boons from them to commit grave crimes, they give them an opportunity, as knowers of all and as part of their duties, to indulge in their own passions and delusions so that others can learn from their evil actions and live virtuously to abide by the laws of God. At the same time, they also make sure that such actions by the demons would not lead to chaos and disorderliness of the worlds.

The *Puranas* illustrate many instances where the three gods go overboard in granting generous boons to very wicked demons, knowing well that they would most likely misuse their powers and create chaos. The demons take full advantage of their generosity and seek very destructive powers that are difficult to counter. In the end, it results in serious conflagrations between gods and demons requiring their direct intervention.

Some of the most notorious demons mentioned in the *Puranas* are in fact great devotees of either *Brahma* or *Vishnu* or *Siva*. They love God, but their love is tainted with egoism, selfishness and evil desires. Therefore, out of ignorance and egoism, they misuse their spiritual powers and eventually meet their end in the hands of the very gods they worship.

The *Puranas* also mention that in most cases the demons, which die in this fashion, eventually attain immortality because of their intense devotion.

Some contradictions of Hinduism

In the following discussion, we review a few well-known contradictions of Hinduism that become evident when you study its scriptures or beliefs and practices. Their presence should not to be construed as its weakness but strength and the source of its resilience.

To the discerning minds, they reflect its indefatigable tolerance towards the contradictions and pairs of opposites inherent in life itself and in God's creation, unburdened by the weight of knowledge or our moral sense of right and wrong, which we use in the crucible of our limited wisdom to cast out relative judgments and opinions about a complex world.

They reflect its readiness and openness to embrace even the most sinful of the sinners and give them an opportunity and hope to redeem themselves from their ignorant and deluded past. They remind us of life's endless possibilities and of our vulnerabilities in a world in which nothing seems permanent and certain.

Life itself is full of contradictions. So is the phenomenal world with which we have to cope constantly. Contradictions, ambiguity and conflicts are present in every aspect of our lives. To the unwise, they present themselves as obstacles. To the wise, they reflect the totality of existence in which every phenomenon is both an opportunity and a trap.

Living upon earth is like walking on the edge of a sword. You make one mistake or show a little negligence and it may ruin your chances of liberation for many lives to come.

If you are aiming for liberation, you have to transcend dualities. You have to seek God, the inexhaustible permanence, who alone is one and indivisible. Everything else is subject to change, division, duality, diversity and pairs of opposites.

You cannot travel far in the ocean of life in a rocky boat. You have to look for a support that is not swayed by impermanence.

If diversity characterizes life upon earth, the solutions it offers to resolve the problems we face in our lives also must be diverse. Hinduism responds to the chaotic nature of our lives by offering multiple and diverse solutions that may be applied in different situations by different people with diverse outlooks, knowledge, awareness, wisdom and karmic background.

The solutions arise according to your preparedness and your past actions. Your propensity to good and evil is not an indication of your character or weakness alone, but the very nature of our existence that is built to hold us in its sway.

On the surface, the contradictions and approaches of Hinduism are irreconcilable; but at a deeper level, they resolve themselves into one harmonious whole. They represent but one Truth or the numerous manifestations of one indivisible reality.

Light and darkness, as we know, are the two sides of the same phenomenon that appears differently in different circumstances. It is true in case of gods and demons, knowledge and ignorance, life and death, creation and destruction, one God and many gods and numerous other dualities and pairs of opposites we experience in our lives.

These numerous manifestations of God are like the rays of the sun. They only enhance His glory and His pervasive presence, even if they originate from opposite ends. They complete the circle. They compliment life. They strengthen the hub of the wheel of God's eternal law. They serve Him well by creating in us modifications (*vrittis*) that lead to our bondage and suffering.

Everything has a role and purpose in God's creation. Nothing will ever happen without His will. The gods and the demons in reality work for Him and for the same end, which is to represent the different facets of dharma and creation and put you firmly on the path of liberation by teaching you valuable lessons about virtue and morality in their own good and evil ways.

Both believers (*astiks*) and non-believers (*nastiks*) who take rigid stands about their respective philosophies reflect the inability of the human mind to cope with transcendental truths. The approach truth from different ends and point to the fact that any conclusion we may draw about the world and reality from our experiences with our limited knowledge and conditioned minds would be incomplete, imperfect and inconclusive.

To perceive truth we must climb higher to a vantage point from where we can see truth more broadly with an integrated vision. We must rise above our attachments and imperfections to accept life's contradictions unconditionally in a state of surrender. We must free ourselves from the influence of our *gunas* that drive us into action and bind us to the world.

When our desires subside, our minds become silent and stabilized, and when we suppress the modifications (*vrittis*) that prevent us from seeing truth, we may enter into that awareness in which we may see the contradictions in a different light as complimentary and remain equal to them.

In surrender, we see the totality of life. In accepting the totality of life, we realize the value of contradictions and the pairs of opposites. With the wisdom arising from it and with intelligence opening the doors of discretion, we realize that ignorance is an aspect or a condition of knowledge and it is not absence of knowledge but veiling of it.

The reconciliation of divergent truths into one harmonious whole, which is difficult for a novice to understand or accept, aptly summarizes and concludes what one can learn from Hinduism by studying its scriptures and practicing its doctrines. In essence, it teaches that the One (Truth) manifests itself into many (truths) in the beginning of creation and that the many (truths) in the end slowly resolve themselves into One Truth again! Each person who emerges out of this diversification has to reconcile the divisions and contradictions to return to the point from which everything emerges and diversifies.

In other words, you, the eternal Self, are the source of the contradiction and you, the eternal Self, should be the cause of their resolution and conciliation.

You are the creator of both good and evil and you have to resolve them in the course of your existence upon earth learning your own lessons from them and making peace with them through detachment and renunciation.

Following are a few well-known contradictions of Hinduism that have adherents on both sides of argument. While it may baffle those who are unfamiliar with its beliefs and practices, in Hinduism their source is considered God only.

- One god versus no god
- One god versus many gods
- Practice of sacrifices versus pursuit of knowledge

- The path of knowledge versus the path of devotion
- Saivism versus Vaishnavism
- Purusha versus Prakriti
- Monism versus dualism
- The Vedas versus the *Tantras* and *Agamas*
- The concept of divine nature of humans versus the division of humanity based upon caste and gender
- The concept of renunciation versus the concept of four aims of human life (*purusharthas*)
- The concept of self-control and austerity versus the revelry of gods and the use of sexual pleasure in tantra
- The concept of monogamy versus the practice of polygamy supported in the scriptures and practiced by some gods
- Hindu ethics versus the behavior of gods
- The worship of Mother Goddess versus the treatment of women, the prevalence of *devadasi* system and sati
- Ritualism versus spiritualism
- Buddha as an incarnation of *Vishnu* versus Buddha's own teachings about God, gods and the Vedas

Hinduism truly believes that the paths to God and Truth are many and one may arrive at them by following any path. When one goes beyond the mind and the senses one experiences a reality that is different from the reality we experience in our normal wakeful state. Whatever is within in the field of illusion is also strictly a part of illusion, whether it is a moral code, a particular belief system or a way of doing things. We are prisoners of our own beliefs and illusions. We experience true freedom when we break through the barriers of our mental conditioning and transcend our limited vision, discarding all forms of attraction and aversion to the pairs of opposites.

For that, you need not have to worship God as others do, or seek liberation like others. You can purse your own path, following your own convictions, as long as it is in harmony with your essential nature. You may worship God in whatever way you want. You may even deny Him, because understandably you are in a state of ignorance and delusion. You may regard Him variously as the known or the unknown, or as one without form or with innumerable forms. You may worship Him negatively by worshipping His unpleasant forms. The choice is yours. Ultimately, it is your salvation. Whatever actions, decisions and approaches you follow in your life, you are responsible for them and you will be accountable for their consequences.

Ignorant people pursue ignorant paths. Those who lack discerning wisdom choose perverted methods to seek truth, as people with the predominance of *tamas* do. As we learn from the *Bhagavadgita*, everything in the world is a manifestation of God. He is the goal as well as the means. He is the sacrifice, the sacrificed and the sacrificer. He is the center and circumference of the entire creation.

Therefore, whatever path you may choose and in whatever form you may worship Him, in the end it will lead to Him only. Some of the paths suggested in the scriptures are difficult to follow, like for example, worshipping the Unmanifested Brahman. However, if some people want to pursue it, Hinduism gives them a chance to test their beliefs. Our scriptures give us freedom to worship God according to our knowledge and convictions. They acknowledge that nothing is certain about God or the paths that lead to Him, since He is beyond all rules and restrictions and beyond the known as well the unknown. As one of the *Upanishads* declares, "He who says he knows Him knows Him not, but he who knows that He knows Him not really knows Him"

Rigid approach to theological matters is not a characteristic feature of Hinduism. It acknowledges the limitations of human mind to comprehend absolute reality and recommends relentless pursuit of Truth with purity (*sattva*) and discriminating intelligence (*buddhi*) to go beyond the limited field of perceptual experience. The books and the teachers suggest ways and means to accomplish the highest goal. It is up to the individuals to decide what is best for them.

Hinduism is difficult to define

The many contradiction and disparate philosophies present in Hinduism make it difficult to define. It is not a religion, but it is treated as one for study and understanding and distinguishing it from other faiths. The complexity of Hinduism has also arisen because it is an artificial arrangement, not a natural development.

The word Hindu was coined originally to denote the people of the Indian subcontinent, not the people of a particular faith. Hindustan was the land that existed beyond the river Indus, and those who lived in it were known to the outside world as Hindus. Whatever traditions they practiced were lumped under one denomination as Hinduism. The word has been in use only since the last few centuries as a generic name to denote the traditions that grew in ancient India out of the Vedas or in response to them. In fact, in its long history since the Vedic period Hinduism has been known to its practitioners as *dharma* (religious duty) or *sanatana dharma* (eternal duty).

Ancient Indian society was as complex as it is today, consisting of divergent groups of people following different faiths, worshipping different gods, speaking different languages, and belonging to different social and ethnic backgrounds.

People practiced different faiths and tried to resolve the problem of human suffering in their individual ways or according to their specific traditions.

While their traditions were numerous, distinct and different, a foreigner who visited the subcontinent from outside world would not have missed their common features and unique lifestyles they shared among themselves.

From a global perspective, even today, if you set aside religion and look at the people of India, you will find in them certain characteristics that are hard to find elsewhere.

Dimensions of Hinduism

Hinduism has been enriched by many traditions, which are listed below.

- A scholarly or philosophical tradition based upon knowledge (*jnana*)
- A ritual tradition based upon sacrifices and religious ceremonies (*karma*)
- A *mantra* tradition based upon the use of mental and spiritual energy to invoke gods or manifest our hidden desires
- A *tantra* tradition that aims to transform sexual energy into spiritual energy
- A yoga tradition that aims to suppress the modifications of the mind and stabilize it in transcendental Self through inner transformation and cultivation of *sattva*
- A devotional tradition that aims to secure liberation through the grace of God
- An esoteric tradition known only to a select few and practiced with utmost secrecy
- An ascetic tradition which advocates renunciation of worldly desires and all forms of attachment to experience oneness with God
- A folk tradition that is based upon the beliefs and practices of people living in the rural and tribal areas
- Traditions of bygone eras, fragments of which are now available to us in the scriptures or their derivative works as indirect references

Hinduism has many dimensions and suffers from divisions and inherent contradictions because it never accepted any particular person, god, prophet, theory, dogma or institution as the source of all knowledge and wisdom. You may compare it to a whole museum of art, instead of a single painting, because it represents such diversity and complexity that it is difficult to put all its essential features and elements on a single canvas. Many streams of knowledge and wisdom joined Hinduism in its long history. Whoever joined it brought with them their own set of beliefs and practices and integrated them into the tradition they accepted as their own.

In this, we cannot judge Hinduism with the standards of an organized religion or a rigid dogma. Hindus firmly believe that each individual is responsible for his or her choices, in which past actions and past-life impressions (*samskaras*) play a vital role. Since we do not have the right knowledge, it is not proper on our part to criticize the faith of another or confuse them with our own knowledge and beliefs. Each individual must be allowed to pursue liberation according to his or her inherent nature and dominant tendencies.

The strength of Hinduism lies in its emphasis upon the freedom of each individual in seeking spiritual solutions to the problem of human suffering, its acceptance of diverse pathways to liberation and its glaring indifference to the notion of brining people of other faiths into its fold.

Truly, Hinduism is a living and continuing tradition, containing diverse religious and spiritual beliefs that have been tested for long in the furnace of human knowledge and spiritual wisdom and accepted as valid milestones in the spiritual progress of the civilized world. Just as the world and our civilization evolve and expand, Hinduism also evolves and expands, without compromising its core values derived from the *Vedas*, incorporating new knowledge and truths that become part of our growing and expanding consciousness.

In whatever direction the world may progress, whatever new scientific truths it may unravel and revel in, Hinduism surely has the tenacity and resilience to survive and continue for generations to come, with increasing vigor, wisdom, and tolerance, providing dynamic solutions to the challenges that may arise as the humanity progresses. Definitely, it has an inherent advantage since it does not suffer from the limitations of dogma or the weight of theocracy.

Main Beliefs of Hinduism

Hinduism is comparable to a giant banyan tree that has grown in many directions overtime and yet kept its roots firmly entrenched in the soil in which it was born.

If you are born in a Hindu family, you understand what Hinduism means without much effort as you imbibe its values and beliefs as part of your growing and learning.

However if you are not conversant with it or with the religions that have grown as offshoots of human knowledge and wisdom rather than the gift of a founder or a prophet, it may take time before you realize what it actually means.

For the purpose of this discussion, let us be clear that Hinduism is an artificial name invented by people who did not practice it to distinguish it from other religions they knew. They were not interested in what it represented, but how to separate it from other faiths so that they could present it as a distinct tradition and a comparable religion. This artificial arrangement made the task of defining Hinduism rather difficult and challenging.

For those who have difficulty in understanding Hinduism, we can define it as a set of religious beliefs, practices, philosophies and traditions that originated in the Indian subcontinent several thousand years ago and undergone numerous internal reforms, incorporating beliefs and practices from various sources, yet remaining faithful to its core values and basic philosophy as enshrined in the *Vedas*.

Its primary source is in the *Vedas*, but like a giant banyan tree that has grown in several directions and sprouted secondary roots, it draws its inspiration from various sources and provides shelter to many ancient beliefs and practices whose origins are difficult to trace but which continue to inspire millions of people even today. Hinduism is well integrated in the life of a Hindu. In Hinduism, it is difficult to separate the life of an individual from his or her religion.

Faith is interwoven into the lives of Hindus. It influences every aspect of their lives, their ways of living and thinking, their belief in *karma*, rebirth and liberation.

A Hindu, which is again an artificial word invented by non-Hindus, is one who is born in a Hindu family or who practices Hinduism as a religion or belief system. Most people become Hindus by virtue of their birth in Hindu families as part of their *karma*. Their faith is shaped mostly by the faith of their parents and other members of family.

However, this does not have to be true always. In recent times, a number of people from other religions are converting to Hinduism, driven by curiosity or quest for truth, peace and solace. Hinduism offers what many religions do not, which is freedom to practice one's faith according to one's inherent nature.

One can become a Hindu by conviction or by cultivating faith. Special ceremonies and observances are not required. However, optionally one may seek the help of a priest or a spiritual guru to undergo an initiation ceremony and join the tradition formally.

Today, Hinduism is practiced in many parts in the world and the number of those who are converting to it on their own has been steadily growing. The more educated and spiritual a person is the more likely he or she is drawn to its subtle aspects.

Apart from India and Nepal where it is the religion of the majority, it is practiced in the rest of the countries of the Indian subcontinent. In some countries like Cambodia, Indonesia, and Malaysia, it has been practiced for over a thousand years; while in some like Mauritius, South Africa, Kenya, West Indies, Singapore, UK and Fiji for over two or three centuries. Wherever it has gone for historical reasons, it has acquired a flavor of its own. Present day Hinduism is therefore even more difficult to define.

To understand Hinduism, we have to examine its core beliefs, which are many and some of which are listed below. By knowing them, we can understand its diversity and complexity and realize why Hinduism stands apart from every other religion in the world and why it may be even an injustice to equate it with other religions in the traditional sense of the word.

Belief in Supreme God: Hindus believe in the existence of Supreme Self, who is popularly known as Brahman, but goes by many names. He has manifested and unmanifested aspects. In His manifested aspect, He appears in numerous forms, including *Isvara*, the Lord of the Universe and *Hiranyagarbha*, the golden egg. He is extolled in the *Vedas* as the eternal, inexhaustible, absolute, supreme, Lord of the Sacrifice, Creator, Preserver and Destroyer of the worlds, the Final Abode of the pious and the source of liberation for all beings. As preserver, He enforces His divine laws (*dharma*), ensures the order and regularity of the worlds (*rta*) and makes beings responsible for their thoughts and actions. Hindus worship God in numerous forms, mentally, physically and spiritually, as the Supreme Self and Pure Consciousness as well as incarnations, emanations, deities, symbols and idols.

Belief in the eternal individual souls: Hindus believe in the existence of eternal, imperishable and absolute individual souls who appear in the worlds of God as beings or embodied souls (*jivas*) when they come under the influence of Nature and become subject to its modifications. The individual souls may be either aspects of God or independent of Him. They may exist in various states of liberation or bondage. Even when they are in bondage to Nature, they remain pure and impervious to change and destruction.

Belief in obligatory duties: Hinduism is traditionally known as *Santana Dharma*, loosely translated as eternal religion. Literally speaking *sanatana* means eternal and *dharma* means obligatory duty or duties. Hinduism is all about performing our duties or discharging our obligations. The duties are meant not only for us but also for all other beings in all the worlds, including gods, celestial beings and demons. Even God has duties to perform. He does it to uphold the worlds and set an example to others so that the worlds remain in their sphere and their order and regularity is ensured. Since the basic duties for all the beings are eternal and the same from creation to creation, they are called eternal duties (*sanatana dharma*) and Hinduism is a religion, which speaks about them and enjoins people to perform their duties as a service to God.

Belief in sacrifice: Sacrifices occupy a central place in Hinduism. Sacrifice is considered the source of all creation. For human beings sacrifices are obligatory. Through sacrifices only, gods and humans nourish each other. Through sacrifices performed internally and externally, we attain liberation. Out of sacrifice alone emerged all gods, beings, the *Vedas*, knowledge, wisdom, peace, prosperity, the divisions of society and food. Humans should practice sacrifices physically, mentally and spiritually to establish peace upon earth, promote *dharma* and attain liberation.

Belief in Purusha and Prakriti. Hindus believe that the Supreme Self or the Lord of the Universe (*Isvara*) has a twin aspect, namely *Purusha* and *Prakriti*. *Purusha* is the Cosmic Self and *Prakriti* is the primeval nature. *Prakriti* is considered either an aspect of God or an independent eternal entity. The two are also regarded in Hinduism as Father God and Mother Goddess. Their association results in the manifestation of materiality, diversity, dynamism and beingness. These phenomena are subject to modifications, formations and impermanence. The same aspects are responsible for our beingness and existence in the mortal world.

Belief in the Trinity: Hindus worship God in numerous forms. The most prominent among them are *Brahma*, *Vishnu* and *Siva*. They are lords of their own spheres from where they keep an eye upon the worlds and beings and ensure their order and regularity. They are called the Three Beings (*trimurthis*). They are essentially the purest and the highest manifestations of God who perform His triple functions as creator, preserver and destroyer respectively. These three are present in every aspect of creation.

At the highest level, they are responsible for creation, preservation and destruction of the worlds during each cycle of creation. They are worshipped both individually in numerous forms and specifically as the Supreme Self.

Belief in the existence of gods and goddesses: Hindus believe in the existence of numerous gods, goddesses and celestial beings who inhabit the higher worlds and who can be invoked through prayers and sacrifices. Most of them inhabit the world of *Indra*. The rest of them exist in their own spheres as either lords or their associates. They also exist in the macrocosm of God and in the microcosm of each being as subtle beings. They can be invoked through worship and sacrifices and their help can be sought for our spiritual and material wellbeing.

Belief in liberation and rebirth. Hindu scriptures suggest that a being may either go the world of immortals or to the world of ancestors depending upon its past actions (*karma*). Those who go to the world of immortals are liberated forever. They never return. However, those who go to the world of ancestors, return to the earth after exhausting their merits and take birth again. The sinners, who commit mortal sins or come under the influence of demons fall into the darkest hells and suffer there. Being may return from there and take birth again, but it is more difficult and may take much longer time.

Belief in the power of sounds. Hindus believe in the efficacy of the mantras and their ability to manifest desires with the help of Gods. According to the *Vedas*, the power of God is hidden in the sacred sounds of the hymns. When it is released during sacrificial ceremonies in the form of chanting it travels through space (ether) and awakens the gods to come to the earth and receive their nourishment. Similarly, each *mantra* has a hidden deity and when it is chanted reverently, it awakes and manifests our wishes. The most potent and sacred sound of all is *Aum*, which is God Himself in sound form having the ability to purify our minds and bodies and prepare us for our liberation. The mantras are used in both ritual and spiritual practices of Hinduism.

Belief in the conflict between good and evil: Hindus believe in the conflict between truth and falsehood (good and evil) and the ultimate triumph of truth (good). The demons, gods and mortal beings upon earth are all children of Brahma only. However, they are subject to different degrees of ignorance and delusion. The gods are upholders of *dharma*. They aim to maintain the order and regularity of the worlds in accordance with the laws of God. The demons are interested in occupying the heavens and creating chaos. They may worship God, but usually do so for their own nefarious ends. The beings upon earth possess both divine and demonic qualities according to the predominance of the *gunas* and open themselves to the influence of both.

Belief in idol worship: Hindus worship God in numerous forms. They also worship God and various gods and goddess in idol form and in the form of symbols. In Vaishnava tradition, an idol (*arca*) is considered a manifestation of God Himself having the ability to respond to the devotion of a devotee. The practice of idol worship in Hinduism is justified on many grounds. The chief reason is it is easier to worship God with a form and relate to Him rather than worshipping a formless God. Secondly since God is omnipresent, everything including an idol is worthy of veneration. Thirdly, the idols are not mere statues. They are installed according to specific rituals and infused with the power of God.

Belief in karma: *Karma* means any action performed by the beings upon earth. In Vedic tradition, *karma* means ritual. The ritual portion of the *Vedas* goes by the name *karmakanda*. In a specific sense, *karma* refers to the law of action according to which actions performed by beings upon earth with desires and expectations have consequences, which will shape their lives and destinies. Good actions that tend to promote *dharma* and morality lead to happiness and progress towards liberation while sinful actions lead to suffering and spiritual downfall. The *Bhagavadgita* suggests that when actions are performed without desires and expectations and as an offering to God, they do not bind the beings. This is *karmayoga* or the yoga of performing desireless actions.

Belief in Maya: Hindu scriptures affirm that the world, in which we live, in fact the entire creation of God, is just a projection or a mere illusion. Only God or Brahman is real. Everything else is an appearance like the clouds in the sky. *Maya* or delusion also pervades our minds and bodies whereby we mistake one for another and fail to discern truth correctly. The delusion is responsible for bondage upon earth. Delusion can be overcome by cultivating purity (*sattva*) and intelligence (*buddhi*). When we are free from delusion, we realize that we are eternal souls and work for our liberation.

Belief in the Vedas: Hinduism acknowledges the *Vedas* as God in word form. They are revealed to us by God Himself at the beginning of creation for the welfare of the world. The knowledge contained in them is final and inviolable. You cannot dispute them because their source is God who is truth personified. They are the means by which we can practice and promote dharma upon earth. The *Vedas* are eternal. They exist eternally in the sphere of God. We can use the knowledge of the *Vedas* to ascertain truth, as a testimony in case of dispute, to secure the help of gods, to establish peace and prosperity upon earth and to attain liberation.

Thus, we can see that Hinduism is a complex religion with numerous beliefs, most of which are derived from the *Vedas* and confirmed by other sources such as the *Agamas* and the *Puranas*. Other important beliefs of Hinduism worth mentioning are the six schools of philosophy (*darshanas*), the seven seers, temple rituals (*smartaism*), caste system, the mind and body as the field (*kshetra*), aspects of Nature (*tattvas*), the four aims (*purusharthas*), the four states of consciousness and the four stages (*asramas*) of human life.

Methods of Worship in Hinduism

The methods of worship in Hinduism are as complex and diverse as Hinduism itself. Most methods are structured based on certain beliefs and ancient traditions.

Some involve elaborate and esoteric procedures. They are performed on specific occasions, which only the priests can understand and explain, or perhaps not since the symbolism involved in them is deep and ancient.

Others are simple or elaborate acts of obeisance, performed anytime during the day or night according to one's convenience and interest in the temples, households or public places.

Hindus worship many gods and goddesses in different ways according to scriptural injunctions, local customs and family traditions.

They also worship the highest God in numerous forms and with different names.

They may worship at home, in temples and public places. They may worship physically or mentally.

They may worship one God, many gods or a combination of gods and goddesses.

They may worship them individually or in groups, silently or loudly, austerely or with a lot of pomp and publicity.

In most methods of worship, you will generally find one or more prayers or supplications, physical postures, offerings, praise, expectations, singing, expiation and a formal conclusion.

Some acts of worship may last for a few minutes and some may last for days and months.

The methods usually fall into two classes, those that are performed ritually and ceremonially by priests in the chanting (*sruta*) tradition and those that are performed at home in domestic (*grihya*) tradition.

They are also classified into three main categories: daily (*nitya*), periodical (*naimitta*) and those for fulfilling desires (*kamya*).

The purpose of worship may be mundane or spiritual, for peace and prosperity, to avoid misfortune, ward off evil, achieve spiritual transformation, express pure devotion, seek expiation of sins or fulfill an obligatory duty.

In the *Bhagavadgita*, Lord Krishna declares that four types of people approach Him, men in distress, seekers of material wealth, the inquisitive types and men of wisdom. Of them, He considers the last one the dearest to Him.

In another instance in the same scripture, He also declares that whatever is offered to Him with love and devotion, be it a flower or fruit or leaf, He accepts them unconditionally.

The scripture upholds numerous methods of worship and presents them as the manifestations of God and different ways to reach Him.

No restrictions are imposed upon the devotees how they may worship Him. He is the end recipient of all offerings. Howsoever, one may worship Him or approach Him, says the Gita, eventually they all lead to Him only.

He is the worshipped, the method of worship, the material used in the worship and the object of worship.

He is present in the scriptures, present in the chants, present in the offerings and present in the ritual outcome.

All offerings are received by Him even when people worship other Gods.

However, since He does not intervene in matters of faith, those who worship the gods and demigods go them, while those who worship Him directly go to Him only. In other words, not all methods are equal. Their importance in liberation depends upon to whom they are addressed.

If God is the object of worship, it is better. He speedily rescues His worshippers from the ocean of phenomenal life. Those who worship Him constantly, with their minds fixed upon Him, live in His heart and He lives in theirs. He takes care of their welfare upon earth and helps them in their liberation.

The ceremonial methods of worship usually fall into two categories: the Vedic rituals and the Agamic rituals. The former are performed according to elaborate procedures laid out in the *Brahmana* portion of the *Vedas*. The latter are performed according to the *Agamas*, a collection of tantric texts, usually involving idols.

The *Purva-Mimansa* School explains the importance and the philosophical basis of the Vedic rituals. The *Tantra* schools follow the *Agama* tradition in worshipping gods. The *Devigita* explains that worship is of two kinds, external and internal. The external worship is again divided into two types: Vedic and Tantric (or Agamic). The Vedic worship is further divided into two according to the images used. According to tradition, both Vedic and Tantric methods of worship should be performed by skilled priests who are well versed in the respective scriptures.

Some of the Vedic rituals are considered optional since they are meant to fulfill one's desires (*kamya*), while some are obligatory and should be performed as part of one's duty (dharma).

The Vedic tradition had an ambivalent attitude towards Vedic sacrifices. While some schools argued that the sole purpose of the *Vedas* was performing sacrifices, in some *Upanishads*, like the *Katha Upanishad*, we notice certain pessimism towards empty ritualism.

The most common methods of worship practiced currently in Hinduism are listed below. Their practice is rooted in the past.

While they may present some degree of sophistication in their execution, due to the introduction of modern instruments and methods of communication, such as the use of loud speakers, tape recorders, televisions or other gadgets, each has a long history and significance of its own. It is also now possible to worship the deities remotely by paying nominal fees to the temple authorities and submitting personal information about the worshippers and their family background.

Daily sacrifices

The daily sacrifices are obligatory for the householders. As per the law books of Hinduism, those who take up the duties of a householder (*grihastha*) have to live for others, not for themselves. They should live their lives in the service of others as a service to God and as part of their obligatory duty to uphold *dharma*.

The world does not belong to us. We do not own the bodies, which we inhabit as souls, although we may develop deep attachment to them. Whatever we do and accumulate in this world belongs to God.

Hence, householders are expected to live with humility and perform their five daily sacrifices every day, namely sacrifice to God, to gods, to ancestors, to human beings and to all creatures. They may be performed ritually, symbolically or actually helping others so that the idea of sacrifice is fully expressed through their actions.

The *grihyasutras* also prescribe morning and evening rites to be performed by both students and householders to the Sun (*surya*) and fire (*agni*) gods.

Domestic worship

The most common form of worship practiced in Hindu households is known as *puja*, in which each deity who is worshipped is invited to descend into an image or statue and treated as a guest in the house with utmost respect.

It usually starts with a decision or intention (*samkapam*) to perform the ritual and follows a predictable course. In the simplest forms of worship, the worshippers light a candle or a lamp, make a few offerings of food and submit their prayers and respects to the deity.

The most elaborate method involves making sixteen kinds of services (*upcaras*), which are usually accorded in Hindu families to a visiting guest.

The scriptures compare a guest to God and God to a guest. Honoring guests and treating them with respect is a householder's obligatory duty.

The same courtesy is extended to God when He is invited into the house during worship.

The sixteen services rendered to God are:

1. Prayerful invitation to the deity (*dhyanam* or *avahnam*)
2. Offering a seat (*asanam*) with a welcome prayer (*swagatam*)
3. Washing the feet (*padyam*)
4. Washing the mouth and hands (*arghyam*)
5. Offering water (*acamaniyam*) or a sweet drink (*madhuparkam*),
6. Bathing (*snanam*)
7. Clothing (*vastram*)
8. Wearing sacred thread (yajnopavitam)
9. Applying perfume (*gandham*)
10. Offering flowers (*pushpam*) with eulogy (*astotram*)
11. Offering incense (*dhupam*)
12. Showing light (*dipam*)
13. Offering food (*naivedyam*)
14. Serving betel-nut (*tambulam*)
15. Obeisance with camphor light (*karpura-nirajanam*)
16. Prostration (*namaskaram*), auspicious prayer (*mangalasasanam*) and send-off (*samarpanam*)

It is also customary on the part of worshippers to perform in the end expiatory rites or prayers seeking forgiveness of the deity for any shortcomings on their part in worshipping Him. After the ritual is concluded the remains of the sacrificial food (*naivedyam*) is distributed among the visitors as God's grace (*prasadam*).

Temple worship

In the households, God is worshipped as a guest. In the temples, He is worshipped as the Lord of all. In the presence of the chief deity, in the sanctum sanctorum, the worshippers become subjects while the deity becomes their benefactor and well-wisher.

Visiting temples gives the devotees a rare opportunity to see the deities in their own abode, just as they exist in heaven, and in full regalia, attended and surrounded by a retinue of priests and dutiful servants.

Here God is the Lord, the King and everyone else His worshipper or servant. In the temple premises, He receives the honors and respect due to the Lord of the house.

The idols installed in the temples are treated as the living incarnations of the deities in image form (*arca*).

Each temple is a universe in itself. God is its Lord (*Isvara*). When you enter it, you enter into His Abode. Visiting a temple and standing in the presence of the chief deity is more or less a ritual enactment of entering the Abode of God after death and standing in His presence.

Except in some temples of *Siva*, where direct worship is allowed, ritual worship in the temples is generally done by priests who are well versed in the scriptures.

They perform the rituals strictly according to either Vedic or Agamic rites. Most of them, at least in the old temples, are appointed to the position on hereditary basis.

The temple rituals and services fall mainly into two categories, those initiated by the temple administration as part of regular service due to the deities and those performed at the request of devotees, usually for a fee. The priests offer several daily services to the deities installed in the premises from early morning until midnight.

Every day in the early morning before the sunrise, the priests and even devotees wake up the deities with prayers and supplications. They bathe them, clothe them, serve them food, offer their prayers and worship them until evening. Finally, at the end of the day, they retire them to bed and allow them to rest. When they are resting, no one disturbs them.

On occasions, the gods are also honored with festivities, special ceremonies and public processions during which they are carried in special carriages and chariots through main thoroughfares.

The temples also serve as spiritual centers. They offer several ancillary services to the devotees to inculcate in them religious feelings and uphold dharma. Many educational, religious and social welfare institutions are funded by the revenues generated by them.

Visiting temples is not an obligatory duty, but considered auspicious and purificatory. It is like paying a visit to God personally to express one's love and devotion or find an opportunity to serve other devotees.

Sacrifices

Sacrificial ceremonies (*yajnas*) are central to Vedic religion and by default to Hinduism. They are performed both physically and mentally as per the injunctions provided in the *Vedas* for the benefit of the patrons (*yajman*) who sponsor them and for the sake of gods who depend upon humans for food. They are performed strictly according to the procedure and the code of conduct prescribed in the *Vedas* and the *Srauta Sastras*. One or more priests or groups of priests participate in these ceremonies.

The sacrificial ceremonies are very structured and little is left to imagination. During their performance, the officiating priests make offerings to different deities chanting hymns under the watchful guidance of a head priest, known as Brahman. The offerings consist of various types of grains, clarified butter, cooked food, seeds, firewood and other ritual materials. With chants and incantations, they invoke the gods seeking peace, protection, progeny and prosperity. In these ceremonies, the gods are worshipped ritually and symbolically but idols are not used.

The most common type of sacrifice is the domestic sacrifice. It is performed by householders in their own dwellings, pouring oblations into the domestic fire kept specifically for the purpose. In a more elaborate version, the worshippers set up three to five fires and pour offerings into them chanting hymns addressed to gods such as *Agni, Indra, Varuna, Vayu* and *Mitra*.

Some sacrificial ceremonies are also performed on a large scale in public for the welfare of the patrons, the community and the world in general. Such sacrificial ceremonies may last from a few hours to several days or even months. The altars for these sacrifices are built according to specific geometric patterns. Their construction may take months since the bricks used in them have to be made according to specifications and installed on specific dates and the rituals itself may have to be performed in stages over a period.

Currently, the sacrificial ceremonies are not the preferred method of worship. The complexity involved in performing them, the costs, lack of knowledge and the decreasing numbers of qualified priests who can perform them effectively are few reasons for this decline.

Samskaras

In Hinduism, sacraments (*samskaras*) are meant to celebrate certain important events in life, starting from conception until birth. Most of them are gender and caste specific.

They are performed to mark the progress of an individual upon earth. They add structure and purpose to human life and remind the faithful their obligatory duties upon earth by which they can prepare for their future births or liberation.

Some important sacraments performed in Hindu households are listed below.

1. Ceremony for the conception of a child in the family
2. Ceremony seeking the birth of a male child performed during the third month of pregnancy
3. Ceremony celebrating the birth of a child
4. Name giving ceremony
5. Ceremony at the end of first six months after a child's birth
6. Hair cutting ceremony
7. Initiation ceremony (*upanayana*) to mark the twice born status of a child and the beginning of formal education
8. Marriage ceremony, starting from the time the marriage is fixed until the marriage is consummated
9. Rites associated with the marriage life for the welfare of the couple.
10. House warming ceremony
11. Funeral rites to mark the death of an individual and facilitate the journey of the soul to the ancestral world

These sacraments require time and effort to perform. The method and the manner in which they are performed vary from region to region and caste to caste. They also cost considerable sums of money and put severe financial burden upon the families.

The sacramental ceremonies are caste-specific and obligatory only certain types of people. Hence, not all perform or participate in them uniformly. The birth, name giving, initiation, house warming, marriage and funeral ceremonies are the most common.

Other methods of worship

Apart from the methods discussed so far, devotees may worship God in other ways also, either externally or internally or in both ways, for material wellbeing or for the transformation of the mind and body and liberation. Their continued practice leads to inner awakening and self-absorption.

The earliest form of internal worship was *tapas*, in which the devotees practiced austerities to convert their internal bodily heat into spiritual energy. The methods of classical yoga seem to have incorporated some of its essential principles and practices.

The *Puranas* list nine forms of devotion to God as mentioned below.

- Listening to religious discourses and stories about God from the scriptures (*sravana*)
- Singing devotional songs and prayers (*kirtana*)
- Remembering the name of God (*smarana*)
- Serving at the feet of God (*padasevana*)
- Worshipping God ritually (*archana*)
- Prostrating before an image of God (*vandana*)
- Thinking and acting like a servant of God (*dasya*)
- Cultivating friendliness towards God (*sakhya*)
- Surrendering to God (*atma nivedana*)

The *Siva Purana* suggests that the symbol of *Siva* (*sivalingam*) should be worshipped ritually in 21 different ways, namely *dhyana, avahana, asana, padya, arghya, achamaniya, abhisheka, vastra, bhasma, gandha, akshata, pushpa, bilva, dhupa, dipa, naivedya, tambula, mahanirajana, mantrapushpa, namaskara* and *prardhana*. There are also rules concerning which type of *sivalingams* should be worshipped by the devotees.

The Devi *Bhagavatam* suggests that one should practice external worship of the Goddess until the mind is stabilized in the contemplation of God. Then one should practice internal worship.

The *Saiva Siddhanta* school recommends four methods of worship to attain liberation, namely *charya* (religious and community service), *kriya* (selfless devotional service), *yoga* (postures, meditation and contemplation), and *jnana* (pursuit of knowledge). Of them, the last is considered the best.

Apart from the methods we discussed so far, the following are also the recognized forms of divine worship in Hinduism. They serve the same purpose as the practices we listed above, namely inculcating faith and devotion and strengthening divine qualities.

- *Japa* in which the names of God or sacred mantras are chanted repeatedly
- *Karmayoga* in which actions are performed selflessly and without desires as an offering to God
- *Jnanayoga* in which knowledge of the Self and Brahman are pursued through self-study or with the help of a guru
- *Atmayoga* in which God is worshipped internally through concentration, meditation and self-absorption until the mind becomes still and stable
- *Sanyasayoga* in which desires and worldly pleasures are completely renounced and one lives for the sake of Self alone.

Ritual worship is not confined to the worship of gods and goddesses alone. Hinduism has incorporated the ancient practices of worshipping trees, plants, animals such as bulls and serpents, rivers, lakes and mountains.

In the past, people often indulged in animal and human sacrifices in some extreme methods of ritual worship to declare their faith or appease certain fierce deities. Animal sacrifices are still in vogue. However presently most Hindus are averse to them.

The main purpose of worship in Hinduism is liberation and stabilizing the mind in the contemplation of God. It is way to establish communication with the deities and seek their help to overcome problems, ward off adversity or seek guidance. By worshipping them we remain divine centered and keep our minds filled with the thoughts of God and the importance of practicing virtue and *dharma*. In accomplishing this goal, Hinduism offers many choices and methods of worship in deference to one's essential nature and past *karmas*.

The Hindu Way of Life

"The Hindu man drinks religiously, sleeps religiously, walks religiously, marries religiously, robs religiously." - Swami Vivekananda

Hinduism is frequently described as a way of life, because its beliefs and practices are deeply interwoven in the life of a Hindu the way the nerves and blood vessels are interwoven in our bodies.

It is very difficult to separate religion from the life of a devout Hindu. Both are inseparable. Both complement each other. Both exist because of each other and both would lose their meaning and significance without each other.

Religion is at the center of living for a devout Hindu who uses his religious knowledge to regulate his life and achieve its ultimate aim, which is liberation or establish a firm basis for good life in his next birth.

The reference here is to a devout Hindu because Hindus are a heterogeneous mixture of individuals ranging from the deeply irreligious and perverted to the deeply religious and sincere. For the irreligious, religion does not matter and for the deeply religious, it is everything. A devout Hindu falls somewhere in between, leaning to the side of the deeply religious.

The very act of living in Hinduism, from the time is one born until one is cremated, is regulated by the knowledge enshrined in the scriptures. A devout Hindu uses the beliefs and practices of his religion both consciously and unconsciously to abide by the laws of God and ensure that through his careless actions he would not endanger his spiritual and material wellbeing or that of his family and ancestors.

In the following article, we will examine why Hinduism is regarded as a way of life and how faith is deeply infused into the lives and actions of its adherents, guiding them closely.

In Hinduism, religion (*dharma*) influences the way people live and view themselves. The very act of living is regarded as an obligatory duty and an opportunity to fulfill the aims of creation and participate in God's eternal *dharma*. Tradition holds that religious duty (*dharma*) is the primary aim (*purusharthas*) of human life since it is the foundation upon which one develops the wisdom and discretion to pursue wealth (*artha*) and happiness (*kama*) without compromising the chances liberation (*moksha*).

What distinguishes human beings from animals and others is their knowledge of duties and obligations (*dharma*) to God and creation, abiding by His eternal laws as enshrined in the scriptures. The knowledge is given to them in trust by God Himself with an injunction to preserve it and promote it in total surrender so that they may play their dutiful roles in preserving and promoting peace and harmony upon earth and ensuring the order and regularity of the world.

For Hindus, religion offers the knowledge to perform their expected duties in God's creation and live in peace. It acts as their inseparable companion, guide and philosopher for the duration of their lives enabling them to uplift themselves from the bondage and illusion to which they are subject.

However modern or advanced they may be, whether they believe in God or many gods, religion is deeply rooted in their consciousness and holds its sway upon their thinking and attitude. They cannot escape from it easily even if they choose subsequently to follow another religion.

The religious lives of faithful Hindus, who take their obligatory duties seriously, begin from the time they are born, as if they have come into the world with the burden of their past to fulfill the promises they made to themselves or others in their past lives. Whatever may be their background, their belief in *karma* puts upon them a sense of responsibility to carry forward their family traditions and fulfill their obligations to their parents, relations, ancestors and others.

From then on until they depart from here, they are expected to fulfill their obligations dutifully towards themselves and others during the four stages (*ashramas*) of human life, namely the age of celibacy, adulthood, retirement and renunciation. They cannot avoid or abandon their obligatory duties arising from their birth and the vocations they choose, because their present lives are but continuation of their past ones. They can only ignore them at the cost of their spiritual and material wellbeing.

No one who believes in the ideals of *dharma* and *karma* wants to leave the world with a sense of hopelessness. That awareness and sense of duty remains firmly etched in the minds of the faithful until the end, influencing their thinking and actions, helping them to adjust to the demands of religious life for the sake of their future and accepting their suffering as part of their karmic burden and the means to atone for their wrongdoings.

In Hinduism, the practice of religion is not separate from the act of living. Living is the means, an opportunity, to practice religion and worship God. It is also an opportunity to fulfill one's obligations towards the heavenly beings and the rest of creation.

The sacrifices are meant for the worshippers to nourish gods, ancestors, spirits, and other living creatures and play their dutiful roles as servants of God.

However, rituals are not the only means to worship God. One does it by performing one's duty also. The duties serve as a reminder that religion should not be practiced in specific places or at specific times, but constantly in the very act of living, making one's life a sacrificial offering to God and a means to worship Him in every possible way by doing one's part.

The spirit is whatever is ours belongs to Him and should be offered to Him only. Those who take what does not belong to them incur the sin of theft. Therefore, the moral is, do not hold on to anything. Give everything, at least mentally, so that you do not have to carry the burden of your actions to your future lives.

Whatever you do, the will and the energy to do it comes to you from God and therefore the credit of it and the result of it should go to Him only.

A devout Hindu, well versed in the scriptures, knows that God does not exist in temples and sacred places only. He is present everywhere, in every aspect of our lives, perceptions and experiences. Whatever you interact with is an aspect of God only. Whatever happens to you is a manifestation of God only. Going to the temples is a good practice, but it is not the only way to worship.

God does not exist in temples only, in a particular place or a sacred altar. He exists everywhere and He can be approached in many ways. He can be worshipped not only by performing sacrificial ceremonies and rituals, but also by the very process of living one's life and discharging ones responsibilities towards oneself, one's family, society and religion.

If you have the discretion, you can convert every action of yours into a sacrificial offering and make your life one continuous sacrifice.

The life that we live on earth is divine. Every aspect of it is infused with the presence of God. Hidden behind the diversity and the illusion of phenomena is His golden and immortal presence.

If we are clever and careful enough in our perceptions and observation, we can see His footprints everywhere, and follow them all the way to His Abode.

As we learn from the *Bhagavadgita*, to achieve liberation we do not have to abandon our duties or retire into a forest. True renunciation is renunciation of desires and desire for the fruit of our actions, not actions themselves. You can practice renunciation by cultivating detachment and surrendering all your actions to God as an offering without desiring their fruit. With right discrimination and detachment, we can use every opportunity available to us in our lives to find God and worship Him. We can remove the very causes that bind us to purify us and transform us, and establish a strong foundation on a lasting basis for our spiritual growth and eventual liberation.

Thus for devout Hindus, religion is a way a life, as life offers endless opportunities to overcome their ignorance and delusion to escape from the mortal world. By remembering God constantly, offering Him all their actions, cultivating purity and virtue, making Him the center of their lives, worshipping Him through knowledge and actions, they fill their minds and bodies with the presence of God and sanctify their lives in the service of God.

From them we learn that we can use the pairs of opposites and the dualities of life to cultivate equanimity, sameness and stability. By withdrawing from the phenomenal world, without abandoning it, restraining our senses, we can experience oneness with ourselves and stabilize our minds in the contemplation of God.

We also learn from them that God is not just an old father figure living somewhere in the heavenly regions. It is His symbolic representation only. As the *Isa Upanishad* declares, the whole universe is His abode. He is present everywhere.

As the Lord of the universe, He is the source of all actions, knowledge and abundance. He is present right here, in every aspect of creation, in our minds and bodies and at the very center of our lives and actions.

Since all this belongs to Him, we have the right to perform actions, but not to seek their fruit. Performing actions thus dutifully, we should live our lives upon earth. Then, actions will not lead to our bondage or suffering, but to our transformation and liberation.

Life is an opportunity to bring the illuminating and liberating power of God into our lives and infuse our minds and bodies with His unlimited brilliance and intelligence.

It is an opportunity to cultivate divine qualities and grow spiritually into the likeness of God. It is an opportunity to overcome our ignorance and delusion and know the truth about ourselves.

It is the only opportunity we have to return to our source and live with absolute freedom as eternal and indestructible beings of light and endless delight.

Thus, for Hindus performing their duties with detachment and as an offering to God or worshipping Him in temples and through rituals are karmically the same and lead to the same end.

Self-realization can be achieved by not only renouncing the world and performing austerities, but also living religiously, spiritually, austerely and dutifully like a lotus leaf in a pond.

If we live with a sense of responsibility for the sake of our souls rather than for our minds and bodies, every selfless action we perform in our lives takes us forward in the direction of God.

The idea that religion and living are inseparable is well evident in the manner in which devotees in Hinduism go about their lives and actions. We learn from them that actions and duties are means for wealth and happiness as well as for liberation.

Life offers limitless opportunities to facilitate our spiritual growth. Through actions, you can accomplish your life's goals as well as fulfill your obligations to express your love and devotion to God.

Through actions, you can show your commitment to God and His divine law. You can show this attitude in every aspect of your life, including the practice of arts and crafts.

In Hinduism, art is traditionally practiced as a means to discipline one's mind and body, practice concentration and contemplation and express one's love and devotion to God, the true Creator.

Creation is a form of sacrifice. In artistic endeavor, you spend your energies and artistic talents selflessly and sacrificially to bring happiness and enjoyment to others in whom God is present as their individual souls, Witness and ultimate Enjoyer.

Like God, by performing an act of creation, creating forms, an artist realizes the illusory nature of creation and overcomes his attachment to the life he creates through his desire-ridden actions.

It is the same conviction, the same philosophy, the same approach, which prompts a yogi of dutiful action (karmayogi) to perform his duties with detachment and as a sacrificial offering.

For a Hindu, his present life is but a continuation of his previous ones. Each life is an opportunity for the beings to start all over again to correct their past mistakes, purify their minds and bodies and redeem themselves from their past mistakes and persistent mental impressions (*citta samskaras*) that bind them to the world and prevent them from attaining perfection.

The present life is a precious gift, a blessing from God who is always benevolent and forgiving and who does not want to condemn us forever into an eternal hell.

It is a reminder that we are the creators of our own lives and destinies through the actions we perform, decisions we make and the consequences we reap.

If we want to change our lives, we have an opportunity right now to change our destinies by changing the way we live, think and act.

The philosophy that life is an obligatory duty and a sacrifice makes Hinduism reverberant, practical and relevant to human life and liberation.

It acknowledges the omnipresence of God and His pervasive role in our lives.

It brings Him directly into the center of our lives and puts us in a direct relationship with Him.

It integrates religion with life and life with God. It connects the mind and body to the Self and the Self to its source. It offers an opportunity to the devotees to cross the ocean of life and reach the shore of freedom without being swallowed by the evils of sin or the excesses of life.

For a typical Hindu, religion offers solace as well as salvation.

It is the means to self-expression and an opportunity to worship God variously and find Him in life as well in stillness.

The Role of Dharma in Hinduism

It is difficult to define *dharma* since it has different meanings in different contexts and encompasses a wide range of ideas related to religion, religiosity, duty, divinity, morality and virtue.

There is no word in English or in any other language, equivalent to *dharma*, which conveys its meaning adequately.

To understand it means to understand Hinduism and its subtle nuances.

If you have understood it without conflict or confusion, it is a sign that you have reached a critical stage in your spiritual progress on the path of liberation and understood the true meaning of duty.

In a broader sense all religious knowledge, laws and code of conduct regarding one's religious and spiritual duties constitute *dharma*.

In a narrow sense, it may mean religious duty, obligatory duty, moral percept, usage, practice, custom, conduct, caste rules, virtue, righteousness, justice, piety, religion and sacrifice.

In a philosophical sense, it means essential nature, inherent property, natural disposition or distinguishing feature.

For example, the *dharma* (nature) of fire is to burn, water to flow, earth to bear, wind to blow and space to support creation and the movement of sound.

Dharma also is about how to live and work for one's salvation by following a certain code of conduct or cultivating a particular natural disposition (which is *sattva* in this case). Hence, it is generally understood as religion itself.

Thus, we have *Hindu dharma, Buddh dharma, Jain Dharma and Sikh Dharma*. They not only refer to religious knowledge but also the laws pertaining to the code of conduct and the means to liberation.

The concept of *dharma* implies that conduct and duty are the same, and living and duty are equally the same. Living in a world that belongs to God, you have an obligation to live according to the will of God, as He would intend you to live.

Knowledge of *dharma* is available to us through divine revelations found in the scriptures such as the *Vedas* and the *Bhagavadgita* and through law books called *dharma sastras*, created by men of great knowledge and intelligence, such as *Manu, Apastamba, Gautama, Vashista and Baudhayana,*.

The *Vedas* are considered the heard ones (*srutis*) because their source is Brahman, in contrast to the law books, which are considered memorial works (*smritis*) because they are primarily human compositions or scholarly works based upon the standards and percepts found in the *Vedas*.

They suggest the laws and the ideal code of conduct by which human beings should regulate their lives upon earth virtuously, perform their obligatory duties and earn good merit so that they can achieve either immortality or a good birth in their next lives.

God as the upholder of dharma

While the law books are human compositions based upon the *Vedas*, the primary source of all knowledge concerning *dharma*, including the *Vedas*, is God Himself.

He is *dharma* personified (*dharma-devata*) since He creates, upholds and regulates *dharma* through His innumerable forms and manifestations.

He has His own *dharma* (essential duty), which is to create the worlds and preserve them until the end of the time even though He has no particular desire or interest to achieve anything or attain anything. He does it as His obligatory duty (*dharma*), with detachment, indifference and impartiality, to keep the worlds going in their predictable ways.

To preserve His creation and maintain the order and regularity of the worlds, He establishes code of conduct for all. He also establishes certain inviolable universal laws, such as the laws of Nature, the laws of *karma* (action) and the laws of morality and religious conduct, which He enforces strictly as the Lord of the Universe (*Isvara*) to ensure that things move in predictable ways.

He also formulates and reveals through the *Vedas* and other means the duties, roles, natural disposition (*dharmas*) and proper code of conduct for the beings, the worlds and things He manifests, so that they can stay in their respective spheres, do their part in the Creation and contribute to the order and regularity of the worlds.

He is thus the creator, protector and upholder of *dharma*, which He sometimes conceals and sometimes reveals according to His will. When He conceals, delusion, ignorance and chaos prevail; when He reveals, order, knowledge and liberation follow.

Whenever the order of the worlds is disturbed or when evil forces gains ascendance and create chaos, He responds as part of His duty, either directly through incarnations or indirectly through His aspects and emanations, to destroy evil, protect the weak and the pious and restore order.

Through His actions and manifestations, He sets an example to the beings upon earth how they should live, doing their duties, and work for their liberation.

Dharma as the moral compass

One of the misconceptions of Hinduism is that since it lacks centralized authority people can choose their own code of conduct and live in their own ways.

While it is true that Hinduism gives its practitioners immense freedom to choose their paths and practice religion according to their respective beliefs, it does not discount the importance of virtue and morality in their lives and liberation.

It is wrong to believe that everything done in the name of religion is justified and approved by the tradition. While it is true that the ancient law-books have fallen into disuse longtime ago and no unanimity exists among scholars as to what constitutes the right code of conduct and right methods of worship, the scriptures constantly remind us that we can only ignore at our peril the importance of discretion (*buddhi*) and *karma* in our lives and destinies.

People not only have freedom, but also responsibility. They may follow their own paths, but they have to abide by the rules and restraints that lead to purity and divine qualities.

They have to fear *karma* and the consequences of making wrong choices.

They have to pay attention to their conscience, sense of morality, scriptural injunctions and the lessons they learn from life.

A few hundred years ago thieves, dacoits and robbers used to worship *Kali* and seek her blessings to commit terrible crimes. Some of them even used to perform human sacrifices on a regular basis to appease the goddess. They are tamasic methods of worship invented by perverted minds out of ignorance, delusion and egoism to justify despicable acts. One should be aware of their influence and guard oneself against the confusion and suffering arising from them.

According to our scriptures, we are responsible for our actions and choices. In other words, they enjoin us to live responsibly and dutifully and use out time upon earth in living and realizing the ideals of dharma.

Our actions must be in harmony with the norms and laws upheld by God Himself through His actions and manifestations.

They must promote morality (*dharma*), peace and happiness, order and regularity (*rta*, and lead one towards truth, light, immortality, stability, predominance of sattva, perfection in yoga, knowledge and wisdom.

Contrary to the opinion held by some misguided and miscreant people, Hinduism does not support sexual promiscuity or perversion. Sex is meant primarily for procreation, not for enjoyment. Sexual pleasure (*kama*) is one of the four aims of human life, but it should be pursued as duty (*dharma*) according to the establish norms of human conduct (*dharma*) and moral percepts (*dharma*) and should result in liberation (*moksha*) rather than bondage and suffering.

Moral foundation is very important. It is the basis of every action, aim and goal. Since human beings are subject to ignorance and delusion, they are vulnerable to the evils and temptations of worldly life. Hence, they should resort to *dharma*, the law of God, and use it as a guiding principle to make wise decisions and avoid negative consequences.

A devotee on the path of liberation has many opportunities to familiarize himself with his religious duties and the approved code of conduct.

He can learn about them from scriptures, teachers, family traditions, society and from learned people. He may also learn about them from the suffering of others or from his own suffering.

The scriptures make it abundantly clear that whoever indulges in wrongful and evil actions has to suffer from their consequences in either this life or in future lives.

The epics and the *Puranas* draw a clear distinction between good and evil so that we may learn from the examples they provide about the value of virtue and good conduct. They repeatedly illustrate the consequences of good and evil actions and the need to follow the righteous path and abide by the divine laws.

They show how demons (*asuras*) and wicked people perish in the end when they indulge in delusional and demonic acts and defy the laws established by God, while those who follow Him and adhere to His law are protected and led on the path to salvation.

Through characterization, legends, stories, aphorisms, anecdotes and religious conversations, they appeal to our moral sense and ethical values to lead virtuous and divine-centered lives and escape from the cycle of births and deaths.

Thus, Hinduism is an austere religion in which moral foundation is the basis for fulfilling one's spiritual and material goals. The moral percepts do not have to be common for all, but they must be validated by the scriptures and practiced for achieving liberation.

In this regard, the scriptures are very clear.

Dharma comes before everything else.

It is the basis of life upon earth. It is the foundation, upon which every other aim in life should be fulfilled.

It is vital for the progression of life upon earth from a primitive state of ignorance and delusion to an advanced state of knowledge and enlightenment. When it declines, chaos prevails and evil reins in the world.

Therefore, it is the duty of each individual to live according to the highest ideals suggested in the scriptures and perform actions selflessly and sacrificially to protect and preserve one's *dharma*.

If people fail to uphold their religious duties, the world will fall into evil ways and they commit the sin of following evil.

Hinduism is about our duty towards God

Hinduism is originally known as *Sanatana-dharma*. *Sanatana* means eternal. *Dharma* means religious and moral duty.

What it means is that *dharma* is eternal and its practice in creation is intended to be continuous, not only by God, who is its original source, but also by everyone else, including gods, human beings and others.

Whatever condition or situation may arise in life, our commitment to it and our obligation to follow it should never weaken.

We have to reflect it and infuse it in every aspect of our lives and in every possible way so that in upholding and practicing it we remain on the side of God and earn the right to enter His Abode.

In other words, we cannot be selective in our practice of *dharma*, virtuous in the temples and selfish in our actions or dealings with others.

We have to practice it continuously, even if it means suffering and sacrifice on our part, and perform our dutiful roles in creation in fulfilling its objectives.

When we live in the house of God, which is what this universe is, we have to abide by His laws and do our part in keeping His House in good order. While we enjoy His hospitality, we have to live responsibly, without causing inconvenience to others who also live there. The obligations and duties are eternal, since we are eternal souls. We have duties here upon earth as bound souls and duties in heaven as free souls. We cannot ignore them at any time while we live in the House of God.

Dharma as a way of life

This brings us to another important concept that *dharma* is a way of life. In Hinduism, virtue is an integral part of life and the highest virtue is living dutifully. You are sent to this world to perform certain duties, and by performing them, you keep the world in good order. If you do not perform them, you will incur the sin of causing disorder and suffer from the consequences.

You are not here to enjoy life or pursue your selfish goals, but play your dutiful role in the divine scheme of things. Your duties and obligations never end. As long as you live upon earth, you should keep doing them and honor the code of conduct that is expected of you. Performing your duty is the highest virtue; and what your duties are you will know through discretion, studying the scriptures and practicing yoga.

Living virtuously is part of our moral duty upon earth. It is true that many Hindus today do not care about virtue; but tradition holds virtue as a very important component of human conduct without which human beings cannot bring light and wisdom into their lives and experience peace, and contribute to the peace and happiness of others. You cannot be on the side of God without being godly; it is as simple as that.

Since human beings are vulnerable to evil and demonic influences, they should cultivate discretion (*buddhi*) to know the right from wrong and their obligatory duties. Knowledge of *dharma* available in the scriptures helps them in this regard. They should study them so that they can overcome their delusion and practice their duties without confusion, egoism and selfishness.

Thus, for devout Hindus the scriptures are valuable sources of divine guidance and the means to know their duties and live virtuously, honoring the divine laws and playing their dutiful roles. With the guidance they provide, they can live dutifully, performing their obligatory duties, knowing the difference between action and inaction, and between right action and wrong action, and without inviting their consequences.

Dharma according to the law books

The law books (*dharma sastras*) provide information on how those in positions of authority should regulate society, establish law and order, and punish the violations and how people should conduct themselves in their daily lives, perform their obligatory duties, adhere to social norms, atone for sin and remain committed to righteousness for their spiritual and material welfare.

They inform us how the worlds came into existence, how God manifested beings, what duties and roles He prescribed for them, how time progresses in different worlds, the methods of interpreting and enforcing laws, and the ways to resolve disputes and moral dilemmas.

They prescribe rules and code of conduct for students, teachers, ascetics, hermits, householders, priests, and kings according to their age, gender and caste; and guidelines for studying the Vedas, performing austerities and purification ceremonies, pursuing lawful livelihood, managing inheritance, procreation, adoption, sacrifices, criminal conduct and funeral ceremonies.

These laws are enforced partly by God Himself and partly by the collective effort of gods, *Manus*, earthly kings and rulers, the priests, and everyone else in their own specific ways.

Since the law books are human compositions, they are neither eternal nor inviolable. They are subject to decay, change and modifications. As the times change, so do the laws or our knowledge of the laws, Most of the laws prescribed in the ancient law books are now impractical and outdated. In today's context, they cannot be practiced without discretion and applying common sense and without upsetting the balance and order of society. One should therefore treat the law books as guidebooks and follow them with discretion practicing whatever principles may apply to us in the performance of our obligatory duties.

Whether we follow them or not, it is important to live virtuously, do our part in making the world a safe place and work for our salvation. While the world may change, the principles that guide our duties and responsibilities towards God and creation do not change. Whatever we do, we should not upset the balance of the world or cause pain and suffering to others. It is the most important obligatory duty we can imagine and if we adhere to it, we always remain on the path of righteousness.

Guidelines in case of ambiguity

Although the scriptures and the law books are exhaustive in prescribing guidelines and rules to deal with different situations, due to the complex nature of human life and the rapid pace at which society makes progress, we are bound to experience confusion and dilemmas about some aspects of human conduct and ethical behavior.

One of the traditional methods to deal with this problem is suggested in the *Baudhayana-sutras*. It states that first, one should rely upon the *Vedas*, then upon the scholarly works (*smritis*), then upon the knowledge and experience of adepts (*sistas*) who are well versed in the *Vedas* and scriptures (*sastras*) and who are pure in their hearts and minds, free from evil qualities.

In drawing conclusions, the adepts may rely upon the testimony of the *Vedas* (*sabda*) or the inferences (*anumana*) drawn from them or upon their own experience (*pratyaksha*). If they are still unable to settle the dispute even after all this, then the matter should be referred to an assembly of at least ten blameless people, who have the knowledge of the *Vedas*, sacrificial rituals, *Vedangas* and *dharma sastras*. One may also take the help of five, three, two or even one person of pure mind to determine truth.

When there is ambiguity, the best course to follow is to verify the *Vedas* first and see whether an answer is available in them. If it does not work, one may refer to other reliable sources such as the *Brahma sutras, the Bhagavadgita*, law-books, the *Agamas*, the *Tantras*, the epics, the *Puranas and* the *Vedangas*. If one is still unsure, one may see whether any information can be gleaned from the lives of saints and seers or their teachings. If no solution is still forthcoming, one may consult those who are well versed in the scriptures and known for their knowledge and integrity. Finally, if everything fails, one should rely upon one's own discretion (*buddhi*), intuition or divine guidance.

We know that when actions are performed without egoism and desires and without seeking their fruit, the consequences will not affect you. Therefore, it is always better to perform selfless actions and in cases of ambiguity follow our conscience. Moral dilemmas are mainly for worldly people who cannot overcome their desires and who cannot surrender to God completely. To those who renounce desires, practice detachment, cultivate sameness (*samatvam*) towards the pairs of opposites, surrender to God and fill their minds with His thoughts (*daivatma*), embodying virtue, duty and morality (*dharma*), the law books and our code of conduct serve little purpose. Whatever they do and follow is a moral percept or a law in itself.

Essential aspects of dharma

The practice of *dharma* involves acceptance of certain essential beliefs and adherence to prescribed duties and code of conduct. Human birth is a precious opportunity to attain liberation because human beings alone possess intelligence to accomplish the goal. A being attains human birth only after many lives. Even gods do not have the opportunity although they are immortals endowed with intelligence.

Human beings have the opportunity because they are mortals, subject to change and purification. They can work for their liberation by practicing *dharma*, cultivating purity (*sattva*) and acknowledging their spiritual identity.

The following are some important duties prescribed for them, which they can practice to achieve peace, stability and liberation.

Duty towards God: The *Vedas* and other scriptures unequivocally declare that God is the source of all. He upholds *dharma*. Human beings have an obligation to participate in creation in the service of God and uphold *dharma* at their level, performing their duties with detachment as an offering to Him, living virtuously, honoring the social order, and performing sacrifices to nourish the gods who are dependent upon us. By serving God and obeying His will, they fulfill their role as the dutiful servants of God.

Duty towards the scriptures: The *Vedas* are God's revelation. They are eternal and contain inviolable truths about God, creation and our duties and responsibilities. We have an obligation to uphold the sacred scriptures and practice the knowledge they contain. We also have an obligation to preserve them for future generations, imparting them to deserving students and protecting them from contamination. Through self-study, recitation, and serving knowledgeable people, we should also use the knowledge hidden in our scriptures for our own liberation.

Duty towards gods: The gods are created for the welfare of the world. They assist God in upholding and maintaining the order and regularity of the worlds. They are vital to our spiritual and material wellbeing. The gods also depend upon us for their nourishment. Therefore, we have an obligatory duty to perform sacrifices and nourish them through our offerings. We also have an obligation to remain on the side of gods in their battle against demonic beings.

Duty towards sacrifices: According to the *Vedas*, sacrifice is the source of all existence. Creation emerged out of a grand sacrifice performed by God. Through sacrifices, we establish control over the elements, nourish gods, fulfill our desires and attain peace and happiness. Through sacrificial actions the order and regularity of the world is preserved. We have a duty to perform sacrificial actions either ritually or spiritually for the sake of our welfare and the welfare of the worlds.

Duty towards knowledge: We are born in ignorance and delusion. It is the cause of our bondage. A human being is redeemed by knowledge alone. What distinguishes us from animals is our knowledge. We have therefore an obligation to cultivate knowledge through study and recitation of the scriptures to overcome our ignorance and delusion.

Duty towards family: Your family plays a vital role in shaping your life and destiny and depending upon your role and status in the family, you have certain obligations towards your family members as well as your ancestors. Each member in the family has to ensure its wellbeing and continuity by performing his or her obligatory duties. A father has obligations towards gods, his wife, children, ancestors, guests, friends, relations and the world in general. A mother has similar obligations. Children have an obligation to respect their parents, elders and teachers and educate themselves until they are fit enough to become householders. The family as a whole has an obligation towards other families, society, God and the world in general

Duty towards ourselves: Individually, we have a duty and an obligation to work for our physical and spiritual wellbeing and our liberation. For that, we have to purify our minds and bodies, practice different methods of yoga described in the scriptures to cultivate purity, detachment, equanimity, sameness, intelligence and perform selfless actions in such a manner that we do not incur *karma*. We have to accept our spiritual identity and retrain our minds and bodies to experience self-absorption. We have an obligation to liberate the Self that resides in our bodies through righteous actions, knowledge and wisdom.

Duty towards society. We have an obligation towards society and the world in general because we depend upon them and they are part of God's creation. In truth, they are His aspects only. We have to serve the world and society by helping others, upholding the social and moral orders, performing daily sacrifices, meeting our obligations, promoting virtue and spreading the knowledge of the scriptures for the benefit of those who seek liberation.

Freedom with sense of duty and responsibility

Hinduism may suggest complex and even contradictory methods of worship and approaches to God, but its commitment to *dharma* is supremely one pointed. It gives immense freedom to the faithful, but puts a lot of responsibility and obligations upon them to live in the service of God and for the preservation of life and virtue upon earth. It neither advocates nor upholds philosophies and practices such as atheism and demonic-worship, which contradict the ideals of *dharma*. It projects *dharma* as the primary goal of human beings, since it is vital to their survival and that of the world.

People act according to their knowledge and ignorance, predominant desires and their past life tendencies. Because of lack of knowledge, they may not perform their duties or meet their obligations. A person's faith (*dharma*) is essentially an expression and a consequence of his or her past lives and actions. Therefore, Hinduism advocates leniency and tolerance towards deluded people and their perverted methods of worship. However, it does not validate their methods of worship, reckless and egoistic behavior and demonic qualities.

From the time one is born, one lives in the service of God. This is the first lesson, which every Hindu ought to understand. Their lives are not for their sake. They have to live for the sake of others and in the service of God. They are here not to enjoy life selfishly but to fulfill their roles and obligations in the preservation of God's creation.

Even one's attempt to cultivate purity and achieve liberation is part of this duty only. Non-violence, tolerance, truthfulness, non-stealing, non-covetousness, compassion and similar virtues are important because they are vital to the preservation of life and order upon earth. Hence, they are part of our obligatory duties in preserving God's creation and ensuring its continuity.

If you are disturbing the world, disturbing others, causing them pain and injury or harm, confusing people, creating commotion and disorder in society with your actions, you must know that you are violating the abiding principles of *sanatana dharma*. You are sowing the seeds of your own spiritual destruction, ignoring your duties (*dharma*) as the preserver and upholder of the order and regularity of the world in which you live. You cannot count yourself as a practitioner of the eternal dharma.

As human beings, endowed with knowledge, intelligence and self-awareness, we have a unique opportunity to overcome our ignorance and work for our liberation. By taking shelter in *dharma* and performing our obligatory duties as an offering to God, we should accomplish this ultimate aim of human life and set an example to others to follow. We must know that our duties are part of God's duties and our right to work comes from Him only.

Protecting and upholding dharma

Protecting one's religious faith from distortion and destruction is part of one's obligatory duty upon earth. Our scriptures do not say that we should remain aloof and indifferent when the *dharma* is attacked by destructive elements and demonic people from within or without. Each individual has a duty to uphold *dharma* by practicing it and protecting it.

Our scriptures firmly declare that if you protect you *dharma*, it will protect you in return (*dharmo raksita raksitaha*). Even God responds decisively by incarnating personally or by sending an emanation when evil gains ascendance in the world.

We have a duty and responsibility to uphold our faith and protect it from its enemies. We have a duty to resist evil and keep our homes, families, the world, society and ourselves free from it.

The gods' will decline if we do not remember them or nourish them through our sacrificial actions. Our scripture will fall into disuse if we do not read them or practice them. Our world and society will fall into confusion and disorder if we ignore our duties. We contribute to our own downfall if we do not perform our dutiful roles in society or if we fall into evil ways.

In Hinduism, each individual has freedom to live according to his or her will and desires. However, if the aim is liberation, the scriptures suggest that one should live dutifully performing actions without desires and expectations, and as an offering.

Hinduism encourages the use of knowledge and discretion in choosing one's path, way of life and methods of worship. It approves neither promiscuity nor superstition nor evil and deluded methods of religious worship.

It cautions people to be aware of the dangers inherent in living upon earth and sail safely across the ocean of the phenomenal world using God as the boat and *dharma* as the rudder. You are a follower of *sanatana-dharma* only if live dutifully and selflessly.

God in Hinduism

Hindus worship many gods and goddesses.

At the same time, they also worship one Supreme God, who is considered the Supreme Self, Lord of the Universe and pure consciousness. He is worshipped variously in numerous ways, some of which are listed below.

- As one
- As many
- As Male (*purusa*) and Female (*prakriti*)
- As manifestations (*vibhutis*)
- As incarnations (*avatars*) and emanations (*amsas*)
- As an individual Self (atman)
- As the Lord of the Universe (*Isvara*)
- As the creator, preserver and destroyer
- As a personal God
- As sacred sounds (*mantras*)
- As knowledge, truth and bliss
- As the Highest Abode
- As symbols and images (*arcas*)
- As pure consciousness
- As the Manifested
- As the Unmanifested

God is extolled variously in the Hindu scriptures as Brahman, the supreme transcendental Self (*Paramatma*), the supreme Lord (*Paramesvara*), the highest Father (*Paramapita*), the Lord of the universe (*Isvara*), the great Lord (*Maheswara*), Cosmic Person (*Purusha*), Lord of opulence (*Bhagavan*), best among the Persons (*Purusottama*), the Golden Germ (*Hiranyagarbha*) and so on.

The *Vedas* affirm that God is one, but also many.

He manifests Himself in innumerable forms and shapes. Since He is without another, all diversity that is manifested in the worlds must arise from that singular source only. In no other way things can emerge in creation unless they arise from nothingness.

His One and many aspects have a purpose in creation. Although they are the same in essence, functionally they play different roles and perform different duties.

As the Universal Male (*Purusha*), He joins with Universal Mother (*Prakriti*) who is also known as Nature, Mother Goddess, Matter or Energy, and manifests numerous worlds, things and beings. With unlimited powers and just a small aspect of (*amsa*) of Him participating in creation, He upholds all the worlds, beings and manifestations (*vibhutis*).

He is one and indivisible; yet He has dual aspects. He is both transcendental and immanent, here and hereafter, and smaller than the small and larger than the large.

He is extolled as the Known and the Unknown, the Manifested and the Unmanifested, the Being and the Non-Being, and as Reality and Unreality.

His unmanifested aspect is a mystery even to the highest gods. It is hidden even from His manifested aspect. The *Bhagavadgita* declares that one should not worship God in this aspect because painful is the path for those who choose to worship Him as the Unmanifest (Ch 12.6).

God exists in all and all exist in Him. Nothing is other than Him and nothing is outside of Him. He is inexhaustible, indescribable and indefinable. Hence, the *Upanishads* suggests that we should use the "not, not" approach (*neti*) to exclude what He is not to know vaguely what He is.

Even that may not lead to definitive knowledge of Brahman. Those who think they know Him probably know Him not.

The scriptures describe Him as immortal, infinite, inexhaustible, imperishable, unknowable, absolute, pure, resplendent, supreme, transcendental, independent, and without a beginning and an end.

While He is complete, perfect, indifferent, detached, without desires and expectations, He responds readily with abundant grace (*prasada*) to the calls of His devotees and worshippers and helps them in their liberation.

The one who casts the net of illusion upon the worlds and beings is also the one who grants knowledge and wisdom and helps people to escape from the mortal world, never to return.

All the gods and goddess, things, beings and worlds are His manifestations, emanations, formations, incarnations, powers, projections and aspects only.

In His dynamic aspect, He is *Shakti* (the universal energy). As the Primal Matter and the Universal Mother, and with Her realities (*tattvas*) and modes (*gunas*), She executes His will and manifests the whole creation. She also participates in the act of preservation, renewal and rebirth, by facilitating the progression of the worlds, things and beings from one modification (*parinama*) to another until the end.

The relationship between God and humans is both personal and impersonal.

It is personal from a devotee's perspective when he or she surrenders to Him and worships Him with intense devotion.

It is impersonal from the perspective of Brahman because He is detached and free from desires and none in particular is dearer or hateful to Him. He may respond to His devotees, as part of His duty, rather than personal whim. It also becomes impersonal when devotees practice detachment and renunciation and remain equal to the pairs of opposites.

The *Bhagavadgita* (7.16) identifies four types of devotees who approach God: people in distress, seekers of knowledge, seekers of wealth, and men of wisdom. Of them, Lord Krishna declares that the last ones are the best. He deems a wise person as His very Self.

He is also equal to the offerings devotees make. It is immaterial what has been offered. The attitude with which it is offered is important. Whatever is offered to Him with love and devotion He accepts them.

People may worship Him variously, through rituals, meditation, concentration, austerities, sacrifices, domestic worship (*pooja*), visiting temples and sacred places, chanting *mantras*, singing songs, remembering His names and forms and serving others. They all are acceptable methods of worship.

The concept of monotheism is not new to Hinduism. It is as old as the *Vedas*. References to the indivisible, imperishable and mysterious God are found in the *Rigveda*. The concept is the central theme of the *Upanishads* in which God is extolled variously as *Brahman, Isvara, Hiranyagarbha, Viraj, Sat, Asat, Siva, Vishnu, Narayana* and so on.

It is wrong to assume that the Vedic people were ignorant of universal God and worshipped only lesser divinities. This is absurd argument put forward by some Christian scholars to denigrate Hinduism and present it in poorer light. The *Vedas* speak about one God manifesting variously through a universal sacrifice and individual souls returning to the same source through daily sacrifices and sacrificial actions.

The *Vedas* have four parts, each dealing with a specific subject. Of them, the first two focus on gods and rituals, and the last two on the Self and the Supreme Self. Their manifest content is ritual knowledge (*karmakanda*) but their hidden content (*jananakanda*) is about Brahman and His power to manifest and liberate.

Through the chants and the sounds hidden in the hymns, the *Vedas* unleash the power of Brahman. He is their source with which humans can reach out to gods and seek their help, while gods can receive their nourishment.

If gods help us, peace and prosperity prevails upon earth. When we nourish the gods through sacrifices, they become strong and protect us from evil.

Hence, Brahman as the upholder of *dharma* devised the sacrifices so that gods and humans can thrive in their respective worlds nourishing each other and upholding God's creation.

Hinduism is an open-ended religion, which offers many choices and solutions to the devotees to practice their faith.

Our scriptures clearly state that the pathways to God are many and one may approach Him by following any path.

Those who worship Him go to Him only while those who worship the gods and goddesses go to them. This does not mean He is partial. In the Gita, He declares that whichever deities people may worship, He stabilizes their faith in them.

He is also free from expectations. He reciprocates love with love, but does not show enmity towards those who do not worship Him.

He does not judge His devotees by the offerings they make. Whatever is offered to Him with love and devotion, He accepts them even if it is worthless.

In ancient times, caste inequalities played an important role in religious worship. The *Vedas* and the secret knowledge of the *Upanishads* were taught to a select few.

However, those who followed the path of devotion encouraged people from all backgrounds to participate in religious and devotional services. They emphasized social equality and the need to worship God by all.

The integration of folk traditions and the practice of tantra added a new dimension to the concept of God in Hinduism. The former worshipped village deities, often with animal sacrifices, while the latter worshipped the Mother Goddess as the highest deity, with God as the passive witness, with very unconventional ritual practices that were offensive to those who practice the Vedic rituals.

At the subtle level, God is described as the combination of truth, consciousness and bliss (*satchitananda*).

He is the indweller, the universal womb, the waters of life, and the sole inhabitant of the entire universe.

He not only pervades the whole creation but also envelops it from all sides.

Nothing is outside of Him or exists without Him. In each being, He is the indwelling soul or the embodied Self, the witness, the enjoyer, the silent partner, the hidden Self, the knower and pure consciousness, who discards the body at the time of death and assumes another at the time of birth.

While the Field (*kshetra*) or the mind and body complex undergoes modifications, He remains immutable and untainted by the impurities of Nature.

The ultimate aim of human life is to achieve liberation or union with God. It can be accomplished in many ways.

However, central to all the paths is the cultivation of purity (*sattva*) achieved by performing duty (*dharma*) selflessly, observing rules and restraints (*yamas* and *niyamas*) and practicing breath-control, concentration, meditation and self-absorption.

Of the various paths available for liberation, the *Bhagavadgita* emphasizes three main ones, the path of action, the path of knowledge and the path of devotion.

It also suggests a few ancillary practices that lead to inner stabilization, namely cultivation of intelligence (*buddhiyoga*) with which one can stabilize the mind, the practice of detachment by renouncing desires (*karma-sanyasayoga*) and stabilizing the mind in the contemplation of God or the Self (*atma-samyamayoga*).

Of the three paths mentioned here, the practice of *karmayoga* comes first. By performing actions without desire for their fruit and as an offering to God, the devotees succeed in cleansing their minds and bodies and suffusing them with the predominance of *sattva*.

With this, they overcome their ignorance and delusion, and gain the knowledge (*jnanayoga*) of the Self and the non-self that leads to discernment, detachment and renunciation of desires.

When they achieve perfection on this path, they succeed in stabilizing their minds in the practice of devotion and eventually experience contact with Brahman (*brahmasparsa*).

In Hinduism God is viewed from various perspectives, both in His individual aspects and universal aspects, functionally as well as spiritually.

He represents unity, diversity, all realities and contradictions, from the highest to the lowest and the farthest to the nearest.

He is viewed in terms of His manifestations, relationships and incarnations.

He is worshipped both ritually and spiritually.

The names with which He is addressed are mere reference points for the sake of our understanding.

In truth, He is incomprehensible and indefinable, since He is beyond words and thoughts.

He represents the loftiest ideals, to which humankind can aspire, and the most sublime aspects of our personalities and character.

He is the ultimate Goal (*parandhamam*), attaining which in our individual ways is the very purpose of our lives.

Those who quarrel about His names and forms are the deluded ones who do not recognize His universality or His essential reality.

Truly speaking, Brahman, the God of Hinduism, represents the highest principle and the loftiest vision, which the human mind can ever conceive of.

He is not God of just one world or a few worlds, but represents the entire known and unknown Universes as well as the past, the present and the future of all creation and existence.

The Individual Self - Atman

Unlike Buddhism, Hinduism affirms the existence of individual souls and describes them as blissful, eternal, invisible, indivisible, imperishable, unchanging and beyond the grasp of the mind and the senses.

According to its tenets, it is apt to refer to them as selves rather than souls because they are without form, substance, personality, objectivity, materiality, qualities, modes, features, nature and divisions. A soul is bound when it is subject to these and free when it is devoid of them.

The *Vedas* refer to the Self as *Atman*, the hidden Self, the invisible Self, the inner Self, the real Self, the Enjoyer, the Lord, the Unknown, the Knower and the Witness.

Atman is derived from the root word "*an*" meaning to breathe. *Atman* is that which makes breathing possible, sustains life and actions and keeps the beings alive.

Eternally free and constant, it is undisturbed by the modifications of Nature. It is subject to neither birth nor death nor destruction. Therefore, it is described in the *Rigveda* as *ajobhaga*, the unborn part of the one born.

It is different from and not to be confused with the body or the mind, or with the individuality (ego) which are subject to modifications and impermanence.

Understanding the Self

The Self cannot be known through study or discussion. Those who say they know it, perhaps, do not know; and those who know it, perhaps, may not speak about it definitively.

Because of the difficulties in knowing it, people have misconceptions about its essential nature. As the *Upanishads* declare, the Self is hidden and veiled by impurities. Therefore, it cannot be known until the mind and body are purified. Those who lack discernment because of delusion mistakenly regard their physical selves as the real ones. They may speculate about it but cannot experience it without inner transformation.

Even our physical selves are difficult to know, since they are formed out of the aggregation of diverse components that are difficult to know or reach through ordinary means.

The difficulty of knowing the real Self is even greater since it is beyond the mind and the senses. You may know about it intellectually by knowing what it is and what it is not. Such knowledge may help you in your practice of yoga, but it does not liberate you or give you an experience of its blissful state.

You achieve liberation only when you experience it in deeper states of self-absorption in which the mind and its modifications are virtually absent.

The problem with knowing the Self is you do not experience it in your wakeful state. You may experience it in deep sleep or in a state of self-absorption; but when you return to your normal consciousness, you may not remember much about what happened.

In its outgoing mode, the physical-self remains unconcerned with the real Self while the real Self is always indifferent to the modes and activities of the physical-self.

The two selves are worlds apart, represent two different realities and never meet. Because of this, the Self is incomprehensible to the ordinary self.

To know the Self you have to silence your physical-self (mind and body) and surrender to the will of God. Only then, you experience the Self that is hidden.

Those who achieve it are known as the silent ones (*munis*) because they silence every aspect of their consciousness and beingness. In the absence of the self, we understand from the *Upanishads*, is felt the presence of the self.

Different people interpret the Self differently according to their beliefs, nature and knowledge. This is explained in *Chandogya Upanishad* in the form of a story illustrating how gods and demons understood the Self differently.

It is said that once both *Virochana*, the leader of demons and *Indra*, the lord of the heavens, went to *Prajapati*, their teacher, and wanted him to teach them about the Self. *Prajapati* taught them that the body was the self.

Satisfied with the teaching, *Virochana* went away, believing that the body was indeed the Self. He taught the same doctrine to the demons who accepted it as true and made it their principal doctrine. They live and act accordingly as if the body is the Self and nothing is beyond it.

We have many demonic people living amidst us, who believe in the same doctrine. They live as if there is no tomorrow and indulge in evil actions to satisfy their desires without any fear or hesitation.

Indra was not satisfied with this explanation. He his teacher to teach him more. *Prajapati* gave more answers stating what the Self was; but *Indra* was satisfied with none of them.

After spending many years and learning many lessons, eventually he arrived at the realization that the Self was neither the body, nor the dream self, nor the self in sleep, but the spirit that always existed in pure state beyond them.

The story illustrates that to understand the Self, you have to look at yourself deeply and dispassionately and go beyond your mind, senses and all cognitive experiences to enter into a stateless state of self-absorption where the Self alone remains without duality and the distinction between the knower and the known. At the same time, you must be aware what the Self is not.

What the Self is and is not

The *Upanishads* describe the Self in terms of both what it is and what it is not. In the *Brihadaranyaka Upanishad*, we have a passage (4.5.15) in which *Yajnavalkya* declares that the Self is better described in terms of not-not (*neti neti*) and goes on to say that the Self is not comprehensible, not destructible, not attached, not fettered, does not suffer, and cannot be injured.

The Self is also described as not the body, not the mind, not the senses, not the speech, not the life-breath, not the intelligence, not the ego, not the elements, not the name, not the form, not the known, not limited by time, and not of this world.

The Self is described in positive terms also as eternal, infinite, absolute, ancient, supreme, radiant, free, and independent.

According to the *Yogasutras* (1.24), it is free from *karma* (duty), fructification of *karma*, latent impressions (*samskaras*) and modifications such as aging, birth and death.

The Self is also free from the *gunas* and their influence.

It is incorruptible because the impurities of mortal existence cannot touch it.

The Self remains pure even when it is held in bondage by Nature.

The Self is also hidden in all as the innermost essence (*Chandogya Upanishad*).

When the body dies, it travels to the world of the sun or the moon according to one's deeds.

The *Upanishads* describe the Self as subtle (*sukshma or linga*), smaller than the smallest and larger than the largest.

Some describe it as having the size of a thumb or and others of an atom. Yet, others speak of it as larger than the largest.

In its essence, it is the same as Brahman, the Supreme Self.

It can exist in anything and everything. Hence, it is pervasive (*vyapi*).

Its assumed location is the heart, which is known as *hridayam*, which according to *Chandogya Upanishad* (8.3.5) means in the heart (*hridi*) is this (*ayam*).

The *Upanishads* also speak of the unknowability of the Self since it is different from the known and farther than the known, which cannot be perceived but because of which perception is possible. The difficulty arises because the Self cannot be cognized by any other means but only by itself.

Finally, the Self is different from the physical self or the ego self. The latter is subject to death and decay, where as the Self is free from all modifications.

However, the physical self is part of the embodied Self (*jiva*). It is responsible for soul's bondage upon earth. At the same time, it plays an important role in its liberation and therefore considered important for one's physical and spiritual wellbeing.

Types of souls

In their essential nature, all the souls are the same. All are eternal, infinite and cannot be distinguished from one another in space and time except conceptually. However, some schools state that individual differences may exist among them, with regard to their knowledge, status, state of liberation and purpose in creation.

The monistic schools (*advaita*) hold any attempt to classify souls into one or more categories as intellectual delusion. For them the individual selves are temporary appearances of Brahman who alone is true. Whatever diversity and individuality one may perceive in creation in the form of individual souls or aspects of Nature is just a projection or a mere formation like a cloud in the sky.

The dualistic schools disagree with this premise. They acknowledge the duality between Brahman, the Supreme Self and

Atman, the individual Self. They also acknowledge the distinction between one individual Self and another and between God and His creation.

While the dualistic schools may debate among themselves on the question of whether the distinction between God and souls is real and permanent or notional and temporary, they acknowledge the dualities and distinctions inherent in creation and recognize different types of souls according to their degree of bondage and freedom.

They regard a soul as a dynamic reality (*cetana tattva*) whose essential nature is knowledge (*jnana*) and bliss (*ananda*), in contrast the realities of Nature, which are inert, not self-aware and purely material (*acetana tattvas*). According to them, the individual souls are either bound (*baddha*) or unbound (*mukta*).

The bound souls may exist in different states of bondage in different beings (*jivas*) according to their actions (*karma*). They are dependent entities, in contrast to God (*Isvara*) who is independent.

They may also exist in the ancestral world or in the intermediary subtle worlds in different states of release.

On earth, they exist as embodied selves (*jivatmas*) classified into those born from wombs, eggs, fluids and shoots and sprouts.

Among them, only human beings who are endowed with knowledge and intelligence are subject to *karma* and the rules of *dharma* as prescribed in the scriptures (*sastras*). Therefore sin (*papam*) and merit (*punyam*) arising from their actions accrue to them only.

The free souls (*muktas*) are further divided into, those who are eternally free (*nitya muktas*) and those who are liberated (*muktas*).

According to the dualistic schools the eternally free souls are close attendants of God who never enter into an embodied state except by their free will or when an incarnation of God appears upon earth and God requires their services. They live in the company of God and serve Him. They may be devotees (*bhaktas*) who serve God directly or indirectly as servants of His devotees (*bhagavatas*). They epitomize selfless service and fulfill different purposes with exemplary devotion by playing different roles as willed by God.

The physical self and the real Self

Each living being is a combination of Nature (*Prakriti*) and Self (*Purusha*).

It is supported by God (*Isvara*) and in turn, it supports Nature.

It also houses the real Self, which is different from the visible self, also known as the physical self, the false self, the lower self or the ego self.

It is the field of Nature, which is subject to modifications, desires, attachment, attraction and aversion, name and form and death.

It is also subject to the *gunas* and the limitations of time, space, energy, knowledge and intelligence.

The physical self is a formation around the real Self. It is the vehicle for the Self. The *Bhagavadgita* describes it as the city with nine gates.

It is a combination of gross and subtle bodies. The gross physical body is the outer most. It is formed by food. Hence, it is known as the food body (*annmaya kosa*). It is followed by breath body, mind body, intelligence body and bliss body. All these envelop the Self and encase it.

The Physical self is made up of the aspects of Nature, namely the senses, the mind, the ego and intelligence. Together they are responsible for the individuality and distinction of each living being.

The physical self is subject to the influence of the *gunas* and prone to desires and sinful actions. Because of the activity of the senses, it becomes involved with the world, while the real Self remains in the background as witness.

The real Self does not harm the physical self, whereas the actions of the latter lead to the bondage of the Self. Hence, the *Bhagavadgita* declares that the self is the friend of the self and its enemy. It is a friend when it facilitates liberation and an enemy when it delays it or obstructs it.

Of the four aims of human life, the first three (*dharma, artha, kama*) are essentially for the lower Self and the last one (*moksha*) for the real Self. In fact, the first three prepare each individual for liberation.

Of the two types of knowledge, the lower knowledge helps the physical self in upholding *dharma* and the higher knowledge in facilitating the liberation of the Self.

In the sacrifice of life, the physical self is the sacrificer and the sacrificed. The real Self is the object of the sacrifice, to which the offerings are made.

In the end, the physical self disintegrates and disappears completely, leaving behind a little residue of dominant desires and latent impressions, which act as the seed for the next embodiment of the soul.

The *Mundaka Upanishad* (3.1.1-2) describes the two selves as companions in union who are perched on the same tree of life. Of them, one eats the fruit (of its actions) while the other just looks on without eating. The one, which is engaged in actions and deluded, suffers from grief. It is freed from sorrow, when it sees the other, the Lord who is great and worthy of worship.

The *Mandukya Upanishad* describes four states of consciousness, which one experiences as he passes through the waking state into deep sleep state. These are the wakeful state (*vaishwanara*), the dream state (*taijasa*), the deep sleep state (*taijasa*), and finally the transcendental state (*turiya*) in which one experiences the real Self.

The physical self is fully active in the wakeful state, and partially active in the dream state. It may exist nominally in deep sleep, but in the transcendental state, it will be completely silent or absent, where the real Self alone remains. This last state has no elements. It cannot be spoken of, into which the world is resolved. It is benign and without individuality.

It is the state of the Self. When one enters into it, one become fully absorbed and experiences the formless state of self-awareness (*nirvikalpa samadhi*). What exists beyond the self is the unmanifest (*avyaktam*).

The individual Self and the Supreme Self

The individual Self is considered the Lord (*Isvara*) of the mind and body. The Supreme Self (Brahman) is considered the Lord of the Universe. Both are considered eternal, absolute, infinite and blissful.

However, different schools interpret their relationship differently and express different views about their essential nature. These views fall into three main categories: they are different, they are somewhat different, and they are entirely different.

The first school holds the belief that the difference between the Supreme Self and the individual Self is an illusion. In reality, there is only one entity, which is the Supreme Self. Its appearance as different entities in the objective or phenomenal world is caused by the delusion of our minds just as we mistake a rope for a snake in a dark room.

According to the second school, the difference is notional. The Supreme Self and the individual Self are both the same essentially; however, they are also not exactly the same. Their difference is the same as that between an object and its reflection in the mirror or between the sun and its rays.

According to the third school, the difference is very real. Not only the Supreme Self and the individual Self are different but also one

Self is different from another. The Supreme Self is independent, while the individual selves are dependent upon Him. He is also the cause of their bondage as well as liberation. His grace and blessings play an important role in their liberation. He is truth, knowledge, bliss and purity personified. He is also the ultimate goal (*parandhama*) of all living beings. The entire creation and the individual selves constitute His body, since it exists for Him who is the Supreme Self. He is both its material and essential cause.

There are also some schools, which believe that both the Supreme Self and the individual selves remain in the background as passive witnesses, while *Shakti* (Mother Goddess) manifests the worlds and beings as the dynamic principle.

Self-realization or liberation of the Self

Self-realization is the highest and the ultimate aim of human life.

Self-realization should be the primary goal of every human being.

Self-realization means knowing the Self, or shedding all your other identities so that only your true identity remains.

The Self is the ultimate sanctuary. Everything else in life leads to pain, suffering, birth and rebirth. By taking refuge in the Self and knowing it, one becomes free.

According to the *Upanishads*, whoever realizes his real-Self leaves this world and goes to the world of Brahman never to return.

In Self-realization, one comes to know the true or essential nature of the Self, not notionally or intellectually, but experientially in a state of self-absorption by silencing the physical Self and by suppressing the modifications of the mind (*citta-vrittis*).

The first steps in this regard are withdrawing the senses from the sense objects like a tortoise and cultivating dispassion and detachment. The *Mundaka Upanishad* declares (3.1.5) that self-realization can be achieved by truth, knowledge, austerity and chastity. Those ascetics who have cleansed themselves of impurities and imperfections behold Him. Purity of thought is also important because whatever is thought in a pure mind is easily attained (3.2.10). The help of an enlightened teacher is also important. Cultivating necessary virtues one should approach a learned teacher with sacrificial fuel in hand to acquire the knowledge of the Self (3.1.12) and the teacher should teach him the knowledge in all earnest.

Hindus believe that the individual soul and the universal soul are the two sides of the same reality. *Atman* is *Purusha* who enters the body of a being as a part of His creative process. Since the body is made up of the *gunas*, he comes under the influence of illusion and develops a false identity called the sense of self or the sense of individuality, also known as ego or *ahamkara*.

A devotee's primary concern on the path of liberation is how he may discover his true Self. For that, he has to resort to different means, starting with simple methods of worship, and then moving on to various paths suggested in the scriptures that eventually lead him on the path to the Abode of God.

He has to overcome his ego sense, silence his cravings, and detach himself from his other identities so that his true Self remains.

The scriptures suggest various methods to achieve liberation. They describe two paths principally, the path of gods (*devayana*) and the path of ancestors (*pitryana*), by which the departed souls journey.

The first one leads to the world of immortals and the next one to that of the ancestors. Those who go to the world of immortals never return; but those who go to the world of ancestors have to return to take birth and continue their mortal existence.

The following is a list of various methods suggested in the scriptures to attain liberation. Some of them are preparatory, which transform and purify the seekers and prepare them for the rigors of spiritual life; and some are more advanced methods, which require serious commitment and lead to liberation.

1. Withdrawing and restraining the senses from worldly objects to stabilize the mind and suppress the mental modifications.

2. Cultivating detachment and dispassion (*vairagyam*) to overcome desires and cultivate sameness (*samatvam*) towards pairs of opposites.

3. The practice of abstentions (*yamas*) such as non-violence, truthfulness and celibacy, and rules (*niyamas*) such as cleanliness, contentment and austerity whereby the impurities are destroyed, divine qualities (*daiva sampatti*) are cultivated, the lamp of knowledge is illuminated and discriminating awareness (*buddhi*) is firmly established. This is a very crucial step. Without virtue and discriminatory awareness, immortality cannot be achieved.

4. Renunciation of (*sanyasa*) desires, including the renunciation of likes and dislikes and the desire for the fruit of actions, so that one becomes stable and equal to the dualities of life.

5. Practicing obligatory duties, as an offering to God, without desiring their fruit, whereby one becomes free from *karma*, latent impressions and attachments.

6. Cultivating awareness of the Self by studying (*svadhyaya*) the scriptures, listening (*sravanam*) to religious discourses, practicing concentration (*dharana*), and meditation (*dhyana*) whereby one can stabilize the mind in the contemplation of the Self (*nidhidhyasana*), purify the mind and body and strengthen the divine qualities. This is the yoga of knowledge (*jnana-yoga*). It leads to discernment, enlightenment and absorption in the Self (*samadhi*).

7. Cultivating single minded devotion to God, surrendering all actions to Him, worshipping Him, meditating upon Him, remembering (*mananam*) His names, offering Him all actions, with equanimity and firm resolve, one should stabilize the mind in the contemplation of God. This is the path of devotion, whereby a devotee is speedily rescued from the phenomenal world.

The Self cannot be realized by reading books or by indulging in superficial rituals, but only through self-restraint, purification of the mind and body, withdrawal of the senses and elimination of desires.

The continued practice of various yogas mentioned previously leads to purity (sattva), discriminative insight (buddhi), suppression of mental modifications (vrittis), destruction of impurities (malas), cessation of karma and ongoing permutations of the gunas, freedom from suffering and afflictions (klesas), and the state of self-absorption (samadhi) and self-realization (atmajnan).

In this process, one may experience contact with the Self or even the Supreme Self (brahmasparsa). As the Mundaka Upanishad declares, Truth alone he wins, not the untruth. By the path of gods, he travels to the immortal world.

Freedom from desires is vital. Only those who are free from desires are able to enter the world of Brahman. Everything is a preparation to achieve this austere goal.

Conclusion

A human being is a god in the making. He is limited by the body, which is an instrument of Nature. For the ignorant and deluded, it is the means to enjoy the pleasures of life. Their attachment to it and their identification with it is the prime cause of their bondage.

For discerning persons, the body is a barrier to liberation, until it is purified and transformed into a vehicle of God. They achieve liberation by cultivating witness consciousness, while still in their bodies.

From the vantage point of the Self, a yogi of wisdom perceives the world and its phenomena with detachment and sameness.

Controlling the lower self and established in his higher Self, he transcends his desires and duality to experience self-absorption and oneness with God.

With that, he ends his long journey of life upon earth and his existence as a limited being in bondage to the forces of Nature.

Prakriti, the Mother Goddess

The naked eye cannot miss three basic component aspects of reality: space, matter and the perceiver. The first two are experienced, and in a way exist, because of the last. The first two will exist forever, while the last one will be temporary.

Our ancient scholars studied these three aspects of creation and drew their own conclusions. They argued, debated and discussed about their nature and relationship. The believed that the combination of the first two resulted in the formation of the last. They believed that if the universe had a personality consisting of space filled with pure consciousness, and matter or materiality filled with energy, such combination also went into the making of a being (*jiva*).

In other words, their argument pointed to the possibility that each being was a replica of the universe on a minor scale; and by knowing oneself, one could know the entire universe.

According to them, the body represented matter and the soul inside represented pure consciousness. Thus, life emerged out of the combination of the two eternal principles, consciousness (or ethereal space) and energy (or materiality).

Our scriptures call them *Purusha* and *Prakriti*, the two eternal and highest components of creation. Union between them results in the creation of things and beings. Separation between them results in either the dissolution of the worlds or the liberation of beings.

Purusha is the eternal and indestructible Self. He is described as the efficient cause of creation. *Prakriti* is described as His materiality. It includes every modification of matter and energy that happens in the universe.

In some traditions, Nature is described as the material cause, while in schools of *Shaktism*, which hold Her as the Supreme, She is regarded as both material and efficient causes.

Prakriti is that which exists in its natural state. Whatever is original and pristine in creation is *Prakriti*. It imparts parts, qualities, properties and essential nature to things and beings. Regarding this eternal principle, different views and descriptions are available in Hinduism, which are summarized below.

- Prakriti is primal Nature
- A dependent and dynamic aspect of God
- An independent and eternal aspect of creation
- Source of beingness, materiality and corporeality of all beings
- Natural state
- The mind and body
- Superior to even God
- Source of bondage of beings
- Causes delusion and ignorance
- Veils knowledge and wisdom
- Causes modifications, impermanence and change
- The field (*kshetra*)
- Source of all names and forms
- Mechanical in its actions
- Produces nothing new
- Always constant
- Indestructible
- Creates diversity, duality, desires and attachment
- Universal Mother
- Supreme Energy

The concept of *Prakriti* is well explained in the ancient *Samkhya* School, according to which, *Prakriti* is the source of all creation. By involving the individuals souls (*purushas*) which play a passive and secondary role and subjecting them to its modifications, it manifests duality and diversity.

Its original state is an unmanifested, subtle state (*avyaktam*), in which the *gunas* remain in a state of equilibrium. When this equilibrium is disturbed, it springs into action.

According to *Samkhya*, *Prakriti* is without a cause, which means it is eternal and uncreated. However, it is the source of all material manifestation. In creating things and beings, it actually creates nothing new. It is a mechanical entity. All the effects are already hidden in its causes. Through transformation and modifications (*parinama*), it manifests the effects hidden in its causes and produces things and beings.

Although it is responsible for creation, it does not have any control on the individual souls (*purushas*). Their involvement with Nature is a mere coincidence. Once they are liberated, they never come under its influence again. It is able to manifest things with the help of its sub-natures or constituent realities (*tattvas*), which are said to be 24.

- *Mahat*, the Great One
- *Buddhi*, the discriminating, reasoning and causative intelligence (2)
- *Aham*, the ego-principle (3)
- *Manas*, the mind or the sixth sense (4)
- Five *jnanendiryas*, sense organs (9)
- Five *karmendriyas*: organs of action (14)
- Five *tanmatras*, subtle elements (19)
- Five *mahabhutas*:the, gross elements, namely the earth, water, air, fire and ether(24)

Some do not include *Mahat* in the list. It is the first principle to emerge during creation. It is *Prakriti* in its manifested and dynamic form, in contrast to the subtle (primordial) Nature in which the *gunas* are in equilibrium.

From the *Mahat* manifest intelligence (*buddhi*) as the first principle and then mind (*manas*). Intelligence is responsible for discriminating awareness in beings. It is the higher mind. Not all are endowed with it. Only gods and humans. *Manas*, is the lower mind, which acts as the receptacle of thoughts and feelings.

From higher mind, arise ego (*aham*) and the five subtle senses (*tanmatras*) namely sound, touch smell, color and taste. The rest of the *tattvas* arise from the lower mind (*manas*), namely the five senses, the five organs of action and the five gross elements. Together they constitute the 24 evolutes of Nature, from which beingness arises. Some include the Self (*Purusha*) as pure (*suddha*) *tattva* to make it 25.

The *Samkhya* philosophy was one of the earliest to discuss the meaning and significance of *Prakriti*. Richard Garbe described it as "the most significant system of philosophy that India has produced." Its basic concepts were incorporated later on in other schools of Hinduism, including the *Vedanta*.

We find references to it in the *Bhagavadgita*, the *Yogasutras* and the *Upanishads* such as the *Svetasvatara* and the *Maitrayani Upanishads*. The *Bhagavadgita* presents a modified version of the *Samkhya* Philosophy. In some respects, the *Yogasutras* of *Patanjali* is both an extension and an exposition of the *Samkhya* School, with elements of devotional theism towards the Self (*Isvara*) incorporated in it.

In the original *Samkhya*, there was no reference to Creator God. *Prakriti* was presented as the material cause of creation. The *Bhagavadgita* refutes this idea and considers creation a divine rather than a natural or mechanical process.

It presents *Samkhya* from a theistic perspective, with God (*Purusha*) as the efficient cause and the supreme Source of all creation, with Nature playing a secondary role under His will.

It also accepts many other concepts of the school such as the division of the *gunas*, the bondage of the souls, relationship between *Prakriti* and individual souls, the release of the souls through the practice of yoga and discipline and so on. It also prescribes *bhakti* or devotion as the best means to achieve salvation.

The *Samkhya* philosophy was originally founded by *Kapila*, who lived long before the *Buddha* and even before the composition of some principal *Upanishads* such as the *Svetasvatara, Katha, Prasna* and *Maitrayani Upanishads.*

One of the earliest authoritative works of this school was the *Samkhyakarika,* ascribed to *Isvarakrishna,* who probably lived in the early Christian era. Another important work on it was a commentary written by *Gaudapada,* who was not the same as the *Gaudapada* of the *Mandukya Karika.*

The significance of *Samkhya* lies in that it presents the manifestation of life on earth not as miracle work of God, but as a mechanical and transformative process set in motion by Nature upon coming into contact with individual souls.

The Mother Goddess

In theistic traditions based on the Vedic beliefs, *Prakriti* is venerated as the Universal Mother, Mother Goddess or *Shakti.* If Brahman is comparable to space in the material universe, *Prakriti* is matter itself. Energy is the subtle aspect of matter.

Hence, she is also regarded as the universal Energy (*Shakti*). Energy exists in the universe in various forms. In its grosser aspects it is physical energy and in its subtle aspects it manifests as mind or consciousness, intelligence, breathe energy and sexual energy.

In Hinduism, therefore we worship Nature as the personification of various energies. We pray to Her for the purification of our minds and bodies, so that we can suppress the impure energies arising from *rajas* and *tamas* and increase the pure energy of *sattva.*

The Mother is the deluding power in the living beings. Hence, she is also known as *Maya.* She is also worshipped in the *tantras* as the source of all creation.

They regard *Siva* as the Lord of the Universe and *Parvati,* His consort as the Mother Goddess. In the *Vedas* She is mentioned as *Uma Haimavati,* another name for *Parvati.*

Shakti manifests in various forms. She is associated with every deity from the highest to the lowest. Each of the Trinity gods has an associate *Shakti* as his consort. Thus, *Sarasvathi, Laskhmi and Parvathi* are the associate powers of *Brahma, Vishnu* and *Siva* respectively. Together with them, they participate in creation, preservation and destruction of things, beings and worlds. Each of these goddesses has further aspects, names and forms.

Jiva the Embodied Soul

Jiva is the living entity or the embodied soul. It is used to denote the soul inside a living being that imparts life to it as well as the being itself, which is subject to modifications. All living beings in all the manifested worlds are *jivas*, without exception, even the tiniest ones.

Human beings are also *jivas*, most advanced of all the beings upon earth, but in relation to the beings of other worlds somewhere in the middle of the hierarchy.

Since they are endowed with intelligence and conscious will, with the propensity to cultivate both light and darkness, they alone have the ability to achieve liberation through conscious effort.

Others have to evolve or devolve and attain human birth to attain the same goal. All beings that manifest in creation, irrespective of their cosmic status, are subject to the laws of *dharma* and the modifications of being and becoming.

Only the supreme Brahman in His formless state is eternal and changeless and beyond the state of beingness. In His formless and transcendental state, He is immutable.

The types of Jivas

Some say the number of *jivas* is fixed for the duration of creation. Others say their number is infinite. Some contend that their appearance is an illusion because Brahman alone is real and He alone appears in the individual beings as their inner selves. Others believe that the individual souls are separate entities different from Brahman.

The *Vishistadvaita* School (qualified monism), which draws a very subtle and rather indeterminate distinction between God and souls, divides the *jivas* into three kinds: the bound souls (*baddha*), the free souls (*muktas*) and the forever-free souls (*nitya muktas*). The latter two exist in the world of Brahman as either pure devotees or servants and attendants of God. The bound souls possess bodies that are both gross and subtle.

The gods and higher beings possess subtle bodies. The beings of the darker worlds possess gross bodies. Human beings possess both. Only the human beings and gods are endowed with intelligence, with the ability to acquire knowledge and work for their liberation. The lower beings have to pass through several births and deaths before they attain human birth in a family of pious people and work for their liberation.

The beings upon earth are divided into humans, animals and the stationary ones (*sthavara*) or the plants.

Depending upon how they are born, they are divided into those born from seeds or sprouts (*udbija*), those born from secretions (*svadeja*), those born from eggs (*andaja*) and those born from wombs (*jarayuja*).

Gods, humans and some animals fall into the last category.

Some divinities like *Brahma* and some historic persons like *Sita* and *Draupadi*, are not born from wombs. They are known as *Ayonijas* (not born from wombs). Beings of earth are also classified according to the number of senses they possess.

Some possess only one sense, while the more advanced ones possess all the senses. The mind, which is considered the eleventh sense, is present only in some.

Based upon the composition of the triple *gunas*, human beings are classified into four divisions, priests, warriors, merchants and workers. Priests and scholars (*brahmanas*) have the predominance of *sattva* and warriors (*kashtriyas*) have *rajas*.

Merchants and traders (*vaishyas*) have the predominance of *tamas* followed by *sattva*. The working classes (*sudras*) also have the predominance of *tamas*, followed by *rajas*.

The inner world of a jiva

The *jivas* are bound souls. They are subject to ignorance (*avidya*) and delusion (*moha*). They are repeatedly born because of their desire-ridden actions (*karma*), until they achieve liberation through self-effort or by the grace of God. They are caught in the phenomenal world (*samsara*) and its modifications, which results in their suffering.

Each *jiva* has beingness or corporeality, which is responsible for its limited existence. It is created by the union of the individual-self (*Purusha*) with Nature (*Prakriti*). As the *Gita* declares, established in *Prakriti*, the Supreme Self manifests the worlds and beings. That union is well reflected in each *jiva*.

The Self is eternal, indestructible, inexhaustible and unchangeable even when it is bound to Nature. It does not undergo any transformation even when it is hidden within the body as the Enjoyer, Knower and the Witness.

The Nature (the mind and body complex) of each being is subject to modifications such as aging, afflictions and birth and death. It is the garment the soul wears and discards at the end of each birth.

The Self is free and unlimited, while the *Jivas* are bound to the mechanism of Nature and to the limitations of life, knowledge, awareness and ability.

Nature provides materiality, corporeality and individuality to beings whereby they experience duality, delusion and diversity. As long as they are involved with Nature and its modifications, the individual souls remain bound to the cycle of births and deaths

Each *jiva* is made up of various sub-natures (*tattvas*) of Nature. They are responsible for the divisions, modifications, qualities and functionalities of the human personality.

The *Samkhya* philosophy identifies 23 such sub-natures while some schools of Saivism describe them as thirty-six. The 23 *tattvas* are as follows from the highest to the lowest: intelligence (*buddhi*), ego (*aham*), mind (*manas*), five subtle sense (*tanmatras*), five organs of perception (*jnanendriyas*), five organs of action (*karmendriyas*), five basic elements (*mahabhutas*). To these twenty-three some add the *Mahat* (the great one) and make it twenty-four.

In addition to the twenty-three identified in the *Samkhya*, the followers of *Siva* recognize thirteen additional *tattvas*, namely, *purusha, maya, suddha tattva, isvara tattva, sadasiva tattva*, five *shakti tattvas* and *Siva tattva*.

According to the Hindu conception of human personality, each human being is said to have not one but five bodies, of which the outermost is gross and the remaining ones are subtle.

The outermost physical body is called variously as the gross body, (*sthula sarira*) or food body (*annamaya kosa*). It is made up of the food we eat. As the *Taittiriya Upanishad* (2.2.1) declares, from food are produced all creatures of the earth. On food (earth), alone all beings live and into food (earth), alone they all pass in the end. Food is the foremost of all (*annam hi bhutanam jyeshtham*). Food is eaten; it also eats all beings.

Next to the gross body is the breath body (*pranamaya kosa*), which is made up of breathe (*prana*). It is a subtle body. The body cannot survive without it. Hence, it is also known as the soul of the gross body (*sarira-atma*). It controls our vitality and life-energy. It is the purifier, which connects the gross body with the mental body and stabilizes the mind in concentration, meditation and self-absorption. Hence, in the practice of yoga and in controlling the movements of the mind, breath control (*pranayama*) is considered vital.

The third sheath (*kosa*) is the mental body (*manomaya kosa*), which connects the breath body with the intelligence body. Thoughts, emotions and feelings constitute its food.

The fourth body is the intelligence body (*vignanamayakosa*). It is responsible for reasoning and discernment. Intelligence is the highest faculty of Nature in human beings. It is also called the higher mind. It plays a predominant role in our liberation. Lower beings do not possess this body and hence cannot achieve liberation on their own. It is also called the casual body, because it is responsible for the consequences accruing from desire-ridden actions. It is responsible for both sacrificial actions and selfish actions (*vignanam yagna tanute, karman tanute*).

The fifth and the last one is the bliss-body, (*anandamaya kosa*). It is the innermost, which cannot be reached in wakeful or dream states but only in deep sleep or transcendental states or in a state of self-absorption. By restraining the senses, the mind and the body one can gain access to it.

The culmination of yoga and *samyama* (deep concentration) is reaching the innermost body. It is the very nature of the Self as reflected in human consciousness. Beyond the bliss-body is the inner Self (*atman*). It is the Truth Body. Words return from it not attaining it along with the mind. He who attains it becomes freed from fear. He is not perplexed or tormented by conflicting thoughts. His mind becomes tranquil. *Sankaracharya* proposed that the bliss body and the Self were different, while *Ramanuja* regarded them as the same.

The *Taittiriya* and *Katha Upanishads* provide information on the constitution of human personality. The *Katha Upanishad* says, "Beyond the senses are objects and beyond the objects is the mind. Beyond the mind is buddhi and beyond buddhi is the great self (*mahan atma*)".

In the *Taittiriya Upanishad* (2.2.1-2), we find the progressive states of the human personality: life, life and mind, mind and intelligence, intelligence and bliss and, finally, Brahman.

The *Upanishad* ends with the joyous expression of a liberated soul who has realized the true nature of his eternal-Self, proclaiming that he is food and the resplendent golden light.

The liberation of jivas

The *jivas* are bound souls, different from the liberated souls that exist only in the realm of the highest heaven. In *Saivism* they are called *pasus* (animals).

They *jivas* are bound because they are ignorant and deluded by the power of *maya* (Nature). They are conditioned and limited by the impurities of the *gunas* and suffer from duality, attraction and aversion to things, desires, attachment, egoism and impermanence.

In the embodied state, the Self is not tainted, but it remains enveloped in a fog of ignorance and a state of inertia. A false self (the ego) assumes its identity and acts as if it is the real Self.

The *jiva's* identification with its body and mind is the sole cause of its bondage and suffering. When it realizes that it is an eternal Self and the body is a mere formation, it is qualified for liberation.

Beings are bound to the wheel of *karma* through desires. Desires are responsible for afflictions (*klesas*) and modifications of the mind (*vrittis*). Dominant desires and thoughts fructify as latent impressions (*samskaras*). They accompany the soul to the next world as causative consciousness (*karanacitta*) and act as the seed for one's next life.

Desires arise from attachment, which is caused by the senses acting under the influence of the *gunas*. Only by restraining the senses, suppressing the impure *gunas* with the help of *sattva* and with detachment, one can escape from this loop.

A replica of the universe is hidden within each being. It is more so in the human beings, who represent the universe (manifested Brahman) in its microcosmic aspect. The door to Brahman is therefore one's own self. By studying oneself, knowing oneself and withdrawing into oneself, one can reach the Supreme Self.

In the *Katha Upanishad*, Lord Yama declares the same to the young *Nachiketa* suggesting that through self-contemplation (*adhyatma-*

yogadhigamena) wise men realize the most ancient God and leave behind them both joys and sorrows.

The knowledge of the Self comes by probing into oneself. Our beingness is a microscopic replica of the universal Beingness, which is Brahman in His qualified aspect (*saguna*). Hence by knowing the Self we reach the Universal Self.

Our scriptures affirm that the divinities that exist in the universe also exist in the human personality in subtle forms. They participate in the internal sacrifices we perform daily. They witness our actions, share our joys and sorrows and depending upon how much sorrow or suffering we give them through our actions and attachments, we reap the rewards and punishments of our own deeds.

Those who do not share their sacrifices with gods suffer. Those who offer their actions (sacrifices) to them and take only the remains of their sacrifices qualify for liberation.

Our actions and attitudes matter in our liberation. If we identify ourselves with our names and forms, we remain bound to the world, ignorant and deluded. If we assume doership for our actions, we suffer from *karma*.

If we identify ourselves with our inner Selves and live with that awareness all the time, with our minds firmly fixed upon God or the Self, we become one with Him.

Before we accomplish this highest goal, we have to work for our transformation consciously, with faith (*sraddha*), firm resolve (*dhrita*) and devotion (*bhakti*) of pure (*sattvic*) kind. With their help, the freed souls travel along the path of gods (*devayana*) to the world of immortality.

At the center of each *jiva* is the Self (atman), pure and eternal. It is unchanged even when it is involved with Nature and bound to it. Its reflection in the intelligence (*buddhi*) creates in us self-awareness and the ability to discern things.

When the senses are restrained and mind and body are purified and stabilized through self-transformation, one is able experience the presence of Self within himself and become absorbed in it. Until then one has to remain encircled by the elemental body and caught up in one's own beingness.

The Incarnations of God

One of the unique concepts of Hinduism is the incarnation of God. In no other religion, we find this concept. Other religions have prophets and messengers of God, who are deputed to the earth with specific instructions to deliver His message to the humanity, while He remains in the heaven keeping a distant watch.

The purpose of an incarnation

An incarnation is a direct manifestation of God, in which He retains most of His powers and descends into the world to take birth as one of the mortal beings. Its purpose is essentially maintenance of the world, restoration of order and regularity (*rta*) and keep the worlds free from darkness and evil. In purpose, it is similar to that of parents directly involving themselves in the problems of their children by personally visiting their homes or a high-ranking official taking charge of a local office to set things right. In an incarnation, God Himself is the message and the messenger. He conveys it in numerous ways, through His words, actions, decisions, relationships, adventures and miraculous powers. Living here like a mortal being, He subjects Himself to the conditions of earthly life and leading an exemplary life, He performs extraordinary deeds to root out evil. Having finished His mission upon earth, He leaves behind great memories in the collective consciousness of the world to serve as an inspiration and provide guidance for His future devotees.

In an incarnation, God participates in the events of the world actively. Instead of remaining in the background as a passive witness, He provides a living of example of how one can live upon earth righteously and serve the aims of *dharma* without compromising one's spiritual goals and destiny.

The meaning of incarnation

Avataram means descent or descending. Occasionally God may descend into the earth plane in response to our prayers, sacrifices or meritorious actions to bestow their blessings receive our offerings or witness events. God or His Power may descend into our world for various reasons. Occasionally, He may respond to our prayers and come personally to bestow His grace. He may visit our homes in response to our rituals. However, in these cases, His descent is temporary and partial. limited in both purpose and intent.

They are not considered incarnations. In an incarnation, which is more prolonged, direct, personal, and physical, God descends directly into the earth consciousness and assumes a mortal body usually for a lifetime so that He can stay here and do the work for which He descends. In the process, His devotees get a rare opportunity to meet Him in person and see His divine powers in action. They also get an opportunity to learn from His virtues and participate in His actions as His servants, students, admirers, friends, relations, critics, associates and devotees.

Avatar also means manifestation, appearance, recasting or translation. The entire creation and everything in it is a manifestation of God. Their purpose is to create duality, delusion and pairs of opposites and subject us to various modifications. They reflect His power and glory in varying degrees. He manifests in the darker worlds also, where evil reigns, while He is fully concealed. However, most of these manifestations are His projections or temporary constructs in which He is veiled fully or partially. They cannot be called incarnations.

An incarnation is part of God's eternal duty

The purpose of an incarnation is inherent in God's duty (*dharma*) as the preserver and upholder of the order and regularity (*rta*) of the worlds and beings He creates. If creation has to run its due course and if the divine laws that He uses to regulate the worlds and beings have to work as ordained, He has to remain attentive and responsive and ensure that everything is in its place and works as willed. If God does not do His duty, the worlds will fall into disarray. Chaos will spread. Things do not behave normally or naturally according to their propensities; and people blinded by ignorance and delusion will ignore their obligatory duties and fall into evil ways, causing social disorder degradation and moral decadence. God has to ensure that creation will run its course despite the actions of intelligent beings, who are endowed with a will of their own. Therefore, He makes it His duty (*dharma*) to keep His Creation in order. Whenever the moral and social order of the world declines due to the ascendance of evil, He descends into our world to restore balance and destroy evil.

Why God incarnates upon earth only

Of all the places in the universe, He chooses the earth because it is here both good and evil have an equal chance to thrive and establish their superiority over other worlds. It is here they receive nourishment. It is also the only place, where beings have gross bodies. If we fall into evil ways, chaos will erupt in the other worlds also, since the demons can invade other worlds through our subtle minds. Depending upon whom we serve and which way we go morally and spiritually, we give credence to good or evil in our world and elsewhere. Therefore, God always chooses the earth for His incarnations.

Incarnations of Lord Vishnu

As far as the incarnations are concerned, among the three gods, namely *Brahma*, *Vishnu* and *Siva*, only Lord *Vishnu* incarnates. Since He is the Preserver, He alone has the responsibility to maintain balance, order and regularity of the worlds. Sometimes he does it by fighting directly with the demons and sometimes indirectly through incarnations, emanations, aspects and minor manifestations.

According to the Puranas, Lord *Vishnu* incarnated upon earth several times in the past. He incarnates in each cycle of creation. We have no account of those incarnations. In the current time cycle, He was destined to incarnate ten times, of which nine had already taken place. His last and tenth incarnation known as *Kalki* is expected to happen in future at the end of the fourth and current epoch, known as *Kaliyuga*. There is no unanimity among scholars as to when exactly it is likely to happen.

Regarding His past incarnations also, there is no unanimity. The most commonly accepted incarnations are His incarnations as fish (*matsyavatar*), tortoise (*kurmavatar*), boar (*varahavatar*), lion-man (*narasimhavatar*), dwarf (*vamanavatar*), *Parasurama*, *Rama*, *Balarama*, and *Krishna*. Some lists include the *Buddha* as the last incarnation instead of *Balarama*. The following is a brief description of each incarnation.

- **Matsya:** This incarnation as a giant fish (*mastya*) was meant to save *Manu* (the first-born), the *Vedas* and the seven seers from a great deluge and save the world from falling into ignorance.
- **Kurma:** In this incarnation as a tortoise (*kurma*), He saved the sacred mountain named *Mandara* from sinking by supporting it with His back, while the gods and the demons joined hands to churn the oceans and extract the elixir of life (*amritam*).
- **Varaha:** In this incarnation as a boar, He slew a terrible demon called *Hiranyakasipu* to save the earth from submerging when the demon inundated it with floodwaters.
- **Narasimha:** The purpose of this incarnation was to save one of His devotees, *Prahlada*, from his father *Hiranyakasipu*, who was a demon and who had enmity with Vishnu. Because *Prahlada* was devoted to Lord *Vishnu*, the demon punished his own son with great cruelty. To save him from torture and set an example, Lord *Vishnu* emerged out of a pillar in the form of a man-lion (*narasimha*) and slew the demon, tearing him apart.
- **Vamana:** In this incarnation as a dwarf (*vamana*), He manifested to help *Indra*, the leader of the gods, to retain his lordship over the heaven and save him from Bali, a powerful and pious demon king who grew in stature and strength and was posing a threat to his position as the lord of the heaven.
- **Parasurama:** In this incarnation, he took birth in a priestly family to restore balance and order in society by destroying the warrior clans (*kshatriyas*) who had grown arrogant and neglected their duties as the upholders of *dharma*.

- **Rama**: In this incarnation, he was born in a princely family as Lord *Rama*, and lived as a perfect human being. He slew the demon king *Ravana* who had become a great tormentor and saved the world from his evil and destructive actions.
- **Balarama**: In this incarnation, He appeared as the brother of Lord *Krishna* who was also an incarnation, killed some ferocious demons, probably introduced new methods of cultivation, and facilitated agriculture by changing the course of the river *Yamuna*. Plough was his weapon. Some lists do not include him as an incarnation.
- **Krishna**: In this incarnation, He slew many demons, played a central role in the *Mahabharata* war and cleansed the earth of evil kings and warriors, codified the knowledge and philosophy of Hinduism in the form of the *Bhagavadgita* and emphasized the importance of duty, devotion, knowledge and intelligence in human life.
- **Kalki**: This incarnation will appear at the end of the current epoch (*kaliyuga*) to destroy the evil, restore balance and usher in a new era of truth and justice.

Incarnations are full-fledged manifestations. Apart from them, Lord Vishnu also incarnates partially from time to time to work out a specific problem or set right some aspect of creation. In these, He descends into the world with partial powers (*vibhutis*) to fulfill the chosen purpose. Some well-known partial incarnations are *Hamsa, Satvata, Yagna, Dattatreya*, and *Vedavyasa*.

In some cases, He also manifests in an embodied state with residual powers or greatly reduced powers. They are known as residual manifestations (*amsavataras*). Their purpose is also the same: help restore balance or impart some teachings. A few well-known residual manifestations are *Kapila, Hayagriva, Dhanvantari, Mohini* and *Naranarayana*.

Partial and residual manifestations of Lord *Vishnu* are not incarnations in the strictest sense of the word although their purpose is the same as that of an incarnation, which is restoring order and regularity. However, some scholars tend to consider them also as incarnations because their essential purpose is the same.

Incarnations of Brahma, Siva and Shakti

We do not hear much about the incarnations of either *Brahma* or *Siva* because preservation of the worlds is not their main responsibility. As the creator and the destroyer respectively, both play an important role in creation, but they are not required to incarnate upon earth to perform them. Followers of *Siva* reject the idea that incarnations are required at all for the preservation of the world. In their opinion, God is omniscient and omnipotent and His will is inviolable. Since He decides as well as knows well in advance the fate of the worlds and beings, He does not have to incarnate particularly for situations, which He can control anytime by His sheer Will or plan.

In Saivism, therefore, we do not find any reference to incarnations. However, as part of creation, Lord *Siva* manifests variously in numerous forms and with various names. They are both pleasant and fierce according to the duties involved and worshipped by His devotees with great passion and devotion.

Incarnations of Lakshmi

Whenever and wherever Lord *Vishnu* incarnates, His consort, *Lakshmi*, also incarnates upon earth to assist Him in upholding *dharma*. Since she loves Him and is inseparable from Him, when he incarnates upon earth she follows Him dutifully and incarnates upon earth.

Thus for each incarnation of Lord *Vishnu*, an associated incarnation of the goddess is mentioned in the scriptures. They are listed below.

- *Padma* or *Kamala*, the consort of *Vamana*
- *Dharani* consort of *Parasurama*
- *Sita* wife of Lord *Rama*
- *Rukmini* the chief queen of Lord *Krishna*

- *Varahi* consort of Lord *Varaha*
- *Narasimhi* consort of Lord *Narasimha*

The Significance of incarnations

God pervades the worlds as its Lord as well as its inhabitant. He is hidden in all. He upholds all and envelops all. No place here or hereafter is devoid of Him or free from His lordship. The question then arises is if God is so omnipotent and omnipresent, why does He need to incarnate specially? He can restore *dharma* and perform any task He wishes to do without the burden of carrying a human body that is susceptible to death and disease?

The question is legitimate. Logically speaking, God can do whatever He wants since He is not bound by anything. However, as the upholder of the order and regularity of the worlds, and to set an example, He defines His own duties and sets His own limitations by adhering to the laws He creates. The laws are meant to regulate the worlds and ensure that causes produce their predictable effects. They are meant for practice not for breaking. If God Himself breaks His own laws for the sake of some higher end, others may follow His example and do it themselves. Therefore, when things go out of control and a crisis emerges, God plays by the rules and comes into the world in a mortal body to execute His will and resolve the problem.

God does exist everywhere, but in creation, He remains mostly in the background, veiled by the power of Nature. In the manifested worlds, He does nothing directly, other than being a witness, and allows the beings to live their lives according to the laws established by Him. However, beings in different worlds that are endowed with intelligence and individuals wills may disrupt the normal working of Nature and the course of creation in pursuit of their desires and attachments. When their number exceeds, divine intervention becomes necessary to set things right and allow the creation to run its course.

In darkness, we need light to see things clearly. In a world of utter darkness, we need the light of God. When you enter a darkroom and open a window, darkness instantly disappears the moment the first rays of light hit the floor through the opening. The same happens in a world darkened by evil when an incarnation descends into it and floods it with His rare brilliance.

Wherever an incarnation goes and leaves His footprints, that place becomes pure and sacred (*parandhamam*). Whomever He touches and blesses gains liberation. Whatever knowledge has been lost, forgotten, and polluted with perverted philosophies, He brings it back to the humanity and gives them a fresh chance to redeem themselves.

An incarnation gives the world hope in the triumph of truth. He restores the faith of people in God and goodness and reminds them of their essential purpose. He renews *dharma* and restores faith. He pulls the earth out of the mire of darkness and recharges it with His radiant power and divine knowledge.

One may ask, why God has to descend personally and why cannot He send a messenger or a prophet instead. A messenger may deliver a message. He may help people overcome their ignorance. However, He cannot bring down the full power of God or manifest His consciousness upon earth the way an incarnation can.

A prophet or messenger may help us fight our own battles against evil and impurities; but He cannot wage a war against them on a grand scale. Only God is endowed with the power and the brilliance to do it. A candle is helpful in darkness, but in a limited way. When the brilliance of the sun shines upon earth, we know how effective it is against darkness. God is like the Sun. When He descends upon earth, darkness has no place to hide.

It is the same with the power and brilliance of an incarnation. When He is present amidst us, He purifies the earth like no one else. With each incarnation, our consciousness, takes a quantum leap. Our knowledge and wisdom increase. Our capacity to assimilate complex thoughts and bear with the burdens of life increases exponentially. Our collective consciousness and our collective *karma* receive a generous boost.

A similar process similar to that of an incarnation may happen rarely in the microcosm of an individual. Sometimes, because of the merits gained in the past lives or the efforts made in the present life, devotees may open themselves to the grace of God whereby His power and brilliance may descend into them. While He may not be physically present in them, He speaks through them, listens to them and acts through them. Worshipping them is equal to worshipping Him. Such rare individuals often enter our lives as part of our previous karmas to enlighten us and liberate us.

It may also happen to the practitioners of yoga, when they enter into the advances states of self-absorption. When their desires subside, minds fall silent, egos surrender, and intelligence is filled with the brilliance of *sattva*, the power of God may manifest in their consciousness and give them the experience of oneness with Brahman. It is like God incarnating in the little universe of a being. As our tradition confirms, such subtle incarnations of divine power manifested several times in the past in the microcosm of the individuals.

The possibility of God incarnating upon earth in a mortal form gives us the assuring the feeling that we are not alone in the universe and we have the Supreme Self watching over us and protecting us from evil. It also helps us to live dutifully and responsibly. An incarnation also serves as a teacher and role model for those who are religiously inclined or ripe for liberation. We can learn from His life and actions and follow His example to lead a divine centered life.

Karma – Meaning and Significance

The concept of *karma* is India's unique contribution to the world. Hinduism, Buddhism and Jainism, the major religions of the world, which originated in India, all acknowledge the universality of the law of *karma* in their own individual ways.

According to Jainism, *karma* is not just a metaphysical law, but also a real substance, which flows into people and attaches itself to them like an impurity as they engage in various actions. People are born repeatedly until they rid themselves of the karmic substance.

According to Buddhism, *karma* is an eternal law, which is responsible for the births and deaths and the suffering of beings in the phenomenal world (*samsara*). While no one is free from the law of *karma*, people may minimize its negative impact by living righteously, practicing the Four Noble Truths and the Eightfold Path.

According to the three religions, the law of *karma* is applicable to everyone, to not only humans but also all living beings, including plants, animals and microorganisms. Whoever performs actions, out of desires, attachment and egoism, has to pay the price in the form of suffering arising from the consequences of such actions.

The concept of *karma* is inherent in the Vedic idea of sacrifice. The Vedic people were aware of the concept, but it was a closely guarded secret. It became public knowledge only during the later Vedic period. The Vedic people had an ethical sense about the mortality and immorality of actions. They were conversant with the nature of *dharma* (duty) and its ramification.

For them the sacrifices constituted *karma*. They considered the *Samhita* and *Brahman* portion of the *Vedas* containing the invocations and procedural details about sacrifices the karma-section (*karmakanda*) and the remaining two, the *Aranyaka* and *Upanishad* portion as the knowledge-section (*jnanakanda*).

They believed that by invoking the divinities and performing sacrificial ceremonies in the prescribed manner, one could secure a good position in life or attain a good next birth. Those who earned good merit and died during a particular period of the year, went to world of the immortals and stayed there permanently, while the rest went to world of ancestors and returned to the earth to take birth again.

The origins of karma theory

The consequences of not performing the sacrifices according to the procedure established in the *Vedas* were well known to the Vedic priests. Therefore, they exercised utmost care and performed expiatory ceremonies seeking forgiveness for their mistakes.

The notion of actions having consequences, the dangers inherent in performing evil actions, the merit accruing from religious duties were well known to the Vedic people. Therefore, we cannot definitely say that the concept of *karma* was alien to them.

The early *Upanishads* contain some cryptic references to *karma*, which suggest that probably it was a closely guarded secret known to a few Vedic scholars and seers.

For example, the *Brihadaranyaka Upanishad* (3.2.13) contains a conversation between *Yajnavalkya* and *Jaratakarava Artabhaga*, in which while speaking about action, *Yajnavalkya* says that the secret of what happens after death to a person cannot be spoken in public. Then he concludes his speech saying, "A man becomes good by good actions and bad by bad actions."

The concept of *karma* was also known to the ancient Hindu sects such as Saivism, Bhagavatism and *Samkhya*. Saivism recognized *karma* as one of the three impurities responsible for the bondage of individual beings (*jivas*). The other two were egoism (*anava*) and delusion (*maya*). It emphasized that only by the grace of *Siva* or a *guru*, individual beings caught in the snare of delusion (*maya*) could free themselves from the impurities (*malas*) of life and attain liberation.

Fate versus free will

For a long time, different traditions and schools of philosophy in ancient India debated on the question of whether it was fate or free will, which shaped the lives of people upon earth.

Some schools argued that everything in the world was predetermined and people had no ability to create their own destinies.

Others argued that beings had the ability to control their destinies through their own actions. The former were fatalistic. The latter believed in *karma*.

The *Ajivaka*s, an ancient Indian sect, believed in fatalism. Their leader was *Gosala*, who is believed to be a contemporary of *Mahavira*, the last Jain *Thirthankara*, and the Buddha. They argued that the world, the lives of people and all the events followed a predetermined course or a set path (*niyati*) that was inviolable and inescapable. Therefore, people should live passively, give up seeking and striving, and let life take its own course.

The *Ajivaka*s lived as life happened to them, without trying to make things happen. Theirs was a defeatist philosophy, which advocated renunciation of effort and individual will.

Those who upheld the *karma* theory acknowledged the role of fate partially, but they also believed that beings had the ability to exercise their free will, perform suitable remedial actions and change the course of their lives.

The atheistic traditions, which believed in *karma*, acknowledged the role of free will and individual effort while the theistic schools also recognized the role of God (*adhidaivam*) in changing our destinies.

They believed that desire-ridden actions, ignorance, delusion and egoism were responsible for the suffering of individual souls and their bondage to the mortal world. For them fate was a product of one's own actions and what might look like the intervention of chance was actually the result of previous actions performed by individuals either in their current lives or in previous ones.

In other words, although individuals were born with predetermined destinies because of their past actions, they had the ability to change them and live differently.

While fatalism created despair, *karma* gave hope to people about their future and empowered them to change it if necessary. At the same time, it made them accountable for their lives and actions and reminded them of the dangers inherent in living irresponsibly or immorally.

In this conflict between the two, the fatalistic schools eventually lost their ground. People preferred to believe in *karma* and their ability to pursue their dreams and change their destinies rather than following a fatalistic philosophy that provided neither hope nor solace. The law of *karma* gained upper hand and became an essential component of Indian religions and all major schools of philosophy.

Hinduism, Buddhism and Jainism all acknowledge *karma* despite their fundamental difference about God, creation and liberation. Even Sikhism, which is the most recent of all Indian religions, accepts the role of *karma* in shaping our lives and destinies.

Today, if we have to identify one concept that is deeply ingrained in the consciousness of Hindus, and for that matter a vast number of Indians, which influences their thinking and actions minutely, it is undoubtedly their belief in the law of *karma*.

They may not think about it constantly in their day-to-day lives, but it is deeply ingrained in their consciousness and it influences their lives and actions minutely as a strong undercurrent.

Hindus believe in the law of *karma* and its abiding nature. Whether they are literate or illiterate, they believe in it and acknowledge it. It gives them faith and the forbearance to accept the injustices and inequalities of life with certain resignation and stoicism and absorb the shocks and despairs of life without losing hope in their ability to work for a better future.

The meaning and purpose of karma

Karma means any action. "Kar" means organs of action and "ma" means producing or creating. Literally speaking, *karma* is that which is created or produced by one's bodily organs (*karmendriyas*).

However, *karma* does not mean only physical actions. All actions performed by us constitute *karma*, whether they are intentional or unintentional and physical or mental.

Actions performed by groups and by individuals in association with others also create consequences for the individuals as well as the groups.

Both intentional and unintentional actions are part of one's *karma*.

We also incur *karma* when we instruct others or compel them against their will to perform actions according to our desires and wishes. We are responsible for the *karma* of our children if we ignore our duties and let the children fall into evil ways.

Those who occupy commanding and leading positions, should therefore be careful about what they intend to achieve through others. Their actions and decisions can really lead to negative consequences, if they oppress people, neglect their duties and responsibilities towards other people or cause them undue pain and suffering through immoral and demonic actions.

Thinking plays an important role in our lives. Hence, mental actions also constitute *karma*. Thoughts have the ability to manifest reality and create consequences. With your thoughts, you can affect and influence the lives of others. Good thoughts lead to good consequences and negative thoughts lead to negative consequences. In fact, every action begins first as a thought only.

Hence, for all purposes, thinking is part of one's *karma*. The *Yogasutras* suggests that since thoughts lead to the modifications of the mind and from them consequences arise in the form of afflictions (*klesas*) and latent impressions (samskaras) one should restrain the senses and stabilize the mind in the contemplation of the Self (*Isvara*).

Ancient seers had the ability to manifest their thoughts. According to our tradition, the Vedic *mantras* can be used to manifest our desires. Depending upon our mental attitude and inherent nature, our thoughts may act as either blessings or curses.

As per the law of *karma*, we have to exercise great caution in what we think and keep our minds pure to the extent possible by focusing our thoughts upon God constantly.

The *karma* incurred by a person through his actions determines the course of his life upon earth and his progression into the higher worlds.

Since *karma* is very much a self-correcting and self-regulating mechanism, our actions have the potential to mitigate our suffering or intensify it.

Karma is meant to teach us lessons.

If we learn quickly, we will make progress towards perfection.

If not, we will be presented with much harder options until we realize our mistakes and correct them.

Good deeds lead to inner peace and happiness while bad deeds result in negative consequences for us and all those who are influenced by our thoughts and actions.

Types of karma

Hindu scriptures list various types of *karma*. Primarily, they fall into two categories, past actions and present actions. Past actions may be actions performed in the past in the current life or in the previous lives.

Both the past and present actions may fructify in the current life of a being or in its future lives. They may be producing consequences right now or may do so in future before the end of this life or in future lives. Since *karma* is ongoing, we continue to incur *karma* as we indulge in desire-ridden actions.

Our scriptures recognize the following four types of *karma*.

- *Sancita karma*: It is the sum total of *karma* accumulated by an individual in his or her previous lives. It is the baggage from one's past, which everyone must carry. It is the burden of your past, your lot, which you carry forward from life to life until it is full exhausted. You can call it your fixed deposit *karma* account. You will not achieve liberation unless you exhaust it fully or give it away to God unconditionally through sacrificial actions.

- *Prarabdha karma*: It includes whatever *karma* has manifested or fructified from the accumulated actions of your past (*sancita karma*). It also includes whatever has been manifesting currently and becoming part of our destinies. For example, the fact that you are born in a certain family, with certain features and personality is part of *prarabha karma*. It is what you have got as part of your destiny by birth, by chance or by the turn of events. Depending upon your current actions, it may or may not lead to further *karma*.

- *Agami karma*: This is your future *karma* arising from your current actions, which will fructify in future. It includes whatever *karma* you are creating right now, which may fructify at some point in future either in the current life in future lives. This is your current *karma* account. At the end of your current life, you will be transferring the entire balance from this account to your the fixed deposit *karma* account (*sancita karma*).

- *Kriyamana karma*. It is whatever that manifests from your current actions in this very life. This is the *karma* whose consequences are not added to *sancita karma* but experienced right now or in the future, but in any case in this very life. We can see this particular *karma* in action in our lives as we reap rewards and punishments for the actions we perform and the decisions we make.

Action and inaction

The solution to the problem of *karma* is not inaction or avoiding actions altogether. The *Bhagavadgita* makes it very clear. Both action and inaction have consequences, especially when they are motivated by desires, egoism or some selfish intention.

From the standpoint of *karma*, what we do or do not do intentionally in our lives matters and we may reap consequences from both. We are aware of the implications of doing nothing when a situation warrants a remedial action or the implications of avoiding our obligatory duties for one reason or another.

In life, we pay the price for our irresponsibility, carelessness and negligence. Even in practical matters, if you avoid a problem or do not resolve it in time, it may become a crisis.

During the *Mahabharata* war, *Arjuna*, a warrior by profession, wanted to avoid fighting and abandon his obligatory duties because he did not want to kill his own friends and relations.

Lord Krishna advised him against it since inaction was not the right solution to avoid the consequences of unpleasant actions.

What we do in this life intentionally is as important for our future as what we do not do intentionally. Both produce positive and negative consequences according to the choices we make.

If we shun evil actions, we may earn good *karma*. However, if we shun good actions or if we do not stand against evil (*adharma*) when it is due, we may suffer from the consequences of our complicity and cowardly actions. In both cases, the act of avoiding is in itself an action done with some intention.

Therefore, we have to pay attention to our intentions. We have to remember that here in this world we have an obligatory duty and moral responsibility to uphold righteousness for our sake and for the sake of society. We must be clearly aware of the nature of action. The *Bhagavadgita* makes it clear in the fourth chapter that one should have a clear knowledge of what is action, what is inaction and what is wrong action, because mysterious are the ways of action (4.17). In the next verse, it declares that a wise person sees action in inaction and inaction in action. He is an accomplished yogi who has succeeded in performing actions without attracting their consequences (4.18) since he knows clearly that actions do not bind us, but desires and intentions do. Actions do not produce *karma*. Our desires do.

References to karma in the scriptures

References to *karma* are found frequently in the Hindu scriptures. They identify desires, not actions, as the root cause of our bondage and suffering and caution us against actions performed with specific desires and motives.

The scriptures leave no doubt about the inviolability of the law of *karma* and its universal implications for all beings, from the highest to the lowest, including gods and celestial beings.

Karma is an offshoot of *dharma*. Any action done for the sake of *dharma* without desire upholds *dharma* and produces no consequences.

Those who live dutifully and morally with detachment and with the spirit of renunciation avoid the consequences of their actions and achieve liberation. Others continue to swim in the ocean of life and remain bound to the waves of births and deaths.

Upanishads

The *Upanishads* focus mainly on transcendental reality and the nature of *Atman* and *Brahman*. They also speak about sin and salvation. We find in them some of the earliest references to *karma*, the importance of good deeds and their implications in our lives.

The Vedic people had knowledge of *karma*. For them *karma* meant any sacrificial action that was performed in accordance with the *Vedas*. They regarded all sacrificial actions (*karmakanda*) as dutiful actions (*karma*) that promoted *dharma* and ensured the order and regularity of the worlds. Its knowledge was lower knowledge since it guaranteed a place in the world of ancestors only, compared to the knowledge of the Self, which guaranteed a safe journey to the world of immortals along the sunlit path (*uttarayana*). All the same, both were important (*Isa Upanishad*) for them since the former led to the latter and with the help both alone one could cross the phenomenal world and enter into the light of Brahman.

One of the earliest references to *karma* is found in the *Brihadaranyaka Upanishad*. In the following verses, it recognizes the importance of performing good actions and not having desires. The verse clearly recognizes that actions have consequences and they do matter in the life of an individual.

"Accordingly as one does so he becomes. The doer of good becomes good, the doer of evil becomes evil. One becomes virtuous by virtuous actions. Others become bad by bad actions. Others, however, say that a person consists of desires. As is his desire, so is his will. As is his will so is the deed he does. Whatever deed he does that he attains." (4.4.5)

"Now a man who does not desire, who is free from desires, whose desires are fulfilled, whose only desire is to be with the Self, his vital functions do not depart. He is verily Brahman and to Brahman alone he goes. (4.4.6)

These two thoughts do not cross the mind of the knower of the Self that he has done something evil or he has done something good. He transcends both thoughts and he is not burnt by anything he has done or not done. (4.4.22).

The *Upanishad* also quotes a Rigvedic hymn in reference to *karma* (4.4.23), which states that the greatness of Brahman is not increased or lessened by His actions. One should know how it happens. When one finds it, one is not tainted by evil actions. The following verse (4.4.6) from the same *Upanishad* deals with the consequences of actions performed by people out of desire. According to it, deeds attach themselves to the soul and go to the other world upon its departure, where they determine its further existence.

The object to which the mind is attached, the subtle self goes together with the deed, being attached to it alone. Exhausting the results of whatever works he did in the world he comes again from that world to this world for (fresh) work. This is for him who desires. But he who does not desire...his breaths do not depart. Being Brahman he goes to Brahman."

In the *Svetasvatara Upanishad*, we find many verses that deal with the subject of *karma*. They declare that the embodied self wanders in this world, and assumes many forms and lives according to its *karma*. The following two verses declare the importance of deeds (5.7) and their consequences (5.11).

"He who has qualities (gunas) and doer of fruit bearing actions (phala-karmakarta) is the enjoyer of the consequences of his actions. Assuming all forms according to the triple qualities, he the lord of the vital breaths (pranadhipa) wanders about according to his actions."

"Because of thoughts, touch, sight and passions and because of the availability of food and drink there are the birth and growth for the individual soul. The embodied soul assumes various forms in various places according to the nature of his deeds."

The Bhagavadgita

The *Bhagavadgita* provides a comprehensive solution to the problem of *karma*, identifying its causes and suggesting its remedies.

It has entire chapters devoted to the yoga of action and yoga of renunciation of actions. It declares that *karma* arises not from actions but from desire-ridden actions that bear fruit. The root cause of desires is the activity of the senses.

When we perform actions out of desire or when we desire the fruit of our actions, or when we perform actions with expectations and intentions, we incur *karma* and suffer from the consequences of such actions.

It suggests that the remedy to the problem of *karma* is detachment, absence of desires, renunciation of the fruit of one's actions, surrendering to God and offering all our actions to Him as a sacrifice. The starting point for this is restraining or withdrawal of the senses.

It declares firmly that our right is to action only. God is the real doer, to whom we should offer all our actions and their consequences.

As the true servants of God, we should live dutifully, without abandoning our duties and responsibilities and uphold *dharma*, performing our actions with detachment.

We should cultivate knowledge and intelligence to overcome our ignorance and delusion and use them to escape from the influence of Nature.

The *gunas* are responsible for our desires and desire-ridden actions. We should understand the nature and influence of the *gunas* and cultivate purity (*sattva*) so that we can stabilize our minds in the contemplation of God and experience oneness with Him.

We must surrender to God completely and unconditionally with devotion and live our lives in His contemplation and service.

The following two verses reflect this philosophy (4.23-24).

"For the liberated person, who is free from past attachments, whose mind is established in knowledge, actions performed for the sake of a sacrifice are completely dissolved.

"The act of offering is Brahman; the oblation is Brahman; and the burnt offering poured into the fire of Brahman by Brahman. Brahman is surely attained by him who performs actions fully absorbed in Brahman."

The Puranas

We cannot fail to notice the symbolic representation of desire in the *Puranas*. Both directly and allegorically, they describe how desires motivate people and gods alike in performing their actions with far reaching implications for themselves, the worlds and others.

The gods are pleasure-loving beings. They are driven into action for the sake of pleasure and food. The demons are driven by passions and evil intentions. They try to upset the balance and the order of the worlds to settle their score with gods whom they despise as their eternal enemies, ever since they deceived them and denied them immortality. Humans beings suffer frequently from the actions of both.

In the epics and the *Puranas*, desire is the perceived enemy, which deludes the beings and forces them to act in strange ways.

Desire was the great serpent *Vrata* that Indra slew.

Desire was the dark serpent *Kali* whom Lord *Krishna* tamed by dancing upon its hood, symbolizing His complete mastery over all forms of desires arising from the five senses.

Desire was the lust in the form of *Manmadha* (god of love and lust) whom Lord *Siva* reduced to ashes with His third eye when he tried to corrupt his mind.

Desire and blind ambition made *Dhritarashtra*, the father of the *Kauravas*, to remain partial to his sons even when they indulged in evil actions and tried to deny their cousins, the *Pandavas*, their legitimate right to rule.

Desire again was the reason for *Kaikeyi's* demand that Lord *Rama* should retire to forests and allow her son *Bharata* to ascend the throne.

Desire ruined the life of *Ahalya* and brought disrepute to the wives of *Rishis* when they succumbed to the temptations and machinations of lustful gods.

Desire made *Varudhini* defy tradition and seduce *Pravarakhya*, a sincere disciple of her father, whom she was supposed to treat like a brother.

It was so with *Yami* also, who proposed an incestuous relationship with her own brother *Yama* who was known for his judgment and commitment to *dharma*.

Even *Brahma*, the creator, could not escape from the pangs of desire when he created goddess *Saraswathi*, the goddess of learning, and proposed to marry her.

When Lord Vishnu appeared as a beautiful temptress (*Mohini*) during the churning of the oceans (*sagaramanthanam*) both gods and demons swooned at her sight. Even Lord Siva could not contain his lustful thoughts upon seeing Her.

It was because of desires, the gods and demons engage in regular fights. It was out of desire to achieve immortality both gods and demons churned the ocean to extract the elixir of life.

Desire is the multi-headed serpent *Adishesha* on whose coils Lord *Vishnu* rests with a serene visage, while His consort, *Lakshimi*, the Goddess of wealth, whom everyone reveres for wealth, sits at His feet and serves Him dutifully.

True to the tradition, the *Buddha*, *Mahavira* and later *Guru Nanak* identified desire as the root cause of human suffering, even though they differed fundamentally in other aspects and their respective approaches to salvation.

Renunciation of Desire

Actions by themselves do not cause bondage.

It is the attitude with which we perform our actions that leads to it.

Good actions do not necessarily always produce good consequences, since our lives and actions might be influenced by our past *karmas* also. Our morals and values are relative. Killing a person in the battlefield is valor; but killing the same person in other circumstances is a mortal sin.

Thus, the intention and the context in which we perform our actions are important.

Equally important is the attitude with which we engage in actions. Work done with an egoistic attitude, assuming oneself as the doer, leads to bondage and suffering.

The solution to the problem of *karma* is acquiring the knowledge and discretion to know the truth about actions and perform them with detachment and an attitude of renunciation. The knower of truth about actions knows that actions by themselves do not bind us, but the desires hidden in them.

God Himself engages in actions, but He is not bound to them because He is free from desires and expectations. He does His work dutifully. The *Bhagavadgita* suggests that we should follow the same approach.

We should renounce our desires and attachment and live freely doing what is due and letting life happen, without expectations, with the understanding that we are mere instruments in the hands of God and that by serving Him through actions, we can establish a firm foundation for our liberation

Is Karma a fatalistic philosophy?

Does belief in *karma* inculcate among people a fatalistic attitude?

On the surface, it looks like it makes people fatalistic and prompts them to live with a sense of resignation that whatever *karma* has been incurred in the past has to be lived and endured.

However, this is not true. If you truly believe in *karma*, you know that you can change your life through your actions and create your own destiny by the sheer power of your will. You also know that you can work for your salvation by knowing what sets you free from your own *karma*.

Belief in *karma* should make people more responsive and dutiful towards their duties and obligations and motivate them to live responsibly as good human beings doing their part in serving their families, others and the world in general.

If you know the implications of *karma*, you will do your part in God's creation and fulfill your obligations, without complaining and throwing the blame upon others for your misfortunes.

You will be acutely sensitive to the happenings in your life and try to connect them to your past.

From it, you will learn the lessons life has to teach you and realize the need to live ethically and responsibly, avoiding the pitfalls that ensnare people and lead them to their downfall.

You will listen to your conscience more sensitively and do what is good for you and others.

You will not blame others for your problems or expect them to resolve them for you.

You will not live and act like a victim of your circumstances.

Nor you will try to victimize others, as you know the consequences of such actions.

Most importantly, as you understand the mechanism of *karma* and the way it keeps you engaged with the world, at some point in your life, you turn to God to offer Him all your actions and make Him the object of your veneration. You reach this point and become free from the shackles of *karma*, when you realize that your duty (dharma) is to live for others and for God, but not for yourself and begin to perform actions with that attitude.

Thus, belief in *karma* makes you more human, more responsible and dutiful. True believers in *karma* would not blame anyone or anything for their difficulties. They know that they create their lives and destinies through their own actions. They also know that while their options to deal with their past are limited, they can work for their betterment and create a new beginning for themselves through their actions and their relationship with God.

This makes them feel optimistic and hopeful about their future and their next lives. It also broadens their vision and thinking and makes them look at their lives in a larger framework spanning over several lifetimes.

The Concept of Maya in Hinduism

Hinduism has given to the world, a unique concept known as *maya* or illusion. The word *maya* is used to denote magical power, illusion, delusion of the mind, and Nature or the Mother Goddess.

In a literal sense, *maya* is that which goes forth (*ya*) from the Primal Mother (*ma*) or Nature. It is a reference to the womb as well as to creation, in which Nature plays an important role as the support or the Field.

Maya also means not (*ma*) That (*ya*). Brahman is often referenced in the *Upanishads* as That. That refers to the Ultimate Reality. What is not That is the alternative reality, different and distinct from it. Its source is Brahman, but in its essential nature, it is not Brahman.

References to the word are found in the *Rigveda*, *Atharvaveda* and the epics *Ramayana* and *Mahabharata*. The word has both positive and negative connotations. In a negative sense, it means deceit and fraud and in a positive sense, it means magic and illusion.

Maya, the magical power

The earliest references to *maya* are found in the *Rigveda* (10.177) and *Atharvaveda* (8.10). They allude to the magical powers of the demons (*asuras*) and the gods (*devas*). The demons misuse the power to deceive and distract, while the gods use them to defeat the demons and protect the worlds.

Human beings do not have this power, but they can gain magical powers with the help of the Vedic *mantras*, austerities, yoga, the grace of God and sacrifices.

The concept is further elaborated in the epics and the *Puranas*. The demons use the power to upset the worlds and create chaos, while the gods use it to restore order and stability and save the worlds.

The warriors in both the epics, *Ramayana* and *Mahabharata*, had the power to use magic to unleash the most destructive weapons with the help of magic. *Ravana, Indrajit Marici and Ghatotkatch* possessed extraordinary magical powers, which made them almost invincible, while *Arjuna, Drona, Bhishma and Karna* had magical bows and weapons with which they could delude their enemies or make them unconscious.

Magic was also responsible for the war between the *Pandavas* and *Kauravas*. The Kauravas usurped the kingdom of the *Pandavas* by using deceit and magic in a game of dice, which forced the latter to go into exile and realize the evil nature of their cousins. When the *Pandavas* built their new capital, they employed an architect from heaven to build a special palace called the hall of illusions (*mayasabha*), where actually the seeds of the *Mahabharata* war were sown.

God as the Magician

Lord *Rama* did not use magic in His personal life. He was rather a victim of magic used by *Ravana*. However Lord *Krishna* did. He possessed great magical powers with which He amused His devotees and destroyed His enemies. He appeared to all women of *Brindavan* simultaneously. With His magic flute, He enthralled all the animals and bystanders. As a child, He showed to *Yashoda* the whole universe in His little mouth

References to God as a great Magician (*mayavi*) are found in the *Upanishads*, the *Bhagavadgita* and the *Puranas*. The *Svetasvatara Upanishad* declares that everything that emanates from Brahman is enveloped in *maya* (4.9). Nature is indeed *maya* and its wielder is the great Lord Himself (4.10). He presides over all wombs and in Him everything is manifested and dissolved.

The magical powers of God are affirmed in both Saivism and Vaishnavism. Magic is the means by which God creates the worlds for His own enjoyment and amusement. For Him it is a play (*lila*). For that, He employs His dynamic power (*shakti*) in various ways to mirror Himself in the things and beings He creates. He uses His immense power to manifest, preserve and destroy the worlds and beings He creates. He uses it to reveal truth as well as conceal it, to extend Himself and retract Himself, and to expand the worlds and withdraw them.

He uses His vast powers to not only delude people but also grant them knowledge and wisdom when they are ready for liberation. The worlds rest upon His magic. The worlds exist because of His magic. In creating them, He employs five different powers: mental power (*cit-shakti*), will power (*iccha shakti*), knowledge power (*jnana shakti*), acting power (*kriya shakti*) and the power of bliss (*ananda shakti*).

While He uses His revealing powers to manifests the worlds, He uses His veiling powers to conceal Himself and remain hidden in them. By limiting the knowledge, intelligence, ability and life of the beings, He subjects them to the impurity of *maya*, whereby they become bound to the world and Nature.

The world as an illusion

If creation is the result of God's magical power, it logically follows that whatever He creates magically must be an illusion. While ordinary magic lasts for a short time, God's magic lasts for eons, thereby giving us the impression that it is real and everlasting. Since no one really outlasts creation, no one really knows its true nature, except through the testimony of the scriptures and the teachings of the masters. From them we learn that although the world, which is part of His magic, gives us the illusion of continuity and stability, in reality it is but a temporary construct produced by His manifesting power and His direct involvement with Nature.

Since He uses magic to produce the worlds, His power personified as *Shakti* or *Prakriti* (Nature) is also known as *Maya*. This concept has been elaborated subsequently in the *Upanishads* and in various schools of *Vedanta*.

The world is real only in a limited sense. Since our lives are short, we will never be able to know it otherwise. However, we can draw some conclusions about it true nature based upon our own experience of the instability and impermanence we perceive in the phenomenal world.

In *Vedanta*, one of the six schools of Hindu philosophy, we find two divergent views regarding the nature of creation. One holds it as a temporary phenomenon or an appearance (*vivarta vada*) in which reality is veiled by the superimposition of an alternate reality whereby we mistake truth for falsehood and vice versa.

This view is upheld by the proponents of the school of monism (*advaita*) of which *Shankaracharya* was the foremost. According to this school, Brahman alone is real. The individual souls and Nature are mere formations or appearances. They are projections that appear at the beginning of creation and withdrawn into Brahman when the worlds are destroyed. Because knowledge is veiled, we consider them true.

The other view holds that creation is a transformative process (*parinama vada*) in which the worlds and beings manifest because of the modifications arising within the domain of Nature induced by the will of God. This view is upheld by the followers of qualified monism (*Vishishtadvaita*), which regards God (*Isvara*), individual souls (*cit*) and Nature (*acit*) as the three ultimate and eternal realities. While God is independent, the other two are dependent realities. They are distinct from God but never separate from Him. Together they constitute His universal form.

Nature is both eternal and indestructible. During creation, it undergoes transformation from a subtle state to a manifest state whereby the effects hidden in their causes manifest to create duality and diversity, which we experience through our senses. If creation is a transformative process, so is dissolution during which the effects subside into their causes and Nature returns to its subtle and primeval condition. Its gross material forms disappear, but never destroyed.

Whether creation is a projection or superimposition or a transformation, we will never know empirically. However, we know from observation that the world will not last forever and like a dream, it lasts for a while and then disappears.

Delusion of the mind

Maya manifests in us as ignorance and delusion caused by the veiling power of God whereby we fail to discern things correctly or perceive the reality concerning them. Because of ignorance and limited knowledge, we also mistake truth for falsehood and illusion for reality. We will be proportionately free from these imperfections to the extent we cultivate knowledge and wisdom.

We know from experience that the world around us and the world we experience are not always the same. We cannot draw reliable conclusions from our experiences unless we pay adequate attention and look at things deeply free from desires and attachments. We may consider our phenomenal existence as true because we are subject to delusion and cannot discern the truth hidden behind apparent reality. Our perceptions and experiences are part of the illusion to which we are subject. The scriptures warn us not to take our senses literally or depend upon them blindly, because our knowledge and wisdom are colored by our desires, attachments and egoism.

The world is not real except in a limited sense or from a particular standpoint. What is real in wakeful state undergoes change in the dream state and disappears in a deep sleep state. Sometimes we see the truth; sometimes we infer things and sometimes we make up things because of mistaken notions, faulty perception or ignorance.

To perceive truth we have to cleanse our minds and bodies of the impurities that are present in us, such as the *gunas,* so that we can see the truth hidden within ourselves and behind the appearance of things without the interference of the mind and the senses and without the duality between the knower and the known. We must become absorbed in the essence of things, transcending our limited awareness and the experience of duality and separation. With knowledge and awareness and through the practice of various yogas, we must cultivate discernment to know how delusion clouds our behavior and keeps us chained to the cycle of births and deaths.

The following are some of the ways in which delusion influences the beings upon earth.

- Because of delusion, beings take their physical bodies for real and fail to discern their true selves hidden deep within them.
- They consider themselves different and distinct from the rest of creation.
- They fail to perceive their inseparable connection with God.
- They act in selfish, ignorant and egoistic ways whereby they incur *karma* and remain bound to the cycle of births and deaths.
- They develop attachment to the sense objects through repeated contact and suffer from attraction and aversion to the pairs of opposites
- They become involved with the world and remain bound to it.
- They lack discernment and indulge in desire ridden actions
- They take credit for the actions and achievements and fail to acknowledge the role of God in their lives and destinies.

As long as we thinks that we are individually different from the rest of the creation and work for our own ends, protecting, furthering nurturing and defending our own egos and interests, we suffers from delusion and remain upon earth bound to Nature reaping the consequences of our thoughts and actions.

Overcoming maya

The purpose of human life is to realize the truths concerning our world and our existence by cultivating discernment (*buddhi*) and with that knowledge and wisdom to work for one's liberation. The world is an aspect of God that lasts for a certain time and then disappears. Its roots are in heaven. We cannot see its inseparable connection with God or His hand in its creation because we cannot perceive the truths that are beyond our minds and senses. Since we believe the world to be true, we become involved with it and indulge in selfish actions that lead to rebirth and bondage. We ignore our obligatory duty (*dharma*) which is to live in the service of God and serve the aims of God's creation rather than live for own selfish aims.

The delusion is also responsible for our dependence upon our senses and our inability to see the truth beyond them. The senses draw us towards the sense objects. Through repeated contact with them, we experience attraction and aversion to them, which results in attachment. When we indulge in desire-ridden actions out of attachment to sense-objects, we become mentally unstable and vulnerable to suffering, selfishness and egoism.

Hence, our scriptures suggest that restraint of the senses is the first step to regain control over our minds and bodies and achieve liberation. This is done by withdrawing the senses from the sense objects into the mind, the mind into intelligence and intelligence into the Self. At the same time, one should aim for inner purity. Both the mind and the body should be purified with discipline, yoga and austerities. When one is free from impurities, one becomes aware of the true nature of the world and one's own existence.

As the *Bhagavadgita* suggests we should realize the Self through the self and with the help of the self. It is only through self-transformation we can end the delusion of our minds and go beyond our limited awareness and existence.

Rebirth or Reincarnation in Hinduism

Belief in rebirth or reincarnation (*punarjanma*) is one of the well-known characteristic features of Hinduism. The scriptures affirm that each embodied soul (*jivaatman*) caught in the phenomenal world (*samsara*) reincarnates upon earth repeatedly according to its past deeds (*karma*) and dominant desires (*samskaras*) until it attains liberation through spiritual reawakening and returns to its source, which is Brahman, or to its original eternal, absolute State.

Until then, it remains in the embodied state, bound to Nature and clouded by ignorance and delusion caused by the impurities arising from the *gunas*, the ego and desire-ridden actions. In the deluded state, it assumes many forms and passes through many births and deaths until it is liberated.

The concept of reincarnation is well document in the *Vedas*. Its earliest references can be found in the *Upanishads* such as the *Brihadaranyaka Upanishad*.

The *Bhagavadgita* (2.22) sums up the concept of rebirth succinctly when it declares metaphorically that for an embodied soul, the body is like a garment. Just as a person discards worn out clothes and puts on new ones, the soul discards worn out bodies and wears new ones.

The body is a temporary construct, which is perishable and vulnerable to modifications such as injury, aging, sickness and death.

A soul is imperishable, inexhaustible and free from such modifications even in an embodied state. When it inhabits a body, it is like two realities coming together and coexisting in the same space without ever coalescing.

The happenings in the phenomenal world do not change the Self even a little. Amidst the modifications of Nature, desire-ridden actions and the ever-changing events of life, it remains in its pristine state, untouched and untainted by all the conditions to which life is subject.

Nature keeps it in bondage. That is all it can do. It holds it in the prison of the body but it can never touch it. Amidst the waters of life, the Self remain pure like a lotus flower.

It is also said that the Self neither acts nor causes anything to act.

All actions arise from the mind and body or aspects of Nature, but never from the soul.

According to Hinduism, the soul's bondage to Nature is a willful act of creation intended by the Creator Himself. Under His will, Nature keeps her hold upon the individual souls and engages them in actions and in the process of creation to create diversity, bondage, ignorance and delusion.

Each embodied self has to live many lives and undergo many experiences before it attains perfection and returns to its original state of absolute freedom.

Bondage of souls

According to some widely acknowledged theories of creation available in Hinduism, life manifests upon earth when individual souls come under the influence of Nature and become involved with it developing material bodies and objectivity. Their mortal existence continues, as long as they remain as embodied selves subject to Nature and its modifications, driven by desires induced by the *gunas* and enveloped by ignorance and delusion. In a state of bondage, they progress from one life to another, assuming various forms, according to their actions, past life impressions and predominant desires.

After many births, they attain human birth and get a chance to work for their liberation through selfless actions and sacrificial duties using their knowledge and wisdom. Those who succeed in this effort reach the world of Brahman and attain immortality. The rest continue their existence upon earth until the end of the creation.

However, human birth is not a straight ticket to liberation. The beings have to work hard to qualify. Those who lack discernment may find it hard to overcome their attachments and animal passions. If they fall into evil ways and engage in sinful actions, they may even degenerate into lower life forms as worms and insects or even descend into the darkest hells and languish there for a long time. Therefore, human birth works both ways. It is both an opportunity and a hurdle for those who seek liberation.

The making of a jiva

The embodied selves are also known as *Jivas*, meaning the living beings, or those endowed with life-breath (prana). They come into existence because of the union between the Self (*Purusha*) and Nature (*Prakriti*). Nature is also known as the Field (*kshetra*) and the Self as the Knower of the field (*kshetrajna*). Their coming together is necessary for life to exist upon earth.

In each, the Self is the psychic or spiritual entity made up of pure intelligence while Nature manifests as the body or the physical self. The soul is passive, eternal and indestructible. Nature is active and indestructible, but subject to modifications in its parts and aspects.

The soul is the inner Witness (*sakshi*) and the Enjoyer of all experiences, perceptions and modifications that arise in the field (body); but does not desire things or actively participate in any modifications of Nature. Unlike the soul, Nature is divisible. It has many component realities or sub-natures (*tattvas*), which are responsible for the diversity among the beings and things. They manifest in a being to create the illusion of individuality (ego), or the false self, which acts as if it is the real Self.

The component realities of Nature are intelligence, ego, mind, the triple *gunas*, the five elements, and the fifteen senses. Together, they constitute the field or the physical self. The physical self and the real Self together constitute jiva or the embodied self. The *Jivas* are subject to desires and modification, induced by *gunas*, whereby they become subject to *karma*, rebirth and suffering. When the body dies, the soul leaves it and goes to either the immortal world of Brahman or the ancestral world depending upon its past deeds.

Rebirth vs. immortality

Those who live righteously and transcend their desires and attachments through self-purification become immortal. They go to the immortal world and never return. There is no rebirth for them, even in the next cycle of creation. The pious who do not qualify for immortality, go to the world of ancestors, where they stay until their karmas are exhausted and then return to take another birth.

The rest who indulge in sinful actions, ignoring their duties and wasting their precious opportunities to work for their salvation, go the world of *Yama* or hell and suffer there until their sins are washed away through suffering. The heaven and hell offer two contrasting options for the humanity. The ancestral world is a temporary solution. It does not resolve the problem of rebirth, while it prolongs the suffering of beings.

Thus, rebirth is for those who cannot escape from the law of *karma* or who do not know how to perform actions without inviting consequences. For them, since they lack knowledge and discretion *Karma* acts like a self-correcting mechanism. They learn the hard way through pain and suffering, until they realize their sinful ways and begin to work for their salvation. Usually all embodied souls have to undergo numerous births and deaths in their bound state until they resolve their imperfections and escape forever from the control of Nature.

The unfolding of Nature in life

The concept of reincarnation is based upon the premise that although God is the Creator, He does not manifest everything instantly. He does it in phases over great epochs of time, remaining as the Witness and Enjoyer, allowing Nature to manifest its aspects in a multitude of beings and giving them an opportunity to evolve through self-transformation according to their wills, desires, knowledge, intelligence and individual actions (*karma*). In creation, Nature manifests things and beings through a gradual mechanical process building bodies around the individual souls in a phased manner until they are deeply embedded in materiality, delusion and ignorance.

Life evolves upon earth through the aggregation of the component realities of Nature (*tattvas*). They are responsible for the diversity we see in creation. The *Samkhya* School dwells deep into the working of Nature and its mechanism. It suggests that Nature is a preprogrammed entity, a blind mechanism, an automaton, without having a will or purpose of its own. It is not the creator in the true sense of the word. It creates what is already present or imprinted in its vast intelligence (*mahat*) as latent impressions, thoughts, desires and ideas according to the predominance of the *gunas*.

Under the influence of *sattva* it produces divine and resplendent things and beings. Under the influence of *rajas*, it produces world and beings of exceptional beauty, talent and vitality. Under the influence of *tamas*, it produces dark worlds and demonic beings. Whatever it manifests or intends to manifest exist in it already in a seed form. All the causes and effects are present in it in various states of dormancy, becoming or being. They manifest when the causes are triggered. The impetus for the trigger may come from the will of God (*daivikam*), the law of Nature (*bhautikam*) or the desire-ridden actions of the beings themselves (*adhyatmikam*).

Since these processes take a long time, the beings have to go through several lives and phases of transformation before they develop all the aspects of Nature. Thus, in the domain of Nature, nothing new is produced. It reproduces what is already present and brings forth beings and their qualities in its own timeframe. Beings evolve to the extent Nature unfolds in them its component realities. In the highly evolved beings, Nature manifests fully and in the lower life forms, it manifests partially or minutely.

The evolution of life upon earth

A study of the *tattvas* and their gradual differentiation from the indeterminate primal Nature (*mula-prakriti*) suggests that Nature unfolds its component realities in the beings gradually, starting with the differentiation of basic elements and ending with the appearance of intelligence. In creation, intelligence is the last to manifest. The whole process from the beginning to the end takes a long time and happens incrementally, through a gradual awakening of one component after another. With regard to the gunas, *tamas, rajas and sattva*, this is the order of manifestation. The lower life forms are driven by inertia (*tamas*) and the higher life forms are filled with the brilliance of *sattva*.

In the beginning stages, only the elements (*mahabhutas*) are differentiated or activated. In this primitive state, the first to appear are the inanimate objects or the material things consisting of the five elements, followed by semi-animate life forms. They possess some dynamism (*caitanyam*) arising from attraction and aversion, which distinguishes them from the inanimate objects. However, except for limited movement and some biological activity, you can consider them borderline life forms.

In the next stage, the senses manifest and join the elemental body, providing the beings with perceptual ability and the ability to interact with their environment. Even here, their manifestation is gradual. First, beings appear with one or two senses. Then, come beings with more senses. Finally, as in case of human beings, all senses appear, including the mind, the eleventh sense.

In the next phase, Nature unfolds further and manifests beings with an internal organ (*antahkarana*), consisting of the mind, the ego and intelligence, which is responsible for a distinct personality or individuality. At this stage, beings possess some individuality and rudimentary intelligence, which they use to interact with the world and fulfill their desires. Although they possess some intelligence, they are mostly guided by their instincts and impulses rather than intelligence. Most of the animals fall into this category.

The intelligence that human beings possess takes time to manifest upon earth. It happens after many births, when the *tattvas* fully unfold and beings develop the ability to make their own decisions and regulate their own through willful and intelligent actions. Intelligence manifests fully only in those who cultivate purity (sattva) and overcome their delusion and ignorance.

Thus, we learn from the above description, that creation not as an instantaneous, magical or miraculous process but a gradual transformative process that happens in phases over a long time involving the will of God, modifications and diversification of Nature and the actions of the beings themselves. It happens both at the universal level in which beings manifest with progressive levels of intelligence and at the individual level in which beings undergo self-transformation until they develop knowledge and wisdom to work for their liberation.

Life evolves upon earth gradually through the modifications and transformation of Nature, while beings evolve individually through their own actions, knowledge and intelligence. They evolve according to the levels of purity (*sattva*) they achieve. The will of God begins the process. The activities of Nature play an important role in the early stages of evolution, until beings develop their own individuality and intelligence. In case of higher beings, their own actions play an important role in shaping their destinies and spiritual transformation.

Human beings are at the end of this long line of evolution upon earth. However, in relation to the beings of other worlds, they stand somewhere in the middle, with the gods above and the demons below. At the lowest end of this chain is the primeval Nature or pure energy that remains unmanifest and undifferentiated, while at its highest end is the absolute and supreme Brahman of indescribable intelligence with His

Manifested Aspect setting in motion the whole process and His Unmanifested Aspect hidden and unknown. Those who want to climb this ladder of intelligence and consciousness need to practice yoga and undergo inner transformation to overcome their impurities and stabilize their minds so that they can discern things more clearly and overcome their ignorance and delusion.

Karma and rebirth

Dharma, karma, and rebirth are interrelated. *Karma* arises from dharma and rebirth becomes necessary when the *karma* incurred in one life cannot be squared off in the same life. Even the manner in which a person dies has implications for his or her afterlife and next life. In fact, the nature of *karma* is such that it can never be squared off in one life. The shadow of *karma* follows us, life after life, until we learn to neutralize the fruit of *karma* with spiritual knowledge and self-transformation.

According to our scriptures, those who live for themselves and perform actions selfishly to satisfy their own desires are born repeatedly. However, those who perform their actions dutifully for the sake of God, as an offering, with the spirit of renunciation and surrender, are freed from their consequences. God takes responsibility for their lives and actions; and when they depart from here, frees them from the cycle of births and deaths.

Actions performed according to the tenets of *dharma* ensure a good next life and progress towards liberation. Those who violate God's eternal law have to reap the negative consequences. One cannot avoid rebirth by being selective in actions or by avoiding them. This is stated very clearly in the *Bhagavadgita*. To avoid rebirth and the consequences of *karma*, obligatory actions must be performed dutifully however unpleasant they may be, without seeking their fruit.

References to rebirth in scriptures

The *Upanishads* and the *Vedas* contain several references to rebirth. The earliest references to life after death are found in the *Samhitas* of the *Rigveda*, which describe the world of *Yama* where people go after they depart from here and where life is more joyful and perfect compared to the life of suffering upon earth. The best way to reach it is through sacrifices. Those who indulge in wicked actions are punished by *Varuna* who casts them into a dark abyss.

Reference to the world of the ancestors where life is temporary and the world of immortals where the souls exist forever are also found in the *Rigveda* (10.88.15). The *Upanishads* present a more advanced and detailed version of these rudimentary beliefs about life after death and the ascent of the souls to the sun or the moon.

The *Brihadaranyaka Upanishad* clearly states that those who know Brahman or realize that they are eternal Selves become immortal. For the rest, suffering only awaits.

When a soul leaves the body, says the *Upanishad*, his intelligence departs with him. His knowledge (*vidya*) and actions (*karma*) take hold of him and so do his memories (*purva-prajna*). Like a leech that leaves one body and latches on to another or a caterpillar that leaves one blade of grass and moves on to another, the soul leaves one and draws itself to another. Just as a goldsmith takes a piece of gold and turns into a beautiful shape, the soul makes for itself another beautiful form like that of his ancestors, celestial beings, gods, *Prajapati* or Brahman himself.

The same *Upanishad* also states (4.4.1-6) that the subtle self (*lingam*) goes to the other world with the objects to which the mind is attached, together with the deeds, and after exhausting the results of its works, returns to this world for fresh work. One escapes from the cycle of births and deaths and becomes immortal only when all the desires in the heart are cast away. The body without the soul is very much like the slough of a snake cast off by it.

The *Upanishad* also speaks of the two paths, the path of Brahman by going which the departing souls never return and the other path by which those who give charity and perform sacrifices go to the ancestral heaven and return. Those who do not go by these two become worms, insects and snakes (2.2.16).

The same paths are mentioned in *Prasna Upanishad* (1.9), *Mundaka Upanishad* (3.2.6), *Kausitaki Upanishad* (1.6) and *Chandogya Upanishad* (4.15.5 & 5.3.2), which further states that those who perform pleasant actions are born through pleasant wombs in families and those who actions are evil take birth through evil wombs (5.10.7).

References to rebirth are found in the *Katha Upanishad* also, which declares that a man ripens like corn and like corn is born again (1.6). Lack of discretion leads to rebirth (2.7).

The Bhagavadgita is essentially about how to avoid rebirth and the consequences of *karma* by performing actions without desires and attachment. It reminds us of our spiritual nature and the fact the body is like a garment, which the soul keeps wearing and discarding from birth to birth.

The eighth chapter discusses the two paths mentioned before, the consequences of remembering God at the time of leaving the body, and how the multitude of beings are born again and again during each time cycle. It also states that those who attain God are never born again.

The *Yogasutras* provide a comprehensive solution to the problem of rebirth by suggesting self-purification through the eightfold practice of yoga to root out desires and modifications whereby the mind becomes stabilized in the contemplation of the Self, the latent impressions are burnt away and the possibility of rebirth is eliminated.

Ignorance, attraction and aversion, and the ego are responsible for the afflictions of the mind (*klesas*) and soul's bondage to the earth and Nature.

The *klesas* determine the stock of *karma*, which may be experienced in this life or in future lives.

They also determine the type of birth, span of life and the enjoyment of a being upon earth (2.12).

These can be eliminated through the yoga of action (*kriya-yoga*) consisting of self-discipline, study and devotion (pranidhanani).

Liberation is achieved by cultivating uninterrupted discriminating intelligence (2.27) which arises in one's mind when the impurities (*asuddhis*) are removed.

The scripture also declares that when covetousness (*aparigraha*) is removed one develops the knowledge of births (2.39).

The epics and the *Puranas* contain many stories about rebirth. Great souls and even gods are born upon earth in consequence of their actions. Apart from one's own actions, curses and blessings play an important role in determining one's next birth.

For example to take revenge against *Bhishma*, a princess named *Amba* received the blessings of Siva and took birth in the family of *Drupada* as *Sikhandi* and participated in the *Mahabharata* war. *Bhishma* himself was born because of a curse.

Significance of reincarnation

As we have discussed before, creation happens when pure consciousness or supreme intelligence descends into matter, which results in the emergence of embodied selves. The body is like a sheath or a secretion formed around the soul. It happens over a longtime until Nature manifests its full potential. This gradual flowering of intelligence in Nature or the unfolding of all of its potentials is facilitated by rebirth. Reincarnation gives the beings an opportunity to evolve, transform and liberate. It helps them progress from a state of ignorance and delusion to a state of awareness, knowledge and intelligence, guided by discretion and individual will. Those who misuse their actions, knowledge and wisdom are reborn until they learn their lessons, while those who use them to overcome their desires and attachment attain liberation. During this whole process, while Nature undergoes transformation, the inner Self remains pure and undisturbed.

Each birth is an opportunity for an embodied soul to continue its journey towards liberation or fulfill its dominant desires. With each birth, it gathers the weight of desires as well as the light of knowledge and wisdom arising from its previous experiences. Its destiny depends upon the choices it makes and the course of action it chooses. Only at the end of several births, it realizes the need for liberation to overcome its suffering and bondage. Rebirth is therefore an opportunity we give to ourselves to learn from our past and renew our journey to the world of Brahman.

Evidence for Reincarnation

The concept of reincarnation is not recognized in western traditions. They do not believe in the very concept of soul's liberation but only in its emancipation from sin. They believe in soul's ethereality in contrast to the Vedic description of the individual Self as pure consciousness without qualities, substance and attributes. According to them, the souls are born in sin on earth and they cannot get rid of it through pious actions. However, they can go to heaven by atoning for their sins and by declaring their faith in God and their allegiance to His Law.

Despite lack of appreciation outside Indian religions, evidence is gathering in favor of reincarnation of soul. Research in paranormal experiences and past life regressions prove that the memories stored in the subconscious may often contain memories of past lives. It is now possible to guide individuals through hypnotism to regress into their past lives and wake up dormant memories, images and impressions of their previous lives. The practice is also used in certain meditation techniques practiced in Buddhism.

The pioneering work done in this field by enlightened masters and psychics like Edgar Cayce confirm beyond doubt that reincarnation is not just a theory or imagination, but a definite reality. Their experiences and findings prove that some of the most troubling problems in our current lives such as incurable phobias and diseases may have their source in some disturbing events of our past lives.

The implications

The concept of reincarnation reinforces the belief that life on earth did not emerge suddenly, but evolved gradually, involving great epoch of time and a vast multitude of beings. During this process, the static and inert consciousness of matter yielded place to the dynamic movement of life and consciousness. The animal tendencies gave way to human reason and humane thoughts. Extending the same logic, we may further conclude that this part animal, part human and part divine being, has the potential to evolve further and escape from the hold of Nature.

If you study the components that make up the personality of human beings, you will realize they have aspects that are grosser and denser and cannot be purified and transformed in a limited lifespan. A hundred years of life upon earth is not sufficient for a being to learn valuable lessons and progress from a state of ignorance to knowledge and intelligence, unless one is willing to undergo intense self-purification process and take extraordinary steps to practice renunciation, devotion and detachment.

It is even more difficult for lower life forms to overcome the snares of the phenomenal world in one lifetime. For that, they need higher intelligence and inner purification, which may take time. Beings have to evolve progressively through innumerable births and deaths before they can be free.

From inertia to activity, corporeality to consciousness, ignorance to awareness and self-knowledge, attachment to detachment, delusion to discernment, impurity to purity, unreality to reality, darkness to light, death to immortality, this is the forward movement of life in creation. This multifaceted and complex transformation of beings cannot happen in a few years. God's creation is opposite of His essential nature. It is not what God is in

His unmanifested state. Without diversity and duality, creation would be static, with no scope for change and movement.

It is true that God is hidden in every aspect of His creation. However, that which is visible and sensible is not His true self. It is His false or illusory self. It has to become silent and pure to reflect His divine qualities and allow the Self to shine. The inexorable law of karma plays a significant role in this transformation.

It is the correcting mechanism, the chisel. It polishes the negative self, the lifeless stone, relentlessly, until it is transformed into a deity and installed in the temple of God as His manifestation. An awareness of this very mechanism is an important step in the evolution of a being.

Creation and evolution need not universally be progressive always. Since *karma* operates on the principle of trial and error, sometimes a being may regress into lower life forms due to negligence and mistakes.

Therefore, one cannot take one's liberation granted even after reaching perfection in the practice of yoga. One should not rest until the impurities of the mind and body are completely removed and one attains perfection in the practice of yoga.

Each living being has to find its own way, sailing in the boat of its own *karma*, in a sea of worldly phenomena (*samsara sagaram*), through trial and error and self-effort, with the soul remaining as its silent, witnessing companion.

Gods and Goddesses in Hinduism

It is difficult to characterize Hinduism as a polytheistic religion because Hinduism recognizes both the unity and diversity of manifestation and views God as not only One but also many. The one God appears as many and the many gods and goddesses in their highest aspect are but the same One. This is the theme, we find constantly in all the scriptures of Hinduism.

One God and many gods

Seeing all in one and one in all is one of the dominant virtues the Upanishads highlight when they speak of Brahman, the Supreme Universal Self. They speak of Brahman as the one indivisible, indefinable, indescribable, absolute and infinite Self. He contains within Himself all the complimentary and contrasting aspects of life. He is both what is and what is not, one and many, manifested and unmanifested, being and non-being and the smallest of the small and the largest of the large. This vision of God as the sum total of everything that exists here and hereafter is very well reflected in Hinduism in its concept of God, the structure of the universe and methods of worship.

In Hinduism, people worship numerous divinities both ritually and spiritually, such as *Brahma, Vishnu, Siva, Lakshmi, Parvathi, Saraswathi, Indra, Varuna, Mitra, Agni and Vayu.* At the same time, they also worship them as aspects of Brahman only. Brahman is not usually worshipped directly in domestic or temple rituals. He is usually worshipped indirectly in the form of other gods or internally in meditation and contemplation. While He is the ultimate recipient of all offerings, they are usually made through various divinities and personal gods whom people worship.

Apart from divinities, in Hinduism people also worship many animate and inanimate objects such as conch shells, water pots, round stones, trees, plants, rivers, lakes, snakes, hills, planets, stars, constellations, the sun, the moon, spirits and ancestors. They also worship saints, yogis, seers and sages. In the Vaishnava tradition, devotees worship the images of God (*arcas*) as if it is His living incarnation having His potency. While some may scoff at these practices as primitive and backward, the practice reflects the deep-rooted conviction in Hinduism that the Supreme Universal Being pervades the whole universe and He is hidden in every object and aspect of creation. If He is present everywhere and in everything, logically everything is worthy of worship. The same conviction guides the devotees in Hinduism to view the whole world as the sacred ground of God and life itself a precious opportunity to envision Him everywhere and in everyone.

Methods of worship

In Hinduism, the divinities are worshipped variously according to *Vedic, Agamic and Tantric* methods of worship. As the name implies, the methods are derived from the scriptures they follow. During worship, they are propitiated with *mantras, yantras and tantras. Mantras* are prayers and incantations. *Yantras* are specific symbols and diagrams representing the deities and their powers. *Tantras* are esoteric rituals centered on the worship of body and bodily parts or on Nature and its aspects.

The deities are worshipped both externally and internally. External worship involves rites, rituals and sacrifices practiced according to well-established procedures. Internal worship is practiced through various techniques of yoga such as meditation, contemplation, prayers, songs, Vedic chants and austerities. The methods of worship include daily sacrifices, domestic worship, elaborate sacrificial ceremonies, temple rituals and sacraments. The deities are worshipped daily or on specific days in a week, month or year. In some elaborate methods of worship, deities are worshipped continuously for days and even weeks.

Hindus also worship to mark or celebrate specific events in the life of an individual such as conception, pregnancy, birthday, beginning of education (*upanayanam*), marriage, birth of a child, pilgrimage and death. During these various forms of worship, the devotees may worship many deities, a particular deity or an aspect of God. The methods of worship may be either rigidly structured according to established procedures laid out in the scriptures or freeform according to one's convenience and conviction. Presently, most methods of worship in the temples and households follow the *smarta* tradition, in which gods are propitiated most personally and devotionally with various types of offerings, such as food, water, clothes, light, incense, prayer and so on.

In Hinduism, the temples are meant to preserve, promote and facilitate traditional forms of ritual worship by trained priests. In the temples, devotees get an opportunity to worship the deities in their own Abode and make them offerings through the mediation of the priests, minimizing the effort and the possibility of making mistakes. In the temples, it is customary for the devotees to offer prayers to a few attendant gods installed in the premises before visiting the sanctum sanctorum and offering obeisance to the main deity. After they worship the main deity and receive blessings and remains of the offerings (*prasadam*) through the priest, they visit the remaining deities in the premises to offer their prayers. Many devotees allot a special place in their houses to install their favorite deities and offer them regular worship. In choosing their deities, they usually follow their family traditions, advice of gurus, caste rules or their own beliefs.

Polytheism is an important component of Hinduism. While some intellectual may berate the practice, worshipping God in numerous forms has its own symbolic and spiritual significance. The practice continues, despite awareness movements initiated by several reformers and religious institutions in the past.

Present day Hindus to worship their favorite deities and personal gods both in their homes and in temples. They celebrate festivals with a lot of fanfare to declare their faith. The express their love and devotion to God in numerous ways. They participate in sacrificial ceremonies, devotional activities, community service, charities, and similar activities to declare their faith. Hindus are very possessive about their gods and treat them as part of their families. Their memory is deeply interwoven in their consciousness. In traditional Hindu families, children are usually named after their favorite deities.

There is a certain purity and innocence in the methods of worship practiced by the deeply devoted. They worship God with deep conviction that He is one and many. They worship the divinities not only as aspects of God, but also as real entities that inhabit the higher worlds of God's creation and help us in our material and spiritual wellbeing. They communicate with them in the most personal terms and worship them with highest regard and veneration.

The pantheon

The Hindu pantheon is very complex, which runs like a family tree that is 10000 years old. According to a popular belief, Hindus worship over 30 million gods. However, this number should not be taken literally. It is used mainly to suggest that Hindus worship a complex array of gods and goddesses. In truth, no one really knows or no one has actually counted the total number of gods and goddesses worshipped in Hinduism. The number is difficult to determine considering that each god has numerous names, forms and aspects and devotees worship both the popular gods and local deities. Besides, many popular divinities of ancient times are now forgotten or their names have been changed or replaced by newer ones.

Hinduism regards these numerous divinities as not only distinct but also aspects of one Supreme Self. Neither the idea nor the practice is new. For example in the *Brihadaranyaka Upanishad*, *Yajnavalkya* responds to a question on how many gods are there with the answer that there are thirty-three. When he is asked again, he says six. When asked again, he replies three, and then says one and half and finally one.

The implication is clear. Although there are multiple gods, in their essence they are one. Just as you cannot comprehend the universe in a single image, you cannot comprehend or envision God in a single form. In the *Bhagavadgita*, we find the universal form of God consisting of numerous hands, eyes, feet and forms. Thus, the Hindu pantheon truly represents the immensity and the diversity of God's universal form and His numerous manifestations. Worshipping God numerously and in multiple forms is not only a declaration of our faith and conviction in His universality but of our inability to comprehend His universal form singularly.

In fact, although there are numerous gods, actually Hindus worship few very significant ones who are listed below.

- Brahman, the highest Supreme Self
- Vedic gods and goddesses
- The Trinity, Brahma, Vishnu and Siva
- Shakti or Mother Goddess
- Attendant and associate gods and goddesses
- Saintly persons, gurus, seers and sages

Brahman

Brahman is the highest God of Hinduism. He is extolled in the *Vedas* as the universal Self who pervades the whole universe and beings as pure consciousness. He has both manifested and unmanifested aspects. The latter is beyond the limits of all knowledge (*vidyas*).

In His manifested aspect, He appears variously and brings forth the worlds and beings as part of His creation. In the beings, He appears as the individual Self (*Atman*). As declared in the *Bhagavadgita*, no one knows His limits or immensity. He upholds the entire creation with just a little aspect of Him.

His material aspect is primal Matter or Nature (prakriti) with which He manifests the world and beings and gives them materiality and corporeality. At the end of each time cycle, He withdraws the worlds and beings into Himself and dissolves them. Since He creates, upholds and destroys the worlds, He is considered the creator, preserver and upholder of creation. He is also known by various names, which remind the devotees of His immense powers, greatness, qualities, duties and roles.

Although He is not worshipped directly during sacrificial rituals or domestic worship, He is considered the ultimate recipient of all offerings, the chief Priest (*brahmana*) and Creator (kavi), who presides over sacrifices, rituals and devotional services. Because He is the original and highest aspect of every divinity in the Hindu pantheon, it logically follows that all honors and offerings go to Him only. Those whom we worship as our personal gods are His aspects only, who uphold His Law (*dharma*) and manifest His will.

The Vedas are all about Him. They declare that those who attain Him are liberated forever. The *Upanishads* extol Him as the end of all or the Highest Goal (*parandhamam*). They suggest that those who aim for liberation should worship Him internally through meditation and contemplation and achieve union with Him in their meditative and transcendental states so that they are freed forever from the earthly bonds. They extol Him as *Aum*, the Lord of the universe (*Isvara*), Cosmic Person (*Purusha*) and personal God (*Siva* or *Vishnu*).

Brahman is both known and the unknown. Even gods do not know Him really, because He is the First, above all and without a beginning and an end. Brahman is not worshipped and not usually mentioned in religious conversations or ritual worship. However, He is the invisible God and the silent Partner in all our actions and rituals. The power to pray and the power to concentrate in prayers arise from Him only and go to Him only.

A complete book on Brahman by this author is available for those who want to know about this unique God of the *Samhitas* and the *Upanishads*.

The Vedic gods and goddesses

The Vedic deities are the oldest of the Hindu pantheon. The progenitors of the human race are part of this group of divinities.

They are worshipped during the Vedic rituals, sacraments and sacrificial ceremonies. The prominent ones are *Indra, Agni, Soma, Vayu, Varuna, Mitra, Surya, Usha, Yama, Aditi, Aswins, Prajapati, Saraswathi,* twelve *Adityas,* eleven *Rudras, Maruts, and* eight *Vasus.*

Gods of bygone eras and previous time cycles who exist in the highest end of the heaven are also part of this pantheon. However, their names are not known. They are only mentioned in the *Vedas* as gods who preside over the primal sacrifice Brahman performs in the beginning of creation with Himself as the sacrificer and the sacrificed.

The gods are immortals. They live in *Indra's* heaven and use the language of archaic *Sanskrit* for communication. They have immense powers over the elements (bhutas). However, they depend upon human beings for food, because even with all their powers they cannot make their own food. The Vedas prescribe sacrifices as obligatory for human beings for this reason only. They declare that it is the duty (*dharma*) of human beings to nourish the gods through sacrifices by making sacrificial offerings of food and in return, gods should help them by manifesting their desires and protecting them from evil powers and adversity.

Indra is the lord of the heavens. He is a god of immense strength, courage and valor. He is extolled in the Vedas as the god who wields lightning as His weapon and who slew the demon *vrata* and released the rainwater from the sky to help the beings upon earth to make food and perform sacrifices.

Agni is the fire god, who is receives the utmost attention in the *Vedas* as the god who brings light and cheer into the homes and hearts of people and who is responsible for our knowledge, breathing, digestion and internal heat. According to tradition, he receives on behalf of all gods the sacrificial offerings made during the rituals and distributes them fairly among them.

Soma the moon god is also very popular in the Vedic pantheon. He is worshipped during *soma* sacrifices, about which currently very little is known. It is believed that in these sacrifices the worshippers extracted an intoxicant ritually by pressing some herbs and used it to enter into altered states of consciousness and communicate with gods and their ancestors.

Other important gods are *Varuna*, the god of law and justice, *Aditi*, the mother of gods, *Prajapati or Brihaspati*, the teacher of gods, *Vayu*, the wind god, *Surya*, the sun god, *Sarasvathi*, the goddess of learning and *Usha* the goddess of dawn.

Apart from them, there are gods of commonality who are worshipped collectively such as the *Adityas*, the solar deities, Rudras, the storm gods, Maruts, the wind gods and *Vasus*, the serpents.

These deities not only inhabit the heavens in the macrocosm of Brahman, they also exist internally in all living beings as centers of light or energy. They participate in the internal rituals of the mind and body and receive nourishment from us by living inside us.

According to the *Brihadaranyaka Upanishad*, if we do not look after them or if we ignore them by not performing our obligatory duties, we incur sin and may take birth as worms, insects and snakes.

The Three Gods

Brahma, *Vishnu* and *Siva* are the most popular gods of Hinduism. Together they are known as the triple deities, the three forms (*trimurthis*) or simply Trinity. They are considered the three functional aspects of Brahman, namely creation, preservation and destruction, having an existence of their own as independent physical entities, but transcendentally united with Him at the most subtle level.

In their essential nature and highest aspect, they are worshiped as Brahman or *Isvara*, the Lord of the Universe, and in their individual aspects, they are worshipped as the three gods have their own worlds forms and names, from which they keep an eye upon the worlds and ensure their creation and preservation and their final dissolution.

The concept of Trinity emerged during the latter Vedic period, with the rise of sectarian movements, namely Vaishnavism and Saivism, and the popularity of devotional movements (*bhakti*), which emphasized devotion to personal God as the best means to liberation. The sectarian movements, which had a long history of their own, introduced the hitherto unknown aspects of the Vedic religion to the common people who were discriminated and neglected by the higher castes and made the religion more vibrant and responsive to their spiritual needs.

Brahma

Brahma is the creator god. He is also known by other names. According to *Vishnupurana*, in the beginning of creation he manifested from a lotus flower born from the navel of *Vishnu* and desired to create worlds and beings. Hence, he is known as the water-born (*kanja*) and navel-born (*nabhija*). In his images, He is shown with four heads facing four directions, which symbolically represent his omniscience and omnipresence.

In some descriptions, he is referred to as the self-born (*svayambhu*) because he was the first to appear in creation from the waters of life. Since all beings are created by him, he is known as lord of the people (*Prajapati*) and the grandfather (*pitamaha*) of all. He is also known as the ordainer of destinies (*vidhata*) because he determines the fate of living beings before they are born on earth. For the sake of *dharma* and nourishment of gods, he reveals the knowledge of the *Vedas* to the humankind. He also imparts knowledge to gods, demons and humans as their father and teacher. Since He is the god of knowledge and revealer of the *Vedas*, *Sarasvathi*, the goddess of learning, is his consort. Among the trinity, Brahma is the least worshipped god. Very few temples are built in his honor and only a few of them survive today. The most well known among them is the temple at *Puskar*, in *Rajastan*. *Brahma* was originally a prominent god in the Vedic pantheon before his importance declined in comparison to *Vishnu* and *Siva*.

Vishnu

Vishnu or *Mahavishnu* is the preserver of the worlds. Currently he is the most popular god of Hinduism worshipped by a vast majority of people. He is worshipped as the Universal Self (Narayana) as well as the Creator and Preserver. He is also worshiped in various forms and with different names ascribed to His incarnations, manifestations and emanations. In his highest aspect, known as *Narayana*, he is regarded as Brahman Himself. In the images, He is depicted with blue color, representing sky, peace, immensity and universality. He is a god of purity, *sattva*. The *Puranas* describe his world as *Vaikuntha*, the Abode of God, where only free souls and attendant and associate gods of *Vishnu* live and which only his devotes can attain. The Puranas also state that in *Vaikuntha*, he rests on a bed made up of the coils of a giant thousand-hooded serpent, *Adisesha*, while it floats eternally in the ocean of milk (*ksirasagaram*). *Lakshmi*, the goddess of wealth, remains seated at his feet serving Him with love and devotion. Garuda, the divine eagle, is his vehicle.

In his pleasant images, he is shown as having four hands, with a large necklace, *Kaustabha*, adoring his neck. Although he was not well known to the masses during the early Vedic period, he became popular subsequently when the Vedic civilization moved eastward into the Gangetic valley. He is worshipped in numerous forms and some of his incarnations are more popular than he is.

Siva

Until Vaishnavism rose to prominence, Lord *Siva* was the most popular god of the Indian subcontinent. He is also perhaps the oldest among the three deities. Scholars believe that the Indus Valley people probably worshipped an aspect of Him. In the ancient world, he was probably worshipped outside the Indian subcontinent also in numerous forms. He is the destroyer, who destroys our sins and delivers us from bondage. He also destroys the worlds at the end of the time cycle. *Tamas* is his predominant nature. He has numerous names and forms.

He was known to the Vedic people as *Rudra*, the red-one or the fierce-one. He is extolled as Brahman in some *Upanishads* such as the *Svetasvatara Upanishad*. In his highest aspect, he is considered the Lord of the Universe (*Isvara*) and the great Lord (*Maheswara*). *Parvathi* is his consort. *Nandi*, the bull is his vehicle. Lord Ganesha and Kumara are his two sons. The Puranas describe Him as the mountain dweller who wanders around in the Himalayas, with *Kailas*, as His eternal abode. His association with icy mountains signifies His lordship and mastery over ignorant minds, death and inertia. "*Si*" means cool (*sital*) and "*va*" means to live (as in *vasa*). *Siva* therefore means, He who lives on the top of icy mountains or who lords over tamasic minds and transforms them with his auspicious (*sivam*) touch.

Siva is worshipped both symbolically in the form of a *sivalingam* and in his iconic form (*mula murthi*) as a god of immense beauty and grace. He is worshipped both as the universal Self and as the destroyer of the worlds and beings, according to the methods prescribed in the *Vedas*, the *Agamas* and the *Tantras*. The *sivalingam* symbolically represents the union between Purusha, the Cosmic Self and Prakriti, the Cosmic Mother. It symbolizes creation, reproduction, life, continuity, diversity, union and existence itself.

Shakti or Mother Goddess

Shakti represents universal energy. If *Isvara*, the Lord of the universe is pure consciousness, *Shakti* is pure primal energy. They are considered the passive and dynamic aspects of the eternal reality, Brahman or the Supreme Self.

However, some traditions consider them entirely independent and eternal. Some even go further and hold *Shakti*, as the Mother Goddess or the Supreme Universal Mother, who is the source of all and personifies universal energy and dynamic consciousness, while Brahman or the Father God remains in the background as the passive enjoyer of the cosmic drama unfolded by the Goddess.

Like Brahman, the Mother Goddess too has both manifested and unmanifested aspects. In the unmanifested aspect, the triple *gunas* rest in equilibrium, while in the manifested aspect the equilibrium is disturbed which leads to modifications and manifestation of diversity.

Shakti is also known *Prakriti* (Nature) or that which is found in its natural state. According to the *Bhagavadgita*, the worlds and beings manifest when *Purusha*, the Universal Male unites with *Prakriti*, the Cosmic Female. The *tantras* consider Her the Highest and the source of all activity (*caitanyam*) and manifestation. They describe the gods as powerless beings who cannot act on their own unless there are united with their associate energies (*shaktis*). Thus, in the Hindu pantheon, we have one or more female deities associated with each god. Each Trinity god is associated with one principal goddess, *Sarasvathi* with *Brahma*, *Lakshmi* with *Vishnu* and *Parvathi* with *Siva*. They also go by different names. Devotees worship them jointly as well as independently. However, in whatever way they may worship them, the offerings are shared by them equally since in truth, they are inseparable and their union is eternal.

Just as the three gods have numerous manifestations or aspects, the goddesses also have several corresponding manifestations and emanations. As popular as the trinity gods, they are worshipped in numerous temples and in various forms by millions of people all over the world. The worship of *Shakti* as the universal Supreme Mother and the Creator of all makes Hinduism unique. In no other religion, except perhaps in some tantric schools of Buddhism, female deities are worshipped with such esteem and veneration. While women are given secondary and inferior roles in most Hindu families and subjected to discrimination and many disabilities, the goddesses enjoy great popularity as aspects of the Universal Mother. They were extended the same respect due to a mother in Hindu society.

The Divine Mother has both peaceful and fierce forms. On the one hand, she personifies love and peace, and on the other, anger and destruction. In ancient times, she was worshipped mostly in Her fierce forms by the followers of *tantra* and *shakti*. It is said that this practice was discontinued after *Sri Sankaracharya* visited the main *shakti* temples (*shakti-pithas*) in the country and introduced benign methods of ritual worship.

As a result, today in most temples we see Her only as the Universal Mother of unbound love. *Ramakrishna Paramahansa*, the spiritual guru of Swami Vivekananda, proved on numerous occasions that through intense worship one could see the Goddess in physical form and close proximity.

The goddess is the favorite of many devotees. She is worshipped in various forms in many temples built in her honor all over the country. She is particularly famous in eastern India where she is worshipped with great fanfare during the *Durga* festival for five consecutive days. In southern India, Mysore in particular, she is worshipped during the *Dasara* festival for ten consecutive days during which the devotees practice austerities to maintain purity. On the tenth day, they worship her as *Chamundeswari* or *Durga*, celebrating her victory over the demon *Mahishasura*.

Attendant and associate gods

Each of the gods and goddesses we have discussed before have aspects, associate deites, emanations and manifestations. Major and minor incarnations of *Vishnu*, and aspects and forms of *Siva* are worshipped with great fervor both ritually and spiritually in temples and in their homes. So are the manifestations and aspects of *Shakti*. Each of them also has several attendant gods. *Ganesha* and *Kumara*, the sons of *Siva*, and *Hanuman*, the devotee of Rama, are very popular gods, with a wide following of their own. They receive offerings and widespread attention during festivals and rituals. The vehicles of *Siva* and *Vihnu*, namely *Nandi* and *Garuda* are also worshipped with equal devotion. The *Jyotirlinga* temples of *Siva* and the temples of *Shakti* are considered very sacred.

Lord *Balaji* or *Veketeswara* of *Tirupati* is perhaps the most popular and richest god Hinduism presently. Millions of people visit his gold plated temple located on the seven hills at *Tirupati* in Andhra Pradesh,. Every day his temple coffers receive staggering amounts of money through the voluntary offerings made by His devotees, which is spent by the temple administration in welfare activities and restoration of old temples.

The Navagrahas

During rituals and on special occasions, Hindus worship many minor deities. The most popular among them are *Navagrahas* and the *Ashtadikpala*s. *Navagrahas* means nine planets or nine planetary gods. *Ashtadikpalas* means eight directional gods who rule the eight division of the sky or the galactic space.

The nine gods are *Surya, Chandra (Soma), Mangala (Kuja* or *Angaraka), Guru (Brihaspati), Sukra, Sani, Rahu* and *Ketu*. The first seven represent the Sun, the Moon, Mars, Mercury, Jupiter, Venus, and Saturn respectively. The last two, *Rahu* and *Ketu* do not represent planets but comets that eclipse the moon regularly out of vengeance. The two are actually demons who joined the ranks of divinities under peculiar circumstances and became immortal. They are propitiated because they are inauspicious deities who can do harm if they are neglected, which is usually not the case with the other deities.

The *navagrahas* are found in most temples, but invariably in the temples of *Siva*. Devotees offer them prayers before or after they visit the main deity in the temple. You may find them installed in specially designated areas according to the traditional rules of temple architecture (*Vastu*) or carved on the doors or walls, where devotees can conveniently perform their worship by making rounds or bowing before each. When they are installed separately, they are placed in such a way that they do not face one another other but look in different directions, with the Sun in the center facing the east. Each of these deities has his own form, vehicle, weapons and significance. Some temples are also built exclusively for them, collectively or individually, such as the *Navagraha* temple in the outskirts of *Ujjain* or the *Sani* temple near *Hindupur*.

They planetary gods are worshipped mainly for their astrological significance. They have the power to ward off evil and the remove misfortune arising from improper alignment of planets at the time of one's birth.

The Ashtadikpalas

The *Ashtadikpalas* rule the eight directions of space as the galactic guardians of the world. They are actually original Vedic deities who have been entrusted with an additional responsibility in the cosmic hierarchy to protect the worlds from evil demons by keeping a watch over a particular direction in the sky. Thus, the eastern division or direction is ruled by *Indra*, western by *Varuna*, northern by *Kubera* and southern by *Yama*. Among the intermediate directions, northeast is ruled by *Isvara*, northwest by *Niruthi*, southeast by *Agni* and southwest by *Vayu*.

The *Ashtadikpalas* are worshipped on important occasions seeking their help in guarding the sacrificial altars and other sacred places from evil, requesting them to keep a watch while the rituals last and act as the witnesses to the auspicious actions the worshippers perform. They also figure prominently in the traditional science of construction (*Vasthu Sastra*), which prescribes rules for building safely both secular and religious structures, sites and monuments.

Saintly persons, gurus, seers and sages

In additions to gods and goddesses, in Hinduism, devotees also worship spiritual gurus, celestial beings, saintly persons and seers, founders of various schools of philosophy, poets and composures of sacred scriptures. They also extend their devotion to objects and places of religious and spiritual significance, considered auspicious or sacred. Prominent among them are the *Alvars* and *Nayanars*, the famous medieval saints of Vaishnavism and Saivism respectively who popularized the devotional movement. Others include *Vedvyasa, Dhanvantari, Agastya, Dattatreya, Patanjalik Hayagriva, Kapila, Maschindra, Ksetrayya, Annamaya, Yajna, Ranganatha, Chaitanya, Varadaraja, Bhangi, Virabhadra, Candesvara,*

Prathamaganas, and Katyayani. In fact, some *gurus* such as *Shirdi Saibaba*, enjoy more popularity than many deities in the Hindu pantheon. In some cases, they are treated on part with the gods of Trinity or even Brahman Himself. Some devotees worship them as aspects or incarnations of Siva or Vishnu.

Apart from them, in many temples, attendant deities such as the guardians of the temples (*kshetrapalas*), guardians of the doors (*dwarapalas*) and those associated with chariots and related devotional services receive offerings from temple priests.

Significance

The gods and goddesses who are worshipped in Hinduism are real entities. They have symbolic significance in the sense that you can invoke them to bring improvements in specific areas of your thinking and behavior. However, they are not mere conceptual aspects of God. They are divine beings, who have an existence of their own in the cosmic hierarchy. If your faith is sincere and devotion pure, they may even manifest in your life or your consciousness and fulfill your wishes or help you in your efforts. This has been confirmed by many devotees in the past.

The divinities are God's creation. There are immortals, who exist for the sake of *dharma* and for that reason they are endowed with greater knowledge, wisdom, purity and ability to control Nature, time and space. They inhabit the higher worlds and play a significance role in executing the will of God and in upholding and preserving the order and regularity of the worlds in all aspects. They also inhabit our minds and bodies and help us in upholding and practicing virtue and religious duties. We have a duty and responsibility towards them, since they play an important role in our spiritual transformation and in purifying and preparing us for our liberation.

We worship them because not only they have their own importance in the divine hierarchy but also they are aspects of God only. Through them, we have an opportunity to worship God variously and declare our faith in Him. Through them, we reach out to the Highest God who is not usually reachable directly.

Hindus worship their deities with the conviction that they are manifestations of the Supreme Self who also exist in our own little universes as energy centers, dominant attitudes, bodily parts, mental faculties and states of consciousness. We nourish them with food and in return, they protect us from evil and grant us peace, prosperity, knowledge and wisdom with which we can fulfill the four aims of human life, namely duty, wealth, pleasure and liberation.

It is difficult to envision Hinduism without its deities and divinities. The Kingdom of God is resplendent with a large retinue of gods and goddesses, who keep it colorful and vibrant with their dutiful presence and attentive response. They remind you that everything in the universe is sacred and is filled with the presence of God. They channel the power and glory of God into your life and consciousness. They keep you on the steady path to liberation. They assure you of divine help when you need them. They speak to you if you are willing to listen and learn. Right now, they are watching you while you are engaged in your thoughts and actions. While critics and some scholars may consider our methods of worship outdated and our allegiance to numerous gods as primitive and superstitious, the gods are here to stay as long as the eternal tradition prevails here and hereafter.

Idol Worship in Hinduism

Before we begin this discussion, let us be clear that Hindus do not have to be defensive about idol worship or to find other expressions to avoid the stigma some people tend to attach to it. For all practical and religious purposes, idol worship is an approved form of practice in many traditions. It is a thousand times better than many wretched acts people commit in the name of religion. Perhaps those who are uncomfortable with it should not practice it all and those who practice it should not care what others say or think about it.

In whatever way we may put it, the fact is Hindus worship God in various ways and they are all approved by our scriptures, and each method has its own history and tradition. As we have discussed before, in Hinduism, devotees worship God in abstract form as Supreme Self as well as in physical form as symbols, images and idols. For those who are visually and emotionally inclined, image worship is very suitable and for those who are spiritually inclined, mental worship is best suited.

By definition, an idol is an object of worship and adoration and it is more appropriate to use it when we worship the numerous forms of God in temples and households.

Worshipping God in the form of idols and images (*murti puja*) is an ancient practice, dating back to prehistoric times. Excavations at most ancient sites uncovered idols used by ancient civilizations to worship their deities. There is nothing modern about mental worship or primitive about idol worship. Both have been in vogue since ancient times and both have been found effective.

Some traditions do not approve idol worship and regard it as an act of superstition or ignorance. However, Hinduism, which is the oldest living religions of the world, has a long history of supporting and promoting the practice as an acceptable method of declaring one's faith and devotion to God. While some may find fault with it, those who practice it consider it the best way to relate to God and experience nearness to Him. They find in it certain childlike simplicity, ease of focus and directness, which may be hard to experience in more advanced forms of worship.

The idols give the worshippers an opportunity to stand before God reverently in total submission, express their devotion in human terms and experience closeness to Him.

The idols may not speak to everyone, but certainly to those who have faith and devotion. This has been proved many times by great devotees in the long history of Hinduism.

Those who practice the yoga of devotion (*bhakti-yoga*) know its value in their spiritual transformation. In the presence of an idol, they feel its transformative energy, sacred presence and purifying influence.

Worshipping God's numerous forms with their hearts and minds, they allow the supreme power of God to work through them, open their minds to higher wisdom and prepare them for their liberation.

The idols also serve them as sources of inspiration whereby they remind themselves constantly of the need to lead virtuous lives and practice *dharma* as an obligatory duty.

Through idol worship, you can give wings to your imagination and let your mind sour heavenwards with prayers and supplications.

In modern terms, an idol is like a wormhole through which with effort you can enter into a new dimension of reality and experience your own infinity and oneness with God.

The *Bhagavata Purana* (11.27.12) refers to eight kinds of images made up of eight different materials that are fit for worship, namely stone, wood, metal, earth, paint, sand, clay and the mind. In other words, you can build a mental image of God in your mind with your thoughts and worship it. In fact, internal worship is considered more effective than physical worship.

Idol worship became popular during the later Vedic period, with the rise of sectarian and devotional movements, which emphasized devotion to personal gods as the principal means to achieve liberation.

While its aims were similar to those of the Vedic rituals, such as establishing communion with gods and securing their help, its methods and approach were more personal and devotional, with lesser dependence upon priests and elaborate rituals to achieve the same.

Developments within Buddhism and Jainism and the rise of Mahayana Buddhism, which emphasized ritual worship of the Buddha, also contributed to its popularity.

It gained further traction with the emergence of temples as the main centers of religious activity where people could worship God and perform devotional services to experience peace and nearness to Him.

Some aspects of idol worship can be traced to early Vedic religion, such as the use of prayers and rituals to invoke the deities and seeking their help and blessings in return for the offerings made.

In its essential aspects, idol worship is a form of sacrifice only in which offerings are made to the deities ritually accompanied by prayers, invocations and sacred chants as part of one's obligatory duty.

An expression of devotion

For devout Hindus, idol worship is a convenient method of expressing their love and devotion to God in the most personal terms. They are ashamed of neither going to the temples nor worshipping reverentially the idols installed in them. For them, it is an approved practice, sanctioned by their scriptures and an obligatory duty. They have no hesitation to stand or prostrate before their gods and speak to them as if as if they are real and attentive.

They may hail from different backgrounds and pray with different mindsets and for different reasons, but their commitment to the innumerable forms of God, which they hold in their minds or their vision, is unquestionable. They worship them with conviction and faith inculcated into their minds by their families and community from an early age.

If the idols remain unresponsive or their prayers remain unanswered, it would not shake their confidence in the deities or their method of worship. They continue to worship them ascribing their failure to their past actions (karma) and seeking their help to overcome their suffering and work for their salvation.

When *Mohammad Gazni* invaded India the last time, and attacked the famous *Somnath* temple, the priests serving the temple did not run away or take up weapons to defend the temple. Instead, in their habitual fashion, they turned to God and kept praying seeking divine help. In the past, their prayers were answered and the invaders were repelled repeatedly; but this time the situation was different. The invaders had an upper hand and they managed to destroy and plunder the temple.

History is replete with instances where idols in Hindu temples were desecrated and vandalized by the freebooters who invaded India during the medieval period with large armies in search of pillage. For some mysterious cosmic reasons, the gods remained silent and allowed the destruction of the temples to continue.

However, these developments did not shake the faith of the Hindus in medieval India in their gods and the idols. They continued to worship them in makeshift temples with renewed faith. In fact, following the invasions and the large-scale destruction, the country witnessed unprecedented resurgence in devotional (*bhakti*) movements, which emphasized the importance of personal devotion and ritual worship as the principal means to achieve liberation. They strengthened the roots of Hinduism in the soil of India and made it stronger and resilient.

Significance

In Hinduism, a vast majority of people from all backgrounds practice idol worship. For them it is neither superstition nor ignorance but one of the most visible forms of devotional services and an effective means to focus their minds in the contemplation of God. It is wrong to equate it with mere idolatry.

Although idols are worshipped, the object of worship is not the idol but God hidden in the image. An idol is not viewed as mere statue or image but a living embodiment of body. The stone or the material used in the making of the idol represents the elemental body of God.

The worship exemplifies the devotees' conviction in the omnipresence of God. If God is hidden in every aspect of creation, it logically follows that He is hidden in the idols also.

Hindus do not worship idols as such but God in numerous forms. It is therefore wrong to equate it with mere idolatry. The object or worship is not the idol, but God hidden in it. The act of worshipping Him in the form of idols and images exemplifies their faith in His omnipresence and hidden presence.

For devout Hindus, God's universality and omnipresence are not debatable points but undeniable truths. If God is hidden in every aspect of creation, it logically follows that everything in creation and every manifestation of God (*vibhutis*) is sacred and worthy of respect and veneration.

The idol used in the worship is a very much a symbolic representation of God. One can relate to it personally or worship it with faith and devotion.

In Vaishnavism, idols are regarded as incarnations of God in elemental form. Each image is a living incarnation (*arca*), which embodies the manifesting, purifying and liberating power of God.

Its power grows in direct proportion to the faith of the devotees and the offerings they make. The reason is obvious to those who understand the deep connection between God and His devotees.

Devotion has such drawing power. With devotion, devotees pull the power of God into the images they worship, since He cannot resist their calls and prayers. The love between them is mutual. When devotees keep praying to an idol constantly and sincerely, God responds to their love by descending into it and remaining in it to fulfill their wishes or help them in their liberation.

A temple becomes sacred not only by the presence of God, but also by the prayers of devotees. Idol worship in Hinduism is justified on this ground. The idols installed in the temples are the living images of God. They are brought to life by pure devotion. They connect the devotees to God and God to His devotees. Through them, you can find your way to the heart of God and eventually to His eternal Abode.

In the temples, the idols are worshipped with the same attitude, as if they are the living embodiments of the deities. They are treated with utmost respect and served with great reverence from morning until midnight as if they are living and breathing entities. The same attitude is shown even in the households, where the deities are worshipped regularly with faith and devotion.

It is difficult to elicit a response from God until we attain a certain level of purity, stability and freedom from sinful nature. It is difficult to pray to God with an impure heart. If idols do not respond to our prayers and supplications, the problem lies with us, not with the objects of our worship.

The deities respond to pure devotion. Idol worship is a living example that the power of God can manifest in numerous ways and if our faith is strong, He communicates with us even through stones and statues. The lives of devotees like *Mirabai, Sant Tukaram, Shri Ramakrishna Paramhansa and Shri Yogananda* prove beyond doubt by worshipping idols with great love and devotion one can establish direct communion with God and receive His attention and grace.

The Vedic Indians worshipped various gods through sacrificial ceremonies and daily sacrifices. They also worshipped them symbolically in the form of symbols, altars and sacrificial materials. However, we do not have evidence that they worshipped idols. The Indus people probably worshipped idols ritually and made them public and private offerings. The practice seems to have entered Hinduism mainly from such sources and gained momentum with the integration of diverse traditions.

It added a new dimension to the Vedic religion, which was primarily ritual-centric and relied upon sacrificial ceremonies to secure the help of gods.

It became popular in the early Christian era with the rise of *Saivism* and *Vaishnavism*, popularity of devotional worship (*bhakti*) and the construction of numerous temples across the sub-continent.

Megasthanese who was deputed to the court of *Chandragupta Maurya* (4th century BCE) as an ambassador mentioned in his book *Indica* that the worship of idols was a popular practice in ancient India. Numismatic evidence shows that ancient Indians were familiar with the images of their gods and goddesses. The *Kushanas* worshipped Siva. The *Guptas* worshipped many deities, especially *Vishnu*. They built many temples in His honor. The *Barasivas* who ruled parts of central and northern India worshipped Lord Siva and built many temples in His honor.

Justification

Hindus worship God both ritually and spiritually, as one and many, with form and without form. In both cases, they may resort to symbols and images to fix their minds in the contemplation of God and experience profound peace and devotion. Worshipping God and His innumerable forms symbolically is an established form of devotional service, which intensifies religious fervor and feelings of religiosity.

It brings vibrancy and vitality into the act of worship and makes it more human, personal and relational. The objects of worship inculcate in the minds of worshippers a deep sense of reverence and respect for gods, remind them of their obligatory duties and spiritual goals, and the need to withdraw from their worldly duties heeding to their inner call for salvation.

Worshipping the deities in the convenience of their surroundings enables them to invite the divinities into their lives and make them an inseparable part of their thoughts and actions. It strengthens their spirituality and prepares them gradually for a life of duty and renunciation. Besides, it is a good *karma*, which helps them remember God or His numerous forms frequently.

If we set aside the excessive ritualism and the naked display of power and pomposity, which some people often display to draw attention to their own importance, we realize that worshipping God in the form of images and symbols is a simple and pure way of expressing one's faith and unconditional allegiance to God and His numerous manifestations.

Whatever may be the method one chooses the intention or the purpose behind the act of worship determines its merit and efficacy, not the act of worship itself. In this regard, the *Bhagavadgita* mentions four types of people who worship God: those who are in distress, the curios minded, the seekers of wealth and men of wisdom (*jnanis*). All the four are good, but among them, a man of wisdom is deemed by Krishna as His own Self.

Wisdom and the pursuit of God for the sake of knowledge and liberation comes to the beings only after several births, when they are tired of worldly pursuits and turn to God and spirituality with deep conviction. The following reasons cited in favor of worshipping God in the form of symbols and images prove beyond doubt that the practice is very much justified.

1. If God is omniscient and omnipresent, it logically follows that everything in the universe, including the idols and images we worship and the temples we visit, is filled with His presence and everything should be regarded as sacred, divine and worthy of worship. Our love and devotion to God should be complete and unconditional and encompass every aspect of Him. A true devotee sees God everywhere, even in the idols and the objects he worships, the people he meets and the objects he perceives.

2. It is a mark of respect extended to God in very personal terms. When we look at the pictures of strangers, me may not feel any connection with them; but if we look at the images of people whom we know intimately, we may be strongly drawn to them. On such occasions, we may not even realize that we are looking at pictures, not real people. It is the same with the idol worship, which gives us an opportunity to connect to God personally. In society, we show respect and admiration to the images and statues of prominent people whom we admire by putting them on public display. If we can do it for mortal beings, we can as well do it for God to show our love and admiration to Him and relate to Him most personally and emotionally.

3. Devotionally, it is more effective to worship God in the form of idols, images and symbols rather than in abstract forms, which are difficult to envision and hold in mind. The *Bhagavadgita* declares that severe is the path of those who choose to follow the Unmanifested Brahman. It is because as the name implies, the Unmanifested Brahman does not respond or manifest under any circumstances even with intense prayers. Secondly, it is difficult for the human mind, which is subject to duality and perceptual reality, to focus upon a formless and abstract notion of God.

4. The practice is approved by the *Vedas*, which are inviolable. In Hinduism, we accept them as verbal testimony to ascertain any truth. Whatever they say, we accept it as an instruction of God. Our tradition upholds the practice because the *Vedas* approve the worship of Brahman and His numerous forms both ritually and spiritually or externally and internally. For the devotees,

therefore, this method of worship is fully justified. The *Puranas*, the *Agamas* and the epics also justify the practice, citing instances of gods, celestial beings and even demons worshipping God in this manner to show their respect or secure boons.

5. It is easier and simple to practice. The idols give us an opportunity to express our love and devotion to God in the very comfort of our homes, temples and other religious places. The Vedic rituals and sacrifices require the assistance of priests and the use of elaborate and established procedures they only know. In contrast, anyone can worship the images and idols without any outside help. You may seek the help of officiating priests when you visit a temple, but you may also worship on your own without their help.

6. The practice strengthens our faith. The idols sanctify our homes and temples. Wherever they are installed, they purify the place and energize it, invoking in us feelings of reverence and devotion. Having them installed in your house is like having God or deities living in your house as your guests and securing their help and protection to the extent you surrender to them and worship them. Their presence also reminds the members of the household of the need to live religiously, upholding *dharma*, practicing virtue and morality.

7. It purifies and stabilizes the mind. The purpose of yoga is self-purification, which results in the predominance of *sattva*, without which it is not possible to with draw the senses or restrain them. Worshipping God in any form leads to the same end. Idol worship is an important component of the yoga of devotion (*bhaktiyoga*) and the best means to open one's heart and mind to divine influence. The idols help the devotees to experience transcendence and feel the presence of God within them and near them. They also help them in concentrating their minds to experience peace, stability, equanimity and self-absorption.

8. It gives the worshippers an opportunity to perform the triple roles creation, preservation and destruction. In creation, God

performs these three functions. During idol worship, the devotees perform all the three. First, they bring the idols to life by inviting God through prayers, supplications, and requesting Him to be their Guest. Their prayers fill the idols with the sacred presence of God. Next, through prayers and supplications again they request God to fulfill their desires or help them in their liberation. This is an act of preservation on their part. Finally, through regular worship, they destroy the impurities of their hearts and minds and also their misfortunes and bad karmas. This is an act of destruction.

9. The practice prepares the devotees for the hardships of life and the difficulties of achieving liberation. To worship an image or a statue with devotion and to continue the practice in the absence of fruitful response, one needs unflinching faith and conviction. Not everyone can accomplish it, without suffering from doubt and disappointment. The idols symbolically represent the difficulty in communicating with God or relating to Him. They also personify the virtues of stability, sameness, firmness (*dhriti*), equanimity, strength, detachment and renunciation. Like God, although the idols are present they are as good as absent, since they do not directly communicate or respond to our prayers. Like God, they might test your faith to the extremes.

Idol worship is an act of faith and surrender

Worshipping God physically in the form of images and symbols makes our prayers direct, effective and one-pointed. It gives us an opportunity to declare our faith and commitment to God in most personal terms. It is a sign of progress on our part on the path of liberation.

If we are willing to worship a statue treating it as a form of God, it is an indication that our faith has matured and we have reached a stage from where we see God in all and all in God. It is an indication that we are willing to forego our preconceived notions, judgment, knowledge and illusions and surrender to God unconditionally. If an educated mind can prostrate before an idol without any hesitation or inner conflict, it is a sure sign of humility and true surrender.

You do not degrade God when you worship an idol. You degrade Him when you question the simple faith of a devotee who sees Him in a stone or statue.

If you think God does not exist there, you limit God to the places of your choice and the methods of your worship. You mark a few places in the universe and declare that God does not exist there or should not exist there. It is egoism.

It is difficult to know God or reach Him in our wakeful consciousness. He is vastly unknown and whatever you know about Him is limited, symbolic and indeterminate.

In the domain of the senses and the mind, it is difficult to establish contact with Him physically except through imagination, contemplation and visualization.

Therefore, for those whose minds are saturated with the thoughts of God, idol worship is a convenient method to communicate with God and express their devotion.

Why a devout Hindu worships idols may not sound convincing to an erudite mind that is steeped in the reality of the world and the practicalities of life. However, for a deeply religious person, it is a way of communicating with his gods and seeking their blessings. It is neither appropriate nor proper to evaluate such methods from the perspective of other religions or their specific beliefs and methods of worship.

In matters of faith and theology, no religion can claim exclusive ownership of knowledge or approach to God. The paths to God are many and many are the ways one can reach him. In spiritual life, knowledge has its own value and ignorance has its own place. What is knowledge to some may be ignorance to others. A person of intellect may not have the same opportunities as an ignorant person to attain God.

In this regard the Isa Upanishad has its own recipe," *Into blinding darkness enter those who worship ignorance and into still greater darkness those who worship knowledge alone... He who knows both knowledge and ignorance together, crosses death through ignorance and attains immortal life through knowledge."* (I. 9& 11).

Evolution in Hinduism, a Perspective

Hinduism believes in the concept of evolution of life on earth. Although it is not the same as the theory of evolution known to modern science, in many ways and in a very fundamental sense, it points to the gradual evolution of life and consciousness upon earth at both the cosmic and the individual levels.

Modern science speaks of physical evolution and the evolution of nervous system, starting with simple life forms and proceeding to more organized and complex beings with well-developed and self-regulating biological and mental mechanisms. Man is so far the known and the ultimate product of this very complex and continuous process.

Hinduism, on the other hand, provides rudimentary knowledge on the physical evolution of life, suggesting vaguely how forms evolve through the aggregation of the basic realities (*tattvas*) of Nature.

It focuses primarily on the evolution of the inner world (*antahkarana*) and the transformation of beings from no intelligence, to lower intelligence, to higher intelligence, as reflected in the humans, and to pure intelligence as reflected in gods and liberated souls.

This transformation is necessary to overcome the delusion and ignorance to which beings are subject. With intelligence comes discerning wisdom and from it the awareness that one is indeed an eternal soul and one should strive for liberation.

The nature of evolution suggested in the Hindu scriptures is based upon the following fundamental premises.

1. Life manifests from supreme intelligence.
2. Manifestation is essentially a projection, separation or transformation of the physical reality from the absolute reality.

3. Evolution is a transformative process confined to Nature and its aspects only. The soul is immutable.
4. Evolution is the long road by which Nature intends to liberate the souls in its own natural way from bondage to the mortal life; but it hardly facilitates the process without adequate effort by individual beings.
5. Liberation is not evolution, but the ending of it.

At the cosmic level are two fundamental aspects, pure consciousness (*purusha*) and cosmic matter (*prakriti*). They are also referred to as Father God and Mother Goddess. Both are eternal and both have manifested and unmanifested aspects or realities.

In its manifested aspect, *Purusha* is eternally constant, while *Prakriti* is subject to modifications and transformation. Consciousness manifests in creation as both the Universal Self and the individual Selves.

 We cannot say, whether they are aspects of the same absolute reality or different, because human beings cannot fathom such mysteries, even with the help of gods.

Nature has several sub-natures (*tattvas*) or building blocks of activity and modifications. They may manifest variously in the beings according to predominance of the *gunas* and their position in the hierarch of creation.

The union between consciousness and matter results in the formation of beings. Life evolves through this union from latent to manifest stage, with effects manifesting by the will of God from their causes that are already hidden in the blueprint of creation resulting in the diversity of things and beings.

Beings manifest in four different ways, from seeds and sprouts (*udbijas*), from secretions (*svedaja*), from eggs (*andajas*) and from wombs (*jarayuja*). Of them, the last ones are the most evolved.

The beings contain all or some aspects (*tattvas*) of Nature according to their position in the hierarchy of creation. Of them, only two types of beings possess intelligence, the gods and humans. Only they are subject to *karma*; and only they can evolve through intelligent effort and actions.

Others, the lower ones, evolve through acts of God (*daivikam*) or mechanical processes of Nature (*bhautikam*).

The beings produced in this manner inhabit 14 worlds of which six are above and seven are below ours (*bhuloka*). The earth is the only place where beings are given an opportunity to evolve through transformation and work for their liberation.

Hence, if gods and demons have to work for their liberation or ascend to higher planes of intelligence, they need to take birth upon earth and go through the transformative process through self-effort and inner purification.

Creation in Hinduism is not an instantaneous magical process. The sub-natures of Nature manifest upon earth gradually through cause and effect until enough diversity is accomplished, and the beings are deeply involved.

In other words, in the Hindu conception of life and evolution, life develops progressively upon earth around eternal and immutable souls, who possess pure consciousness. Through the gradual separation of its sub-natures (*tattvas*) and the flowering of their full potentiality, it subjects the eternal souls to bondage.

Stages in the evolution of life

The first sub-natures to manifest or separate in this process are the five elements (*mahabhutas*) namely, the earth, fire, water, air and ether. Their aggregation results in the formation of materiality and numerous animate and inanimate objects having no life and intelligence.

The inanimate objects that appear as the first signs of creation may have no life (*chaitanyam*); yet they possess the energy of Nature in its most primitive form and do their part in fulfilling its goals. They serve as the basic raw materials for the formation of bodies and beingness and the source of desires, attachment, and feelings of attraction and aversion.

Next, organs of action join the elements to produce rudimentary life forms that are devoid of senses and perception, but have the ability to move and perform certain basic functions. They exist by the force of Nature rather intelligence or consciousness.

The next to manifest along with the elements and the organs of action are the organs of perception (*jnanedriyas*) to produce organisms that have perception and the ability to interact with the world; but possess very limited will and intelligence. In this phase, the sense organs many manifest gradually, resulting in further diversity.

In the next stage, organisms manifest with mind and ego, in addition to the elements and sense organs. They possess movement, perception, cognition, some knowledge and individuality. They still lack intelligence, which manifest in the next state resulting in the self-aware and intelligent beings. Intelligence, like other aspects, also manifests progressively in these beings. The gods are the highest end of this chain and the human beings just below them.

Variations exist in beings not only because of the manifestation of the various *tattvas* but also because of their levels of purity and intensity. Such variations may also exist within each class of beings for the same reason.

For example, while all humans are endowed with intelligence, their intelligence levels may vary because of the impurities (*rajas* and *tamas*) present in them and their progress on the path of liberation. Intelligent beings are subject to *karma*, arising from their own actions.

For this very reason, evolution into higher life forms does not guarantee liberation for the souls. In fact, the more intelligence one has, the greater the risk of going to the dark side. The beings have to cultivate purity and divine qualities to overcome their ignorance and delusion, develop discerning wisdom and escape from the consequences of their actions.

Thus, our scriptures portray evolution as taking place at many levels, vertically and horizontally, from world to world, beings to beings and components to components, in which individual actions (*adhyatmikam*), actions of other beings such as gods, Nature and the world (*bhautikam*), and the actions of God (*daivikam*) play an important role.

Only the highest intelligent beings have the ability to evolve further through self-effort and self-willed actions. The rest have to go through the mill of cause and effect and the mechanical processes managed by Nature.

Since evolution is a mechanical process, guided by intelligence, beings evolve from a state of ignorance to a state of illumination through progressive and successive intermediate states of partial ignorance and partial illumination until they attain full perfection.

In the early stages, consciousness joins matter and brings to life certain life forms that are mostly and vastly inert, unconscious, and driven by the force of blind instinct and natural impulses.

In the second stage, beings develop perceptual ability, ability to respond and adapt to Nature and perform desire oriented actions. In the next stage, they develop individuality, attachment, attraction and aversion, and the ability to direct their wills according to their circumstances and dominant desires. They also experience suffering and afflictions in this phase due to modifications in their minds and bodies.

In the next phase, they develop intelligence or discriminating awareness (*parisilanatmaka buddhi*), which leads to knowledge, memory, wisdom, willful and desire oriented actions, attachments, attraction and aversion, involvement with the world, bondage and ignorance. From here onwards, they possess the ability to evolve on their own, with or without the intervention of Nature, through self-willed actions and intelligent means such as yoga. Their liberation and journey to the world of Brahman depends upon their ability to purify their gross and subtle bodies and get rid of their past life impressions and the fruit of their past karmas.

Natural evolution vs. self-willed evolution

Scientific theories of evolution focus primarily upon the evolution of the physical body; but Hindu theories focus upon the evolution of all aspects of the human personality starting from the most basic elements to the highest intelligence.

In all this, the only constant factor is the Self. It remains unchanged as the center of all life forms, without undergoing any modification or corruption even when it is enveloped by the aspects of Nature.

Science is yet to come to terms with the possibility that man can direct his own evolution consciously and willingly using his knowledge and intelligence whereas Hinduism suggests to that possibility very clearly. Intelligence is the highest aspect of Nature.

Therefore, any evolution or transformation happening in a human being because of his or her own actions is also essentially evolution happening within the domain of Nature.

However, it is reinforced by light of the individual will and the intervention of divine will. In this transformative process, individual actions and actions of Nature and God play a very powerful role.

The vision that we find in the scriptures is much wider and comprehensive. Here Nature is also a powerful agent, playing a very dominant role, but only so long as the individual beings are willing to remain under its limiting influence.

When wisdom and insight prevail, they realize their delusion and liberate themselves from the bonds of Nature by directing their further evolution through self-effort or by emulating Nature.

Thus from the perspective of Hinduism evolution happens at many levels, at the macrocosm, in the microcosm, in the aspects of Nature, in intelligence and in the willingness of each individual to undergo self-transformation.

From unreality towards reality, from darkness towards light and from death to deathlessness: these are the chief aims of the evolution of life upon earth. It primary objective is liberation not bondage, and immortality not survival.

Nature's follows its own way of manifesting diversity by creating beings in progressive states of knowledge and awareness. Human beings can interfere with that process, change it, hasten it or stop it through their actions.

They have both the opportunity and the ability to allow Nature or follow Nature and use its very processes and mechanism to gain control over it or escape from its influence and return to their original state. The effort requires very difficult levels of purity and intelligence, which may take several lifetimes to accomplish.

The transformative process is neither instantaneous nor uniform, neither uniformly progressive nor easily predictable. There is no one particular way by which it can be accomplished. The results are unpredictable and not uniform. The paths are many and so are the techniques and their outcome. There are no certainties in it, except those permitted by Nature and the laws of God. Intuitive awareness and higher knowledge may enable them to discern the possibilities and explore the opportunities.

However, to accomplish it one has to deal with the limitations to which one is subject and transcend them without destroying the spark of hope and the chances of escape. The barriers on the path are many. So long as beings are in love with their own chains and stay caught up in their own distracting dreams, pursuing their desires with faulty actions their chances to emerge into the world of light and freedom, as immortals are very limited. Life offers many opportunities to the beings to learn valuable lessons from their experience. The lucky ones benefit from them, cultivate intelligence and discretion and realize the need to break through the chains that bind them to the earth,

There is no loss on this path. Only delays. By wrong decisions and sinful actions, a being may falter and fail on the path and descend into the lower worlds, or take birth in lower life forms.

However, through self-effort one can rise again and move forward. In this effort, intelligence is vital. By knowing reality from unreality, truth from falsehood, right action from wrong action, and right knowledge from wrong knowledge, one can ensure one's progress towards the Highest Goal.

In this effort, each individual has to rely upon his or her own faith and conviction. Through individual actions and personal merit, one wins the grace of God and the guidance of a *guru*. As the *Mundaka Upanishad* declares, nothing can help an aspirant on the path of liberation except his effort and the grace of God.

Man vs. Superman

Sri Aurobindo, one of the modern seers of Hinduism, envisioned a superior destiny for the human beings. He suggested that human beings have the potential and the needed resources within their own personalities to evolve further into supermen and develop extraordinary knowledge, intelligence, vitality and all round awareness.

With such abilities and potentialities, they would be able to see the reality in a much different light and experience life more profoundly and divinely as an extension of their own vitality and immortality.

He predicted that as more human beings evolve to this level through their actions and the grace of God, they would herald a new world of super humans who will be free from impurities and mental darkness and possess extraordinary abilities and complete mastery over their minds and bodies. He also suggested that if left to Nature, it may take eons to create such beings upon earth, but we can hasten the process through effort and the practice of integral yoga, which aims to purify not only the physical body but also the subtle bodies and integrate them around the real Self.

He wrote, "*To know, possess and be the divine being in an animal and egoistic consciousness, to convert our twilit or obscure physical mentality into the plenary supramental illumination- this is offered to us as the manifestation of God in matter and the goal of Nature in her terrestrial evolution.*"

Aurobindo also believed in both progressive and retrogressive evolutions of life upon earth. One leads to creation and the other to liberation. Liberation is a kind of deconstruction of Nature whereby the soul that joins matter in the initial stages can return to its pristine state and may even exist with a new body that is free from the modifications and afflictions common to the earthly bodies.

Thus evolution followed by involution, or descent followed by ascent, complete the cycle of creation. Thus, what has been created has to be destroyed. What has formed into beingness has to be decomposed. If the birth of an individual is creation, his death is destruction. If his bondage is creation, his liberation is destruction. If his involvement with objects is creation, his withdrawal is destruction.

It is through this repeated process of creation and destruction that the individual beings manifest, evolve gradually in series and stages and eventually return to their source. The One indivisible Self, divides Himself into many, and then through a long and arduous process the many return to the One again. They remake themselves "in the divine image" and become "godhead."

This is the story of evolution in Hinduism. It is the story of evolution through transformation and liberation through evolution.

Creation as a Process

The following accounts and descriptions of creation are based upon the references found in the *Vedas*, the *Puranas*, the epics, the *Bhagavadgita* and the works related to various schools and sects of Hinduism. They are not about how God created the worlds, the narrative descriptions of which you will find in the *Puranas*, but what intelligent or mechanical processes led to the creation of things and beings.

While most schools concur with the opinion that God is the Creator, some schools consider God as the efficient cause only and Nature as the material cause. Some schools go a step further and hold Nature as both efficient and material cause and the source of all creation.

Hindu schools of philosophy consider creation an intelligent and controlled process willed and executed by superior intelligence. All schools postulate that things must emerge from something, not from nothingness or void.

The scriptures interpret the processes involved in creation either directly or symbolically as listed below. According to them creation involves one or more of the following.

Manifestation: The *Upanishads* declare that the unmanifested Brahman becomes manifested. The reason specified is either unknown or some form of desire. The unmanifested Brahman is difficult to worship. The manifested Brahman has again numerous other manifestations such as the ones described in the 10th chapter of the *Bhagavadgita*. As the scripture affirms, there is no end to the manifestations of God in the numerous worlds He creates. Whatever is endowed with purity, brilliance and power is His manifestation only.

Projection or dream: The world is also described in some schools as a projection. A projection is not real. For reasons not clear to us, or perhaps for His sheer enjoyment, God projects an alternate reality from Himself and into Himself. The world in which we live is one of His projections only. You may call it His dream. It is filled with His power, glory and brilliance. It lasts so long as He sustains it and enjoys it as its inner Witness. In the end, He withdraws it into Himself and goes into deep sleep.

Outgoing process: Creation is God's outward involvement with Nature both in the macrocosm of the universe and in the microcosm of each being. The *Upanishads* describe Him as a spider and creation as the spider's web. Everything spreads outwardly from Him as He casts His net of illusion, resulting in diversity in which beings become involved through desires and attachments. The senses are responsible for the involvement and attachment. They are the apertures pierced by God. Through them beings are drawn out and bound to things, resulting in their transmigration. If creation is an outgoing process, liberation is an inward process in which you withdraw from those that bind you.

Union: Creation is also described in our scriptures as the union between the Cosmic Self (*Purusha*) and the Cosmic Nature (*Prakriti*). As the *Bhagavadgita* declares, seated in *Prakriti*, *Isvara*, the Lord of the universe brings forth all the worlds and beings. Their union is well reflected in an embodied self (*jiva*) which is a combination of both. The mind and body represent Nature and the individual Self represents *Isvara*, the Lord. The union is also reflected in *Sivalinga* and in the iconographic representation of Lord Siva as half-male and half-female.

Separation: Creation is viewed as separation because beings come into existence when God and Nature, the two fundamental eternal entities diversify in their own distinct ways. God, the One (*ekam*), is separated into five aspects. Namely time, space, knowledge, passion and power. Nature is separated into distinct realities or *tattvas* whose permutations and combinations results in diversity. Creation also happens, when the individuals souls are temporarily separated from their source, which is God, and brought under the control of Nature. During this process, they are also separated temporarily from knowledge by the impurities that envelop them. Separation also takes place within the field of Nature when diverse components (*tattvas*) manifest separately and the *gunas* become distinct, lose their equilibrium and enter into a state of conflict. The fourteen worlds also become separate from one another and appear as distinct worlds. The earth is separated from the sky and the elements are separated from one another.

Evolution: Creation is also regarded in Hinduism as an evolutionary process in which beings evolve through the births and rebirths from lower life forms to higher life forms endowed with knowledge and intelligence. In this, *karma* arising from one's own actions plays an important role. In the lower life forms Nature plays an important role in their evolution, while in case of human beings it is accomplished mostly through one's own actions (*adhyatmikam*). As the *Bhagavadgita* declares at the end of many lives, one attains human birth and at the end of many lives as a human being, one turns to God and strives for liberation.

Transformation: Creation is also a transformative process in which inert and dark matter joining with souls transforms into living beings. The modifications of Nature are part of this process. The transformation continues as the aspects of Nature manifest in creation gradually, culminating in the creation of human beings, who are subject to ignorance and delusion due to the presence of impurities. In the early stages, their intelligence remains clouded. Influenced by the *gunas* they indulge in desire-ridden actions. Then through the practice of yoga, they transform to emerge as beings of light, knowledge and discerning wisdom that are fit for liberation.

Illusion: According to the *Svetasvatara Upanishad* (4.9), *Isvara*, the Lord of the Universe, is an illusionist (*mayavi*) who casts His net upon the world and subjects the beings to delusion. The schools of monism consider the world an illusion (*maya*) projected by God for the purpose of creation. Beings in delusion consider the appearance of things and beings real, just as they mistake a rope in darkness for a snake. According to this school, Brahman alone is real and everything else, which is essentially His creation, is an illusion. The ego, the false self, is also an illusion. It comes into formation to delude the beings into believing that it is the real Self.

Diversification: Creation results in duality and diversity. The one becomes many. While the diversity is the visible and manifested aspect of creation, its underlying unity in the form of all pervading Self is invisible. The diversity is manifested by Nature with the help of *gunas* and the realities or *tattvas*. Thus, we have classes, divisions and categories of things and beings. We have fourteen worlds inhabited by different beings. We have social divisions and numerous transient phenomena that appear and disappear like waves in the ocean of life. The diversity is responsible for the experience of duality and delusion, attraction and aversion, desires and attachment and *karma* arising from desire-ridden actions, whereby beings are held in bondage.

Descent: Creation is also often spoken as a descending process in which consciousness gradually descends from the highest planes of creation into the lower planes or from God into Nature, resulting in the emergence of living beings and intelligent matter. The concept is symbolically represented in the story related to the descent of the river *Ganga* from the heights of heaven to the earth. The river represents pure consciousness. Whoever is immersed in it is purified instantly. Human beings cannot absorb and sustain that pure consciousness directly. Hence, it flows to us in such a way that first it lands upon the head of Lord *Siva*, who is considered world teacher (*guru*) and then enters our world, which represents earthly consciousness or human consciousness.

Modifications: The Self is free from modifications (*vrittis*), but Nature is subject to them. Life emerges upon earth due to the modifications of Nature only. The three primary modifications are creation, preservation and destruction. They manifest in the beings as birth, life and death. The triple *gunas, sattva, rajas,* and *tamas* play a dominant role in making them possible. In case of living beings, their existence upon earth continues so long as they are subject to these modifications. The mind is the primary source of mental modifications. They are caused by desires, attachment and impurities of *rajas* and *tamas*. The *Yogasutras* declares that the purpose of yoga is to suppress these modifications (*vrittis*) so that one can experience oneness with the hidden Self.

God's play: Creation is described in the scriptures as a play (lila) of God enacted by Him for His enjoyment. Since He was one and alone, He created the worlds and beings for His company and looks at Himself from all vantage points in a state of duality. From the descriptions, we derive the impression that the world is a stage or field in which God and Nature manifest diversity. It may also be part of His dream. God is also described as the Witness and Enjoyer. All this exists for His enjoyment only.

Mystery: The Creation Hymn from the *Rigveda* (10.129) describes creation as a great mystery. It describes how in the beginning there was neither existence nor non-existence. There was no sky, no earth, no water, no death and no immortality. There was darkness and concealed in it indiscriminate chaos. In the depth of that void, appeared That One. Then desire arose. It was the primal seed and from it, all things emerged. However, no one knows for sure when creation happened and how it happened. The One who appeared first, whether He created the worlds or not, perhaps He knows or may not know.

Sacrifice: The *Vedas* describe that creation was the result of a great sacrifice performed in the beginning by Brahman as Cosmic Person (*Purusha*), in which He used parts of Himself as the sacrificial material (energy) to manifest things, the worlds and beings. He created gods and goddesses, celestial beings, humans, plants and animals. From different parts of His body, He created the four different castes. The model of sacrifice is also referenced in other scriptures in which Brahman is described as the sacrificer, the sacrificed and the object of sacrifice.

Temporary: Creation is a temporary process. It does not last long. Only God is eternal, while His manifestations are subject to change, impermanence, modifications and transformation. Just as the day has a beginning, middle and an end, creation also has a beginning, middle and end. Since creation is temporary and nothing lasts here forever, people should not develop attachment with anything here.

Cyclical: Creation is not only temporary but also cyclical. The day of Brahma, the creator god, lasts for billions of years. He creates the world at the beginning of each day. By evening, the worlds are destroyed. Then he goes into deep sleep to wake up next day and start the whole process once again. Each time cycle has four great epochs of varying lengths, at the end of which the worlds are dissolved and the individual souls are withdrawn.

Mechanical: The classical *Samkhya* School regards creation as a mechanical process in which Nature manifests things that are already hidden in it in seed form. According to this school, Nature creates nothing new. It is a programmed entity. All the effects it manifests are already hidden in it in the causes. Thus, creation is a predictable process, the unwinding of a preexisting program, in which God plays no role.

Other views

The *Upanishads* also compare creation to a banyan (*asvattha*) tree, whose roots are in heaven, whose branches are spread out below. On it alone all the worlds rest. None can go beyond it.

Creation is a divine act. Its source is God. Its purpose is not very clear. It is manifested by the will of God, enacted by Nature and enforced or upheld by the power of *dharma*. It seems to mirror His qualities as well as His opposite qualities. It thrives on duality, divisions and diversity. Its fate is not left to the elements or to chance. Individual beings have a chance to escape from it forever. If things go out of control, God incarnates upon earth to restore order.

We are part of this vast creation. Depending upon our actions and attitude, the great powers that manage its processes may hold us in bondage to Nature or help us in our liberation. We are also creators in our own way. We create our lives, we create our actions, we create our destinies, we create our children and families, we create parts of this world and we leave behind memories and impressions in the invisible layers of earth's consciousness. We share with God the joys of creation, playing our dutiful roles to uphold the world He creates.

Creation is a little whimper in the vast silence of the unmanifested Brahman. It is a temporary wave that appears and disappears, or rises and falls in the unending waters of pure consciousness. We are the blessed souls who have been given an opportunity to watch this cosmic drama from inside out.

The Role of Scriptures in Hinduism

To understand a religion, first we have to examine the thought processes that went into its formation and led to its development. The purpose of this discussion is to examine whether Hinduism relies upon any particular text as the basis of its existence and how it manages to sustain the faith of its adherents and continues to grow from strength to strength as civilization marches on and as our knowledge and awareness and the world in which we live keep changing at such an exponential pace.

A religion with many scriptures but few knowers

Hinduism is a multifaceted and multidimensional religion. It is difficult to define it, categorize it and organize its vast body of knowledge into a universally acceptable format.

When we study Hinduism in depth, we realize that in contrast to other major religions, it does not rely exclusively upon any particular scripture or the teachings of a founder.

While, it is derived from various sources such as the *Vedas*, the *Smritis*, the *Agamas*, the *Sastras*, the *Darsanas*, and other scriptures, none of these texts represents it exclusively. It accepts the *Vedas* collectively as the reliable source of truth, but does not rely upon them alone. The truth is, Hinduism may prevail even if some of these texts disappear or fall into disuse.

It is equally difficult to say how far the principal texts of Hinduism are read and understood by its followers. Most of them do not read them at all. Since most Hindus are born into their religion, they learn it as part of their growing and learning. They imbibe it from various sources during their interaction with people and the world. By the time they reach adulthood, the knowledge of Hinduism becomes deeply embedded in their consciousness alongside the knowledge of the world. They may not know its scriptures, but they know what it means to them.

Hinduism is based on many scriptures; but the faith of Hindus is not necessarily derived from their study of the scriptures. Hindus are expected to study their scriptures by self-effort (*svadhyaya*) and recite them as frequently as possible. It is the ideal. However, few individuals really put it into practice. Many Hindus do not study or recite their scriptures that form the basis of Hinduism. They do not know the knowledge hidden in *the Brahmanas, the Aranyakas, the Upanishads, the Sutras, the Darshanas or the Shastras*. They may have some knowledge of the epics and some of the *Puranas*; but it would be mostly anecdotal. Most of them show little inclination to read or recite their scriptures with the same intensity with which people read scriptures in other religions.

In fact, the tradition never intended everyone to study the scriptures. Tradition holds that religious or spiritual knowledge is meant only for those who are ready for it and who are qualified for it. In the past, caste barriers prevented many from knowing certain aspects of the religion, which the law books declared prohibitory and denied to certain categories of people irrespective of their readiness and individual merits.

However, we cannot doubt the faith of the Hindus simply because they do not read their scriptures seriously or do not have access to the specialized knowledge of their religion. Many learn about their tradition directly from their own families and practice it just as their parents and elders practiced before. They may also prefer to practice it according to their particular desires, attitudes and worldviews.

Many go by the teachings of their respective gurus or religious scholars who inspire them or capture their imagination. Some might even read the scriptures of other religions and practice them occasionally without doubting their own faith or feeling guilty. You cannot say that they have committed sin or transgression by practicing an alien faith. In fact, their willingness to practice their faith in such unconventional ways arises from the values they learn from Hinduism itself. Hinduism gives them the freedom to practice their beliefs according to their convictions, even if they are different from the ones recommended by the scriptures so long as they do not interfere with the ultimate aim of human life, which is liberation, and they do not indulge in sinful actions.

At the same time, it makes them responsible for their choices and actions. Beings are bound to their karmas and none can escape from it. People's faith is strong or weak according to their past lives and predominant nature. Nature plays an important role in shaping their lives, actions and beliefs. Eventually everyone may return to the path of liberation, but before it happens each may take several lifetimes and choose different pathways.

If we look at the vast number of Hindus, who are mostly illiterate and who never had an opportunity to study their scriptures or practice them and yet show wisdom and maturity in accepting their suffering and bearing it with certain grace and dignity, we realize the incredible and unquestionable impact of Hinduism upon their lives and character.

When you see in India the cheer and contentment in the faces of the people, despite the poverty, suffering and the struggles they go through and despite the harshness of life, wretched conditions and the painful burden of social and economic injustice, you will understand the significance of Hinduism and its subtle influence upon their thinking and attitude.

People accept their lot stoically as part of their *karma*. They do not question it because internally they take responsibility for what happens to them. People have an obligation to serve others and live selflessly; but no religious authority has been entrusted with the responsibility to enforce it.

It is up to the individuals to exercise their will and discretion and work for their liberation. The tradition's primary focus has always been the individual. Social and economic inequalities are construed as undeniable truths of creation and the reason why one should restrain desires and practice detachment and sameness (*samatvam*) towards the dualities and diversity of life.

Thus, historically the masses were left to fend for themselves. The rulers, who were supposed to be the upholders of *dharma*, did not care what religion they practiced as long as they paid their dues and remained submissive. The higher castes precluded them from religious teaching. At the same time, they expected them to abide by the caste rules and practice their duties faithfully.

In the end, it is up to the individuals, whether they would pursue worldly goals or work for their liberation; whether they would work for their spiritual transformation or come under the influence of evil thoughts and fall into demonic worlds. People may practice tricks and techniques to achieve material success or worship God; but eventually every individual is answerable to God and His eternal and inviolable laws. Thus, the fear of divine justice weighs heavily in everyone's mind and makes them live responsibly.

While the scriptures declare that service to the humanity is service to God, unlike in Christianity or in Islam, no recognized institution is vested in Hinduism with the responsibility to look after the poor and the downtrodden. If some saints and seers and a few dedicated individuals serve them, it is purely their personal choice.

Although the masses are largely ignored and kept outside the purview of organized religion, their loyalty to their family traditions and the faith of their ancestors remains largely intact even today. The tenacity of their faith is exemplary and you will notice it only when you live amidst them, sharing with them their trials and tribulations.

They may practice their faith under different names and in different ways. They may or may not worship gods as per the established procedures, read the scriptures, go to the temples or celebrate festivals. Yet you may find in them the belief system inculcated by their faith and deep and strong, influencing their thinking and actions and helping them to cope with their failures and disappointments.

The community regards the faith of individuals as a personal matter and the consequence of their past actions (*karma*), while the wise ones regard them as beings in various stages of spiritual growth and liberation.

The use and misuse of the *Vedas*

Two main streams of thought prevailed in ancient India regarding the *Vedas*. One groups considered them supreme and inviolable and the other either ignored them or discredited them. The main schools (*darsanas*) of Hinduism acknowledged the *Vedas* as the standard texts (*pramana*) in ascertaining truth. In other words, if the *Vedas* declared something as true, they argued that no further proof was necessary to accept it because the source of the *Vedas* was God Himself and His words could never be faulted.

The other line of thought, which was upheld by the Buddhists, Jains, atheists and some ascetic sects, doubted the *Vedas* or held them in contempt, questioning their supremacy and validity. The extreme among them were the *Lokayatas* or *Carvakas*, the atheists of ancient India, who had a long history of their own as the worst critics of the Vedic religion. They advocated materialism. They argued that there was no soul and no life after death, and people should maximize their happiness while they remained alive without worrying about consequences or afterlife. They were intensely critical of the *Vedas* and the values they upheld. They urged people to ignore them and make the best use of their time upon earth, pursuing their desires and happiness.

If the *Vedas* were criticized by them and others, it was not because the *Vedas* were defective, but because they were ignorant of the Vedas and lacked proper knowledge and understanding of the truths hidden in them. Many factors contributed to this. The foremost among them was the secrecy associated with the teaching of the *Vedas*. As we have already discussed, the caste system prevented many from studying the Vedas or knowing them. Even among the higher castes, specialized knowledge was imparted to a select few. For the priests whose livelihood depended upon performing sacrifices, the knowledge of the *Vedas* was like a trade secret, which they would not divulge except to those who had a right to know it by virtue of their birth, caste or family status. Therefore, in most cases those who criticized the *Vedas* or urged people to disbelieve them had no access them and were not even aware what they were criticizing.

Secondly, in the early Christian era, the Indian subcontinent witnessed the rise of many new languages. They gradually replaced *Sanskrit* as the main language of communication and reduced it to the status of an elite language. This made the Vedic tradition, whose scriptures were composed solely in Sanskrit, rather difficult to study and understand.

Further the changes that took place in Sanskrit lexicon and grammar, rendered many words originally used in the Vedic hymns archaic, which made the scriptures rather cryptic and difficult to understand. As a result, although the priests continued to memorize the *Vedas* and recite them dutifully, they were unable to grasp their true meaning. It led to distortions in their study and interpretation. It also led to the decline of Hinduism, as people lost faith in the Vedic knowledge and sacrificial ceremonies and looked to rival traditions for solutions.

Today, many Hindus do not know what the *Vedas* signify, why the rituals are necessary and what the chants actually mean. Many participate in the rituals and sacrifices rather mechanically, doing what the priests ask them to do. Whether it is a naming ceremony, wedding, conception, pregnancy, funeral or some other religious ceremony, they observe the various sacraments (*samskaras*) and household rituals more out of respect towards their family traditions or out of fear of offending their ancestors and gods. Their lackluster attitude stems from their ignorance and their blind submission to a long tradition without knowing what it actually signifies and what the *Vedas* preach.

Discretion and Dogma in Hinduism

In its long history, Hinduism passed through many phases of growth and decline. It underwent changes from time to time and escaped near extinction through internal reforms in which it would miraculously return to its roots and somehow revive the ideals and values that sustained it before.

Its strength is its core philosophy, which is derived from the *Vedas* and some ancillary texts. They remind people of their essential duties and responsibilities and the liberating power of Hinduism and its expansive vision of the universe as a playground of God and the individual souls.

As it happened many times in the past, Hinduism undergoes transformation from time to time. It is undergoing transformation even now and gradually moving towards spirituality and mysticism of the *Upanishads* rather than the ritual and ceremonial aspects of the *Samhitas* and the *Brahmanas*.

The present-day Hindus are well educated who are gradually awakening to the truths about their ancient religion. This is a positive development, which would help Hinduism to survive the pressures and challenges of the modern world and prepare itself for the future.

Its progress is in line with the growth of our civilization and our increasing knowledge of the world and the universe. It has the depth and diversity to satisfy the curiosity of modern minds who are inquisitive and who are not satisfied with vague answers about life and liberation.

Present day Hinduism offers a broader range of choices to people who are motivated by a variety of religious and spiritual aspirations. It has the depth and the range to cater to the needs of the most ignorant as well as the most knowledgeable ones without compromising its vision or its philosophy. It has the wisdom of the ages, tested for long in the furnace of life, to meet the diverse expectations and aspirations of a heterogeneous mass of people.

Therefore, it is no wonder modern Hinduism has been increasingly becoming responsive to the growing spiritual needs of its people and their hopes and aspirations to lead a balanced and stress free life without ignoring their duties and obligations and excluding themselves from the simple joys and pleasures life has to offer.

It does not offer vague promises or suggest a particular way of life, belief, book or thinking to resolve suffering or guarantee salvation. It adequately responds to the weaknesses of our vacillating minds, the imperfections of our selfish and preconditioned thinking, the illusory nature of the world, in which we live, and the impermanence and unreliability of those aspects our lives which trouble our minds and relationships.

Whatever may be their source, the words in the scriptures are useful only when they make sense to you and when you personally find them useful. It is not the scriptures, but your willingness, vision, preparation and readiness, which renders any scripture useful or useless to you.

The scriptures do not serve all equally. What you may find useful or inspiring may prove different in case of others; and what others may find useful, you may find ordinary.

Since individuals differ in their abilities to respond to their problems and expectations, they would be better served if the religion they practice is sensitive to their specific needs and gives them enough opportunities to grow in the direction of their goals and dreams. Hinduism has such ability. It offers diverse solutions to people of diverse backgrounds. It offers you several solutions and gives you the freedom to choose from them.

At the same time, it makes you responsible for your choices and the mistakes you make in exercising such freedom. It puts you in the glare of your own mistakes and faulty judgments and lets you learn from the darkness of your deeds and the light of your own wisdom.

The *Vedas*, the *Upanishads*, the *Puranas*, the two great epics, the *Darshanas*, the *Sutras*, the *Smritis*, the *Bhagavadgita* and a whole lot of religious literature, still carry a great significance Hinduism and influence the thinking and actions of many of its adherents. However, the religion does not oppress those who may choose to pursue unconventional methods to pursue truth.

In Hinduism, the faithful have the freedom to exercise their discretion or intelligence. They may choose their paths according to their best judgment. They may tread the conventional paths approved by the tradition to avoid taking risks or they may pursue esoteric methods not well known to others and not approved by the tradition. The scriptures may tell you which path may be difficult or painful to pursue, but they will not stop you from pursuing it. The reason is simple. You are responsible for your life and action. You are the source of your suffering as well as your liberation. What you do with your life, is your choice. The scripture guide you and caution you, but leave the decisions to you.

Conventional wisdom has its own value. However, in Hinduism you have no obligation to limit yourself to the dogma or torture yourself with guilt or the fear of sin for not following it. A devotee or an aspirant has no obligation to accept any truth on its face value or follow any scripture blindly, but has the freedom to arrive at truth or draw own conclusions through personal and direct experience. In the end, the tradition holds you accountable for your actions, choices and progress. It recognizes the world inside you, your spiritual nature, and your right to know truth and stabilize your mind in the contemplation of your true Self.

It acknowledges the illusory nature of the world, our vulnerability to ignorance and delusion and our propensity to use or misuse knowledge, including religious knowledge, according to our desires and attachments. Even the *Vedas* are not to be followed blindly without cultivating discerning wisdom (*buddhi*). Much of the knowledge in the *Vedas* is hidden in symbolic form and it cannot be understood without inner transformation and prior preparation. One may rely upon the testimony of the *Vedas* only when it is difficult to establish it through direct experience (*pratyaksa*). A seeker of truth should trust nothing and take nothing for granted. He may occasionally rely upon the authority of the scripture to arrive at truth, but must primarily rely upon his own experience.

As far as transcendental truths are concerned, the knowledge should arise from the Self and lead to the Self. The *Upanishads* and the *Bhagavadgita* are very clear in this regard. They regard the knowledge gained by reading the scriptures as inferior to the knowledge gained through one's own experience. They declare clearly that scriptural knowledge is inferior, which may help an individual gain peace and happiness here, and heavenly life hereafter, but it would not give him salvation. The knowledge of the Self or the Supreme Self alone, gained through inner purification and self-transformation leads to liberation and the Abode of God.

Besides, the mind should be pure, disciplined and empty before true knowledge can gain entry into it. A clamoring and craving mind cannot be stabilized in the silence of the Self. Intellectual knowledge is an obstacle when it interferes with our faith. One should therefore use the knowledge of the scriptures wisely without getting lost in it.

Hinduism in a dynamic world

In conclusion, we can say that although Hinduism does not rely upon a particular scripture or source of knowledge, it considers the testimony of scriptures as valid and reliable knowledge to ascertain transcendental truths that cannot otherwise be known through direct experience.

Hinduism drew its knowledge richly from various sources in the course of its long history, starting from the Vedic times until now.

It underwent many internal reforms and adapted itself well to the challenges it faced. It is still in its expansive phase and adapting itself to the needs and aspirations of the modern world. In the process, it has not compromised its spiritual vision or its religious ideals. Its core values continue to inspire us even today, while its appeal remains undiminished.

In the past, Hinduism derived its knowledge from many scriptures, ascetic traditions, and teachings of many saints and sages. Today, it draws its knowledge from unconventional sources also such as current events, new interpretations of the ancient scriptures, modern teachers, interfaith dialogue, and even science and technology. At the same time, it never loses sight of its ancient wisdom and core values, which stood the test of time and continue to be its main strength.

Hinduism has proven well that it can adapt itself to any environment and attune itself to any situation. It has proven beyond doubt that it can survive the test of time without exclusive reliance upon any scripture, tradition, teacher or founder. We have ample evidence to believe that if there is one religion with which new age philosophies can resonate well, it is certainly Hinduism. What sustain it in this regard are its adherence to eternal values and its willingness to examine truth from different perspectives and standpoints.

Life after Death

Religions are essentially meant to answers questions about the mysteries of life and deaths, answers that we cannot find rationally except through the testimony of the scriptures or the information left by adepts about their own experiences. The answers to these questions distinguish one religion from another. In Hinduism, beliefs about death and afterlife are based on three fundamental convictions. They are common to all sects and schools of Hinduism, including those, which do not accept God or His role in creation, but acknowledge the continuity of life beyond this world.

The earliest beliefs about the subject are found in the Vedas and the same ideas were elaborated and explained further in the subsequent literature. Life upon earth is characterized by change and impermanence, while life in the highest heaven is permanent and eternal. Therefore whatever existence into which beings entered upon their death, was in reference to the mortal beings only and does not apply to gods and other celestial beings. The three convictions about the afterlife existence of mortal beings are:

1. The physical self is distinct and different from the inner Self. It perishes with the death, while the real Self is eternal, immutable, imperishable and indestructible.
2. Actions have consequences. Actions performed by beings shape their lives and destinies. This is the law of *karma*.
3. Beings are born repeatedly until they are liberated. They reincarnate according to their deeds and desires.

A living being is subject to suffering upon earth. Death does not end their suffering. Beings may also suffer in their afterlife, if they do not attain liberation. They go to the ancestral world, where they become food to the gods, and return to the earth to reborn and go through another cycle of mortal existence. Alternatively, they may go to the hell, where the suffering is more intense and prolonged. The Hindu beliefs about afterlife developed overtime in the ancient world as their vision of the world and the cosmos changed.

Two paths

The *Bhagavadgita* and the *Upanishads* mention two paths by which the departed souls would travel: the path of the immortals and the path of the ancestors. They are also known as the bright path that leads to the sun and the dark path that leads to the moon. The pure beings who are freed from desires, attachment, ignorance and delusion and who have stabilized and absorbed their minds in the contemplation of God travel by the sunlit path to the immortal Abode of Brahman never to return. They live there forever. Others go to the world of ancestors, where they stay until their *karmas* are exhausted and their subtle bodies are consumed by gods. Then they fall down to the earth through rains and take another birth according to their past deeds.

Knowledge of these two paths is deemed essential to overcome delusion and the consequences of *karma*. The immortal path is also known as the path of gods (*devayana*) and the mortal path is known as the path of the ancestors (*pitryana*). The immortal world of Brahman is described differently by different sects as *Vaikunta*, *Kailasa*, *Brahmalok* and *Suvah*. According to some descriptions, these worlds are never destroyed, even during the dissolution of the worlds and according to some, they are withdrawn since they are also mere formations projected by God for the purpose of creation.

The last moments of life

What a person remembers at the time of death is also important. The *Bhagavadgita* states that whatever people think at the time of their death, they attain that (8.6). Those who depart from their bodies remembering God attain God only (8.5). While it seems easy to practice this method to escape from the consequences of *karma*, in reality it is not. Since the mind is fickle and cannot be stabilized easily, prior practice is important to remember God in the last moments of one's life. Those who practice yoga, overcome their desires and stabilize their minds stand better chances of remembering God at the time of their death. By virtue of their continued practice, discipline and inner purity, drawing their life breath to the point between their eyebrows and thinking of God alone, they depart from here and succeed in reaching Him.

The *Upanishads* suggest that at the time of death, the soul leaves the body through an aperture located in the top of the head. When it departs, its knowledge and *karma* follow it and so does its intelligence. Latent impressions (*samskaras*) and dominant desires act as the seed for the next life of each being. In pure beings, they are either fully burnt or absent. Hence, at the time of death, their minds remain stable and absorbed in the contemplation of God.

The three worlds

According to the early conception of life described in the *Chandogya Upanishad* (5.2.1), *Brahma* (*Prajapati*) created three classes of beings, demons, gods and the humans. The demons inhabit the nether regions of intense darkness below. They are cruel and deceitful by Nature. The gods live in the heavenly world above and participate in human welfare by supporting our causes, protecting us from evil and fulfilling our wishes in return for the food, they receive through sacrifices. They are light beings who play an important role in upholding *dharma* and the injunctions of the *Vedas*. The human beings live in the middle, in the mortal word. They have the qualities of both and the potential to become divine or demonic according to their deeds. They are also subject to *karma* and rebirth.

Heaven (Svarg)

The world of gods, known as *svarga*, is ruled by *Indra*. Hence, it is also called *Indra's* heaven. In the strictest sense of the world, it is different from the world of sun to which the immortals go. The gods inhabit the heavenly region in the sky and descend to the earth from time to time to receive our sacrificial offerings. The departing souls who leave the earth do not go there, except for a brief visit, although some people wrongly believe so. They go to either the immortal world of Brahman, which is the highest heaven, or the world of ancestors, which is said to be located on the moon.

The departed souls may temporarily go to heaven to witness the wonders there and meet a few divinities, but they are not destined to stay there forever. The warriors who die fighting in the battlefield are expected to ascend to heaven directly, but they stay in a special region called the heaven of the warriors (*virasvarga*), which is again different from the heaven of *Indra*.

Indra's heaven is a blissful world in which the beings experience unlimited pleasure. The gods who inhabit it are immortal beings. They are averse to pain and suffering and therefore do their best to stay free from both. They live in abundance and luxury in palaces made of gold, surrounded by auspicious objects, beautiful sceneries and celestial dancers, listening to the sacred chants from the *Vedas* and heavenly music.

Indra rules this world in the company of other gods, with *Rati*, his wife, by his side. He rides a white elephant known as *Airavat* and protects both the gods and humans from the demons wielding his mighty weapon *Aairavat* (*lightning*). The *Puranas* suggest that Indra's place in heaven or his position as the leader of gods is not permanent. The demons may invade the heaven and create chaos. Therefore, whenever danger lurks, *Indra* and the rest of the gods seek the help of the Trinity. According to our scriptures, Indra does not like the mortal beings who try to attain immortality and go to the Abode of Brahman, which is higher than his world. Therefore, he keeps disturbing them to pollute their minds and slow down their progress.

Hell (Narak)

Unlike heaven, the hell is a dark world, filled with evil doers and their relentless cries of pain and agony, where they are subjected to various types of torture and punishment by the messengers of Yama for the sins they commit upon earth. The demonic world is different from hell, just as the world of *Indra* is different from the immortal heaven to which liberated souls go.

The hell is ruled by Lord *Yama*, who is described in the *Katha Upanishad* as a god of virtue and great intelligence, well versed in the *Vedas* and endowed with exceptional wisdom and discernment. In some descriptions of the *Vedas*, we find that *Yama's* world is the only place to which all departing souls go. However, in the *Puranas* and epics, the world of *Yama* is distinguished from the world of ancestors, as a place where sinners are punished according to the sins they commit upon earth. The punishments are meant to purify the sinners by making them aware of their mistakes and turn them to virtuous and dutiful living.

The *Puranas* narrate that aided by his trusted servants Lord *Yama* keeps an account of the deeds done by the beings upon earth. Nothing escapes their scrutiny, since the god of death is also a personification or aspect of Time (*Kala*). When the sinners enter his world, they are read out their sinful deeds and sent to various regions of hell to undergo punishments. According to the *Puranas*, the punishments given are extremely painful, tortuous and invoke disturbing imagery.

Multiple heavens and hells

In contrast to the early Vedic depiction of creation, which presents a three-tier universe, the *Puranas* describe creation as an endless phenomenon in which worlds appear and disappear like waves in a cosmic ocean.

Creation is God's play (*leela*). Even gods do not know its immensity, origin or dimensions. The manifest universe is dotted with multiple worlds, layers of consciousness and planes of existence, some known and some unknown, some within the field of awareness and sensory knowledge and some way beyond. The worlds are inhabited and controlled by different powers, beings, objects, celestial wonders, deities and mysterious events and phenomena. Apart from them, *Brahma*, *Vishnu* and *Siva* have their own worlds, where each remains seated as the highest and supreme Brahman with immortals and liberated beings who are devoted to them live in their company savoring their presence.

In the *Paingala Upanishad* we find the grandeur of God's infinite creation in the following words, *"Out of the elements thus quadruplicated, He created many millions of Brahmandas (macrocosms), fourteen worlds appropriate to each (of these macrocosms) and globular gross bodies appropriate (to each of these worlds)."*

The *Bhagavadgita* states that all creation constitutes but a little aspect (*amsa*) of God. Some *Upanishads* mention only three worlds the earth (*bhu*), the heaven of gods (*bhuva*) and the immortal world of Brahman (*suvah*). References are also found in the *Vedas* to the three spheres of creation, the lower one where the mortals live, the middle one where the atmospheric gods and celestial beings live and the highest one, which is inhabited by gods such as *Indra, Agni, Vayu Adityas* and *Varuna*.

The *Puranas* mention seven higher worlds of light (*vyahrtis*) and seven lower worlds of darkness (*patalas*), with earth in the seventh position starting from the highest. They are *satya, tapa jana, mahar, svar, bhuvar, bhur, atala, vitala, sutala, talatala, mahatala, rasatala, patala*. It is also said that below the seven worlds of darkness lies the world of *Yama* (*naraka*), which we have discussed before.

Punishment in hell

The *Bhagavadgita* suggests that those who possess demonic qualities and indulge in grave sins fall down to the lowest hells and suffer there. The *Garuda Purana* provides a graphic description of how the sinners are tormented by *Yama* for their sins and the types of sins that lead the beings to hell. It states that those who lack divine qualities, intoxicated with pride or wealth, enveloped in delusion, drawn to worldly pleasures and desire-ridden actions, fall into foul hell.

When such people die after intense suffering, the messengers of *Yama* arrive and drag them away to hell along the path of burning sand reminding them of their sinful deeds. The world of *Yama* does not offer any solace or comfort to the sinners. It is a world without water, without trees, with twelve suns blazing simultaneously in the sky, with all kinds of wild animals and foul smelling impurities, where it is excruciatingly difficult for anyone to endure the suffering.

The *Purana* further describes that *Yama's* world contains 8.4 million hells (types of suffering) of which 21 are said to the most dreadful where the beings are subjected to severe punishments according the sins they committed upon earth.

Alternate theories

In Hinduism, we also hear about other possibilities of existence that awaits the beings after their death. According one version, a departed soul progresses through different planes of existence until he exhausts all the bodies.

This is based on the Vedic belief that a living being has five sheaths or bodies, namely the outer gross body (*annamaya kosa*), the inner breath body (*pranamaya kosa*), mental body (*manomaya kosa*), intelligence body (*vijnanamaya kosa*) and bliss body (*anandamaya kosa*).

When an embodied-self (*jiva*) dies, its gross body returns to its elements (*mahabhutas*) namely, the earth, fire, water, air, while the soul with the remaining four ethereal (subtle) bodies go to the higher planes, where it sheds them one after another overtime according to its previous *karmas*. Once all the layers are shed and the Self remains with its latent impressions, it is born again upon earth to continue its existence.

According to classical yoga, predominant desires, attachments and repeated actions result in the formation of latent impressions (*samskaras*). They form the seed for one's next birth. When a being dies, they accompany the soul in the form of causative memory (*karana citta*), the elements of which determine the course of one's next life. Liberation is achieved only when these impressions are fully burnt in the fire of *sattva* by practicing the various limbs of yoga and stabilizing the mind in the contemplation of the Self.

According to the *Kausitaki Upanishad*, when the living beings die, they ascend to the moon, which is the door to heaven. There they will be asked a question about their identity. Those who do not answer it return to the earth and take birth again as an insect, animal, bird or man, according to their previous actions.

Those who answer it correctly ascend further to the path that leads to gods. On their way along the path, they pass through the subtle worlds of *Agni* (fire) *Vayu* (air), *Varuna*, *Indra* and *Prajapati*. These probably stand for the five worlds where the departed souls shed their subtle sheaths. Eventually, they enter the world of Brahman, and proceed to the City of God. On their way, they encounter many divine beings, wonders, celestial objects, nymphs, messengers and attendants of God. After a long and wonderful journey, finally they enter His Palace and stands before Him. He asks them a few more questions to test their knowledge and devotion. When He is pleased with their answers, He admits them into His fold and gives them a place of honor in His assembly.

The Vedic tradition believed that a man would become immortal by living through his sons and his sons through their sons. The *Kausitaki Upanishad* describes how a father should pass on his tradition (vocation or obligatory duties) to his son at the time of his death. The birth of a son in the family was therefore considered vital to escape from damnation. The scriptures suggest that it is difficult to attain heaven or the ancestral world without a son performing the funeral rites. Those who do not have son should adapt one to avoid descending into a special hell called *Put* or *Punnamah*.

The *Garuda Purana* (7.9) declares that a son is called *putra* because he saves his parents from falling into the hell known as *Put*. It also clarifies who should meet a son's obligations and perform funeral rites if a person dies without a son. The funeral rites are important because without them a departed soul cannot have a proper body in the ancestral world and survive for long.

Some descriptions in the Upanishads allude to the possibility of simulating the journey of a soul to the higher worlds in one's own consciousness through yoga and meditation. By withdrawing the senses, stabilizing the mind and suppressing its modifications, one can gradually ascend into higher planes of consciousness and meet the deities who are present in us and who assist us in our liberation.

The *Vedas* affirm that human beings are made in the image of God (*Purusha*) and the gods and celestial worlds exist in our own microcosm. Gods and demons and the heaven and hell also exist in us in subtle form. Through austerities and inner transformation, we can awaken the divinities hidden in us and with their help travel by the inner sunlit path (*devayana*) to experience union with the Self. We can also seek their help to deal with the demonic worlds that exist in us.

Sri *Aurobindo* suggested integral yoga to integrate the mind and body and prepare oneself to ascend through deeper states of meditation into higher planes of pure consciousness and explore the possibilities and opportunities awaiting the humankind. He indicated that with effort and seeking the help of God and Divine Mother, it was possible for humans to evolve into superior beings having supramental abilities, pervasive intelligence and bodies of light and bliss.

In Buddhism, meditation and mindfulness techniques are practiced to experience the hells and heavens that exist in one's own consciousness. The mind is the seat of the cosmic drama. What happens in the mind has implications for a being's future and destiny. Suffering is hell. Enjoyment is heaven. Our hopes, fears and aspirations create gods and demons and unless we resolve them, we cannot have peace or Nirvana. The gods and demons manifest in our consciousness as our own thoughts, habits, emotions, desires and impulses. When we transcend them and learn not react to them, we enter into a zone of indescribable peace and become free forever from the suffering of births and deaths

The fate of the Self upon liberation

What happens when a person attains liberation? Does the soul continue to exist? Does it disappear? Does it become something else? Different schools answer this question differently. The individual Self is eternally indestructible, inexhaustible and free from modifications, even when it is caught in the cycle of births and deaths. What changes during liberation is its state of bondage.

According to the school of monism (*advaita*), upon liberation an embodied soul ceases to exist as an entity since it overcomes delusion and realizes that Brahman alone is true and everything else is a mere projection, illusion or temporary formation. In other words, according to this school, liberation results in the ending of the very existence of the soul, like a wave in a cosmic ocean that rises for a brief time and then falls back into the vast ocean. When an individual entity (*jiva*) overcomes egoism (*anava*), attachments (*pasas*) and delusion (*moha*) it overcomes the illusion of separation, duality and distinction and becomes one with the Supreme Self, who alone is real.

According to the school of qualified monism (*visistadvaita*), when an individual soul is liberated, it becomes a free soul (*mukta*) forever and never comes under the influence of Nature again. It enters the Abode of God and remains there in His presence, enjoying His company and close proximity and witnessing cosmic events along with Him. On liberation, it becomes like the Supreme Self in its essential Nature, but retains its distinction and duality.

The dualistic schools (*dvaita*) suggest that while some souls qualify for liberation (*mukti-yogya*) from the phenomenal world through effort, some remain bound to it forever (*nitya-samsarins*) and some are destined to go to the nether regions (*tamo-yogya*). In this, the *gunas* play an important role. The distinction between the individual souls and the Supreme Self stays forever. It continues even after an embodied soul is liberated. It remains distinct not only from God but from other souls also.

Conclusion

Thus, we can see that Hinduism offers a very complex structure of the universe, in which heaven and hell are just two worlds, which are not necessarily the only places to which human beings go after death. Human beings may attain heaven, hell, or liberation, in which actions play a prominent role. They may also remain bound to Nature until the end of the worlds. Heavenly existence is not permanent. So also the existence in hell. Souls reincarnate.

Human birth is attained at the end of several lives. Only human beings have an opportunity to guide their lives intelligently and make a conscious and willful effort to escape from the cycle of births and deaths. Death is a temporary phase, a modification and an opportunity for each being to start all over again. Because of desire-ridden actions, a being is caught in the cycle of transmigration until it travels by the path of gods to the world of immortality. Until them, it has to move in circles, learn the lessons and deal with its impurities and imperfections as a prisoner of Nature and a victim of its own thoughts and actions.

Marriages in Hinduism

"It is not, indeed, for the sake of husband (kamaya) that the husband is dear, but for the sake of the Self that he is dear." Brihadaranyaka Upanishad (4.5.6)

It is very difficult to generalize and write about Hindu marriages because the customs and traditions vary from caste to caste and region to region. Globalization of Hindu community has also added complexity to the tradition and made the practices diverse and difficult to generalize. The Vedic marriage system more or less remained the same during the centuries; but Hindu marriages and the social customs associated with it have undergone several changes in the past few centuries. Therefore, only certain aspects of the subject are covered in this discussion to provide a brief understanding of how people view marriages in Hinduism and what purpose they serve. The following are a few general facts about marriages in Hinduism.

1. Marriage is a relationship between two souls

In Hinduism, marriage is considered a sacred relationship not only between a man and a woman but also between two eternal souls. The bond between the two is not confined to one lifetime, but many; and it may begin even before the embodied souls attain human birth. What bring them together are karma as well as fate. Their genders may also change from one lifetime to another. Thus, a husband in one lifetime may become a wife in the next and vice versa. Since Hindus believe in *karma* and rebirth and know the karmic implications of breaking a marriage, divorce rates are relatively lower among them compared to those in the western world.

2. Marriage is a relationship between a man and woman only

The law books clearly affirm marriage as a relationship between a man and a woman. The Vedic marriage ceremonies and the rituals associated with them clearly point to the relationship as one between a man and a woman. Some people claim otherwise, but we do not have evidence that same sex marriage has the sanction of Hindu scriptures or traditional beliefs. The practice of same sex marriage as a social norm is a recent phenomena, foisted upon Hindu society by liberal media, and a clear deviation from established Hindu family traditions. According to the law books and *Grihyasutras*, the purpose of marriage is performance of obligatory duties (*dharma*) and continuation of family lineage through offspring. These goals can be accomplished only by a husband and wife. In a marriage, each partner has a specific role and set of obligatory duties and some of them are gender specific. Even at the cosmic level, creation is depicted as the union between *Purusha*, the Cosmic Male and *Prakriti*, the Cosmic Female. The very symbol of *Sivalingam* signifies their relative importance in life and creation. In many temples, marriages between gods and their consorts are performed ritually. Therefore, it is wrong to argue that Hinduism approves same sex marriages.

3. Marriage should take place with the consent of elders only

This is the established norm. In an arranged marriage, the consent of the bride's father is considered very important. Gifting of the bride by her father or a guardian (*kanyadanam*) is also an important ritual in traditional marriages before the bride and the groom are joined in wedlock. It is customary for the groom and his family to meet the bride's father first and obtain his consent before finalizing the marriage date. During marriage ceremony, the bride's father gives away his daughter ritually as a gift first to the gods and then to the groom with gods serving as the witnesses. These norms are changing now, but sill in most Hindu marriages parents and elders play an important role. In traditional families, marriage is considered not only a relationship between the bride and the bridegroom but also between their families. This has its own downside and often leads to social evils like dowry system, forced marriages and bride killings.

4. The purpose of marriage is upholding of dharma

Marriage is a sacred bond in which both sides have obligatory duties to uphold *dharma* and ensure each other's liberation. After marriage, both husband and wife have to uphold their family values and remain faithful and truthful to each other performing their obligatory duties according to the customs and tradition. As illustrated in the epics *Ramayana* and the *Mahabharata*, they have to stick together through the difficulties of life, despite the hardships and challenges, and live for the sake of one another, family, society and God. For a householder, marriage is an obligatory duty. Its purpose is to ensure the continuity of the family lineage, practice religious duty and serve the interests of family and society. The law books affirm that the institution of marriage was devised by gods for the welfare of human beings. It is meant to ensure the order and regularity of human society. Its primary purpose is procreation and continuation of life upon earth. Sexual relationship between married couple is intended mainly for this purpose. Its secondary purpose is upholding the social order and the religious duty (*dharma*). Its ultimate aim is to facilitate liberation through the practice of *karmayoga*.

5. Even gods honor the marriage tradition

In Hinduism, the institution of marriage is not peculiar to humans only. Even gods marry and live with their goddesses for eternity. According to the *Puranas*, they quarrel, nag and get even with each other just like human beings upon earth, but in the end, they remain inseparable. In the temples, the deities (*arcas*) are married ritually to their consorts in the traditional manner by the temple priests in the presence of their devotees. Such ceremonies are performed either everyday or on specific days by the temple priests as part of their devotional services to the deities. By blessing the divine couple, the devotees who participate in these ceremonies make the deities part of their families. Through their actions and commitment to their consorts, the gods exemplify the ideals and the virtue of marriage for the guidance of human beings who may lack knowledge and discretion or fail to meet their obligations. At times, they may overtly indulge in petty squabbles, as part of their divine play (*lilas*) to exemplify an ideal or accomplish a righteous goal. Such actions are justified on their part, because they are divine beings, having the knowledge of past, present and present and free from desires, attachments, ignorance and delusion. Therefore, we cannot judge them or their actions according to our values and social norms.

6. In marriage the couple's destinies are intertwined

For many, marriage can be a hindrance on the path of liberation since it promotes attachment and selfishness rather than detachment and renunciation. It is, therefore, important to know the negative consequences of marriage life and safeguard oneself from them, living virtuously and dutifully, cultivating detachment and honoring one's obligations. Marriage is the principal means by which human beings can uphold dharma and fulfill the objectives of creation. Without marriage, human beings cannot serve gods, ancestors and other beings. *Manusmriti* (9.8) declares that when a wife conceives, her husband is born again through her. Marriage is not just a mutual contract between two individuals or a relationship of convenience. It a social contract as well as moral expediency, in which the couples agree to live together and share their lives, doing their respective duties, to ensure the welfare of their families, society, gods and the world in general. As the torchbearers of *dharma* and as individual souls, whose lives and destinies are intertwined by their relationship, they should work for each other's liberation.

7. Hindu marriages are characterized by gender bias

In Hinduism, tradition gives more importance to men rather than women with regard to marriages. It is essentially a man's world. It is a man's duty to produce offspring and serve his ancestors. It is a man's duty to protect his wife (or wives) and care for them. It is upon a man's shoulders the welfare of his family, society, the world and beings rest. His wife is more or less, a silent partner, if not a mute witness to the sacrifice of life performed by her husband with herself as one of his sacrificial materials. In the past, women played a subservient role in family matters. Whatever influence she had was mainly through her charm or the good nature of her husband. Unfortunately, the tradition continues in many communities and families even today. Child marriages were common in ancient times. It facilitated older men and widowers marrying younger women before they even reached puberty. It allowed families to free themselves from the responsibility of feeding and protecting young girls. The dictum was a woman's place was in her husband's home and family. The earlier she was married and sent there the better it was for her, her family and her husband's family. Socially and economically, a girl child was considered a burden. This attitude does not seem to have changed much even now in modern Hindu society, considering that not less than a million abortions are performed in India every year based on gender, without any noticeable public protest, and many brides are subject to ill-treatment by their in-laws. Unlike in the USA, no political party is willing to take up the issue of abortions on an ideological basis, thanks to the liberal progressive ideas that confer license upon people to kill babies in the wombs in the name of women's rights and social justice. It is a paradox that in a community that reveres Mother Goddess on a large scale, girl children receive such callous treatment.

In the past, the plight of the widows was even more pitiable. Widows were not allowed to participate in marriage ceremonies or remarry. They were morally held responsible for the premature death of their husbands and they had to carry that guilt and the burden of shame for the rest of their lives. Their very presence was considered inauspicious. Whatever might be the caste into which they were born, the widows were treated on par with the untouchables. In some communities, it was customary to sacrifice the wife of a deceased person on his funeral pyre as part of an ancient custom, a practice that is now considered illegal and barbaric, but not without inviting muted protests from some who still believe in their right to practice such customs as part of their religious freedom or obligatory duties. Under certain circumstances, the law books permitted a childless widow to beget children through the brothers of her deceased husband. However, this practice was not universal. Polygamy was an approved practice. Bias towards women and girl children continues in many parts of India, even among the highly educated and wealthy Hindus. Female infanticide in the form of abortions is a major social issue which Hindu society is reluctant to deal with. In ancient times, in fact until three or four hundred years ago, polygamy was a normal practice. Polyandry was also practiced in certain communities. However, presently monogamy is the standard. In India by law, a Hindu cannot marry another person if married already, unless consent is given by the spouse.

Hindu law books show a clear bias against women in family matters and relationships. The *Manusmriti* (9.1-3) suggests that women should be controlled, and kept under watch since they cannot be trusted. The law books also do not consider gender equality as an important consideration in marriage or society, although they emphasize that in a marriage relationship, each partner has a unique role, which cannot be compensated by the other. They declare the head of the family, who is traditionally a male, as the primary upholder of obligatory duties (*dharma*) and the recipient of all ritual honors, and his wife should serve him as his partner and associate (*saha-dharma-charini*) in fulfilling them. In a traditional household, according to the law books, the woman of the house should play an important role in family and household work, but keep a low profile in social matters. She should avoid outside exposure and contact with men of other families to prevent the family from falling into disrepute. In comparison, her husband is allowed to enjoy greater freedom and authority and command more respect and importance both in the house and society. Life revolves around him. Privileges to the family accrue because of him. His wife enjoys a good status only as long as he is alive. When he dies, she loses everything, her wealth, her identity, her comforts and her status and her right to participate in social and religious ceremonies. Thus, clearly and unequivocally the Hindu law books relegate women to a subordinate position in relationship to men. The status of women in society and the equation between men and women are slowly changing in present day Hindu society, but there is still a large gap. In many families and regions of India, women still suffer from oppression, domestic violence, rape, dowry related deaths and several other disabilities.

8. Marriage is a sacrifice

In Hinduism, marriage has another dimension, which is unique by itself. Marriage is not a mere physical bond between a man and woman or a social practice to facilitate conjugal bliss, but a sacred covenant between them in which gods participate as witnesses on behalf of the bride, to receive the sacrificial offerings and give her in trust to the groom as the fruit of the sacrifice. By joining the couple in the wedlock, the gods ensure that they continue to receive offerings from them in future through sacraments and sacrificial ceremonies that are obligatory for a householder. During the marriage ceremony, it is customary for the priest first to marry the bride to the gods and then present her as a gift from them to the bridegroom. The groom is then made to take an oath with gods standing as the witnesses that he would protect his wife and abide by her for the rest of his life. The idea behind this practice is that a man ought to respect his wife and treat her well as a divine gift since he cannot perform his obligatory duties as the upholder of the *dharma* all by himself. Besides, the belief that he has received the bride in good faith from the gods themselves puts him under a moral obligation to treat her well.

We can notice a clear dichotomy between the treatment of women in the Vedic tradition as reflected in the marriage ceremony and the position taken by the Hindu law books towards women and their status in general. This is clearly, because the law books were of later day origin and the products of the time in which they were composed. By the time they were composed, the Vedic tradition was already in decline and replaced by new traditions based upon rigid caste rules. The law books are manmade intellectual works (*smritis*) in comparison to the *Vedas*, which are considered not-manmade (*apauruseya*) or divine in origin (*srutis*). They loudly proclaim caste and gender bias, which characterized post Vedic Indian society that seemed to have grown distant after 6th Century BCE from the ancient Vedic beliefs and practices.

9. Marriage personifies creation on limited scale

In a Hindu marriage, both the husband and the wife, as the twin aspects of life, personify creation on a limited scale. The husband stands for *Purusha* and the wife for *Prakriti*. Their union results in the creation of life upon earth. In fact, in Hinduism marriage is an obligatory duty for those who want to lead their lives as householders. They are not expected to live for themselves, but for serving God and others selflessly as a sacrificial duty and use every opportunity to work for their liberation. The institution of marriage is meant to facilitate duty and divine service, rather than gratification and self-promotion. By procreating children, they take part in the divine duty of preservation of life and ensuring the continuity of sacrifices to gods, ancestors and others.

10. Caste is a dominant factor in Hindu marriages

In Hindu marriages, caste is an important consideration. The marriage rituals and customs also vary from caste to caste. The partners are chosen based on various criteria such as birth, caste, relationship, family lineage, region, social and economic status, reputation, age, color and creed. However, of them caste is an important factor. People prefer to marry within their castes, since it has been the established norm for centuries and parents, in general, do not like to incur the displeasure or disapproval of friends and family. Inter-caste marriages are not prohibited by the law books. However, they do not accord them the same status as the caste based marriage and do not give the same status to the children born out of such marriages as those born to parents of the same caste. Even now, caste is a predominant factor in Hindu marriages. The number of intercaste marriages is much less and those who marry outside their castes and religion, especially if the bride or bridegroom happens to be from a lower caste, have to cope with many social pressures and disabilities.

11. Type of marriages

The law books identify seven types of marriages. A marriage that is performed according to established norms and in traditional fusion is known as divine wedding. When a couple marries in secrecy, it is called *gandharva* wedding. If money was used to obtain the consent of bride's parents or guardians it is known as *asura* (demonic) wedding. If the bride is taken by force, it is known as *raskhsasa* wedding. If a man marries an unconscious bride, it is called *paisaca* wedding. Presently, the most common forms of wedding are the traditional marriages or registered marriages. The number of live in couples without marriage, which is a recent phenomenon, is also increasing. We have yet to see its longtime repercussions. Marriages by force or kidnapping are less common, but reported in some parts of India.

Hindu marriages in today's world

The concept of divorce is alien to Hinduism, as marriages are meant to last for a lifetime. Neither men nor women can throw away their marital relationships on some flimsy, selfish, or whimsical grounds. Remarriage is permitted only under exceptional circumstances. According to the Vedic tradition, marriage is the means by which a man perpetuates himself through his progeny. A father extends himself into his future life and into the next world through his children. In this process, he is helped by his wife who bears him children through the sacred union in which there is a transfer of sexual energy (*rethas*). In traditional Hinduism, marriage is the best means for the continuation of family and the Hindu tradition, by fulfilling which the two partners in the marriage co-create their future and become qualified for their salvation. The roles of a husband and wife in a marriage are expected to be complimentary, because without helping each other neither of them can fulfill their duties and obligations as householders. The Hindu law books do their best to delineate the roles and responsibilities of both husband and wife in a family to avoid confusion. However, since they have been composed longtime ago, they may not apply to the present day society. Hindu society has to come out with its own solution without ignoring the basic tenets of the religion. The couples have to follow their family traditions and ensure that their actions do not lead to the social disorder. In a traditional Hindu family, married couples have to perform many traditional duties. Some of them are specific to each and some are common to both. In the present day world, the equation between man and woman is changing. With the decline in our commitment to Hindu dharma and in our anxiety to pursue modern lifestyles and uphold progressive, liberal and advanced ideas and ideologies, a good number of Hindus are shunning anything and everything that remotely looks orthodox Hinduism. With the decline in family values and changes in the family structure, there is now a significant overlapping of roles and responsibilities between men and women. In many families, now women are the main breadwinners and taking up the role of the householders in supporting their families. The Hindu Marriage Act passed in India in 1955 also changed the equation between the two significantly. Men still have advantage over women in marriage and social relationships; but in a society where religion is no more central to human endeavor as it used to be, we may see further deterioration in their roles as the protectors and upholders of traditional duties. The traditional beliefs and practices associated with the institution of marriage still hold good in some families. However, we are not sure how long this will continue.

In Hinduism, there are both moving parts and stable parts. The stable parts, which are essentially its core beliefs and concepts, keep the appeal of the Hindu religion intact, while the moving parts, which are essentially its practices and applied aspects, keep it moving and evolving according to the needs of the time. They contribute to its resilience and vitality. Despite all the flux and commotion that is going on in the present-day Hindu society, marriage is still a viable and powerful institution where divorce rates are considerably lower than those of the western countries and where marriages are more stable and enduring. The condition of women is not peculiar to Hinduism. It is a problem of the humanity, which requires a greater understanding and a universal shift in our thinking and attitude towards women in general and gender in particular for it to disappear permanently from the face of our planet.

Teacher Traditions of Ancient India

One of the most unique and ancient traditions of Hinduism is the tradition of *guru* or master. In Hinduism, a *guru* is considered God in human form and given the highest respect due next only to parents. A *guru* is different from an ordinary teacher, who works for a fees and has no interest in your life or liberation beyond his teaching. A *guru* is an enlightened master or a spiritual teacher, who plays an important role in opening the minds of his disciples to the highest truths that are enshrined in the scriptures and prepares them for their lives as well as their liberation.

The word *Guru* is interpreted differently. Literally speaking, it means weighty, heavy, large, great and long. It conveys importance, greatness, respect and excellence. In fact, these meanings point to some important attributes of a great teacher, who is expected to be a person of character, integrity, wisdom and eminence capable of holding our attention and respect. According to one well-known interpretation, *guru* means he who drives away darkness or sheds light upon darkness. Darkness stands for ignorance and delusion. A *guru* removes both.

A *guru* also serves as a father figure. While parents give physical birth, he gives spiritual birth to those who come to him for knowledge. He opens our eyes to the knowledge and wisdom hidden in the scriptures that leads to our liberation. Therefore, those who receive initiation from a *guru* are expected to pay him utmost respect and serve him well so that with the knowledge they gain from him, they can overcome their ignorance and delusion.

Teacher traditions

Hinduism is a complex religion, whose teachings and knowledge cannot be codified or generalized without attracting some controversy. With no central authority and no governing body to codify and regulate its teachings or the conduct of its adherents, it would have been difficult for any religion to continue for such a long time. Yet, Hinduism survived for over six thousand years. Despite the absence of organized leadership and enforceable dogma, it kept its hold upon the masses largely due to the efforts of several ascetic sects and teacher traditions (*guru paramparas*).

For generations, they established and enforced a sound system of succession of *gurus* based upon merit, character and integrity to ensure that teachings of the traditions would be preserved and passed on to the posterity without being lost, distorted or diluted. Their relentless services, commitment to their teachings and personal character ensured that the core teachings of Hinduism and its vital practices were preserved despite communication barriers and constraints in preserving knowledge. In messianic religions, the teachings of the messiahs play an important role. In complex religions like Hinduism, which are not founded by a particular prophet or spiritual person, teacher traditions fill that vacuum. They ensure that the tradition is alive by interpreting and reinterpreting its core principles.

Today, we may not have to rely upon *gurus* and teachers only to preserve the knowledge and wisdom of our scriptures. We can now store and retrieve knowledge in various ways using the modern tools of storage, printing and publishing. We can find the scriptures in the libraries, bookstores, digital media, and on the internet. Anyone, who has the interest or inclination, can find a lot of information (as well as misinformation) about one's faith. Frankly, we do not anymore require the *gurus* to know what information is available in our scriptures. In fact, going to a *guru* for that purpose alone is a sheer waste of his time and our time.

However, a *guru* is still relevant and important. Books may give you knowledge; but a *guru* gives you wisdom that you cannot obtain easily from other sources. He opens our minds to the knowledge that is not found in the books, and provides us with insights into philosophical subjects, which scriptures do not mention. He also helps us personally with his suggestions and advice on specific problems and difficulties we face in our lives. At times, he also protects us from evil influences and bad *karma* by foreseeing things in advance. A *guru* is therefore still important. In some teacher traditions, *gurus* transfer their spiritual energies (*shakti*) to their followers and help them to overcome their weaknesses and deficiencies and hasten their sell-purification.

Life in gurukuls

Literally speaking, a *gurukul* is a place where a *guru* lives with his family and students. Today, many schools and educational institutions in India go by the name *gurukul*, despite the fact that some of them demand hefty sums of black money from the students before they even admit them. The *gurukuls* used to be the places where gurus or spiritual masters used to live and educate young students in various branches of knowledge. They served as both residences for the *gurus* and their families and residential schools for the students to stay and study. Students constituted their extended families. As long as they stayed with them, the *gurus* took responsibility for their education as well as their personal welfare.

They lived mostly in secluded places, away from the humdrum of worldly life, to provide a peaceful environment to their students so that they could study without distractions and temptations. During their stay, the students lived in the care of their *gurus*, performing household duties as part of their learning, in addition to studying and mastering the subjects. Each student spent over twenty years to master all the subjects and return home to begin life as a householder. The schools were private and admission was strictly according to the whims of the *gurus*. Caste and gender played a prominent role, Women were not admitted unless the teaching was about fine arts, spying or related subjects or the students were from a royal family.

The *gurukuls* also served as lodgings for the students. However, for the duration of their stay, they had to secure food through begging only. It taught them the virtues of humility, renunciation and detachment. Even for begging, there were rules such as the students were forbidden to beg from parents and relations or during specific hours of the day. They were also forbidden to accept certain types of food. The students were also required to follow a strict code of conduct. They were to practice celibacy, speak truth, cultivate virtues, obey the master, and never to betray his trust.

Method of teaching

In ancient India, knowledge was treated like a precious commodity and shared selectively. Knowledge was considered secret (*guhya*) or utmost secret (*atiguhya*). In this, caste and family lineages played a dominant role. Knowledge was not imparted unless the students were related or belonged to particular lineages that descended from ancient seers from whom the teachings were originally derived. Some subjects such as the *Upanishads* were considered even more secret (*atiguhyam*) because of their spiritual implications. They were taught only in person. Hence, the name, *Upanishad*, means sitting near. The reasons for such selectivity and partiality in spreading spiritual and temporal knowledge are not difficult to guess. The practice ensured that certain families who were privy to the knowledge retained their monopoly upon their professions prevented unnecessary competition from possible rivals. It complied with the scriptural injunction that knowledge should be imparted to people according to their merit, family background and obligatory duties. As the Bhagavadgita declares, one was not expected to take up the duties (dharma) of another, however superior it might be.

Absence of written materials made the task of protecting the knowledge and passing it on to selected candidates easier. Since written scripts were not available, knowledge was passed orally from teacher to students. Students spent considerable time to memorize what they learned and remember it for the rest of their lives. They memorized entire scriptures verbatim, reciting them day after day until their stayed in their memory firmly. Mastering all scriptures and subjects in this manner was a time-consuming process. It tested the teacher's patience as well as the students' abilities. *Manusmriti* indicates that a student required 36 years to master the scriptures and become proficient in them.

Even after the emergence of written scripts, teachers in ancient India continued to impart education orally for the reasons we have already discussed. Besides, scriptures like the *Vedas* were so voluminous that compared to the costs involved in writing them down and preserving them, memorizing them was more convenience and less expensive. Even after writing was invented, the written script was used in ancient India for limited purposes. Only kings had the wherewithal to employ scribes and convey their messages and royal edicts in writing. As a result, until the invention of the modern press, knowledge was imparted orally and the secrecy associated with the teaching continued.

Despite these drawbacks, the teacher traditions ensured smooth transmission of knowledge, inculcating strict discipline among their students, with adequate built-in safeguards to ensure the purity and continuity of their teachings. They placed great emphasis on the character and integrity vis-à-vis the teachers as well as students. Society expected teachers to main high standards of character and integrity and the students to follow the same. Unlike today's schools, the teachers were not expected to indulge in salesmanship or advertise their services. A teacher had to earn the respect through the students he trained. If the students were satisfied with the knowledge and training they gained from their masters, they would recommend them to others and prefer to send their children to them only for their education and the cycle would continue as long as the relationship lasted. Good teachers therefore had no need to go out into public and look for students. They had to wait for the students to come to them out of curiosity, interest or the obligations of family duty and learn from them following the discipline they enforced.

The *gurukuls* played a key role in preserving the knowledge and practices of Hinduism. They ensured the purity of the scriptures and the continuity of Vedic knowledge, despite the changes that took place in Indian society and the pressures people faced from foreign oppressors and religious persecutors. Staying away from public gaze, they also avoided detection by the Islamic rulers who were intent upon replacing Hinduism with Islam in India. Unfortunately, in course of time, the system degenerated due to lack of patronage and changes in the social and political climate of India.

Types of gurus

In ancient India, two types of teachers imparted education to students, spiritual *gurus* and professional teachers (*adhyapaks*). The spiritual *gurus* imparted knowledge as an obligatory duty for the sake of protecting, promoting and preserving *dharma*. The professional teachers taught for the sake of money and livelihood. They practiced teaching as an occupation and charged money for the services they rendered.

The professional teachers came in different forms. There were men of specialized knowledge, who gave consultation and advice on specific issues; vocational trainers who specialized in the knowledge of specific vocations; and heads of merchant guilds with vast experience and working knowledge of their professions who could train others besides their own family members. There were also merchants, artisans, chemists, doctors, magicians, court jesters, archers, wrestlers, courtesans and other professionals, who trained others, for free or for a fee or under royal instructions. They imparted knowledge and training in specific subjects such as the study of medicinal plants, herbal medicine, fine arts, martial arts, spying, surgery, mathematics, astronomy, architecture, temple building, metallurgy, chemistry, physics, cattle rearing, hunting, cooking and so on. They made sure that their knowledge survived them in people whom they trusted. While the *gurus* were mostly men, women also taught in selected areas such as drawing, painting, cooking, housekeeping, cloth making, dyeing, dance, music, and lovemaking.

In families, parents and heads of families served as teachers. They instructed their children and family members in their duties and occupations. They guided the young, until they went to the *gurukuls*. Kings and nobility took the help of their family priests (*purohita*) and teachers (*rajaguru*) in educating their children. In return, they supported them with royal patronage and reserved for them a seat of honor in the royal courts.

Apart from these, there were spiritual masters, who lived in highly inaccessible places such as caves and ruins in deep forests or in the Himalayas or unusual places like graveyards and treetops. They admitted none as their followers unless they were fully vetted and satisfied as to their sincerity and intent. Unlike the *gurukuls*, their teaching was mostly erratic and strictly on one-on-one basis with no specific agenda or curriculum and depended mainly upon the relationship between the two.

Guru as a symbol

A guru is a symbol of knowledge and authority. He or she does not have to be a living person. One may choose a deity, an idol, an image or God himself and worship him as one's *guru* for knowledge and guidance. It may be someone from the past, an ancestor, a historic figure, a saint, or a seer from the scriptures. He may be even a symbolic or imaginary person because our minds have the power to manifest our thoughts according to our aspirations. Ultimately, in a teacher and student relationship what matters most is faith and commitment.

Nowhere is this better illustrated than in the life of *Ekalavya* and his relationship with his imaginary *guru Drona. Ekalavya*, was born in a tribal family. As per tradition, he was not entitled to learn from a teacher of brahmana caste. Therefore, as an alternative he installed a clay image of *Drona* and under his imaginary guidance practiced archery. In the process, he became a great archer, rivaling Arjuna, the best in the field. When Drona came to know about it, he was not happy because he wanted *Arjuna*, whom he was training personally, to be the best. Therefore, he demanded *Ekalavya* to give him his thumb as the fees due to him (*gurudakshina*) for the imaginary services he rendered. True to his character, *Ekalavya* readily cut off his thumb and gave it to his *guru*. In the process, he lost his ability to use the bow, while Arjuna went on to become a great warrior and participate in the Mahabharata war. Apart from the injustice and social inequalities of the time, the story clearly illustrates the use of imagination and visualization in self-study (*svadhyaya*) with the help of an imaginary *guru*.

Duties of a student

During the prolonged stay of the students in the *gurukuls*, which lasted for two or three decades, the students were expected to perform many ancillary duties, apart from studying the scriptures and mastering the knowledge. In their spare time, they served in the teacher's household, fetching water, cleaning the floor or carrying the firewood. They also served their masters personally by pressing their feat, holding their umbrella, washing his clothes or cleaning his personal items. Such duties and services gave them an opportunity to bond with their teachers, earn their attention and learn from them about household responsibilities, which they were expected to perform when they grew up. It also gave an opportunity to the teachers to observe them closely and help them in their self-development.

The Hindu law books prescribed a strict code of conduct for the students who lived in the *gurukuls*. They were expected to remain obedient to their *gurus*, follow their teachings unconditionally and show their respect not only to them but also to their wives, children and other members of the family. For a student, a teacher and his wife were equal to his parents. Under no circumstances, the students were to engage in any improper behavior with them or other member of the household.

The *gurus* also served as role models and provided their students with many opportunities to observe them and learn from them. At times, they tested their character and integrity and helped them individually according to their strengths and weaknesses. Once a student received initiation from a *guru*, he retained complete control over him until he finished his education and left his place. The relationship lasted for a lifetime and perhaps beyond as the teachers lived through their students with the knowledge and the values they imparted to them.

Gurudakshina, repaying the debt

The gurukuls were not moneymaking factories, unlike today's commercial schools. The *gurus* had character and integrity. They taught knowledge for knowledge sake, not to make profit out of their teaching. Most of them lived in utter penury, yet took care of their students and their education, despite personal hardships. As per tradition, a *guru* was not expected to collect money from his students for the services he rendered. A *guru's* obligatory duty was to teach and teaching others without expectations and as a sacrifice for God was the highest ideal. Therefore, the teachers spent years teaching each student patiently, hardly expecting anything in return, except perhaps good studentship.

However, while the *guru* was expected to teach freely, without expectations, his students had an obligatory duty to repay their debt to him by returning the favor, which they did in the form of complying with his wishes. At the end of education, each student had an obligation to ask his teacher what he wished for and fulfill that wish, however difficult it might be. Whatever a teacher asked at that time, even if it was the most unrealistic and most difficult, a student had the obligation to fulfill. It was called *gurudakshina*, payment to the guru, which provided each student with a chance to repay their debt to their gurus. The practice was essentially a symbolic gesture to on the part of the students to free themselves from the karmic burden they incurred by receiving free education from their *teachers*. The system also offered an opportunity to the teachers to show their character by exercising restraint and freeing the students from debt of gratitude they owed them.

The tradition of master and disciple played a significant role in the preservation of Hinduism. It ensured smooth transmission of scriptural knowledge and religious traditions from one generation to another and contributed greatly to the survival and continuity of Hinduism even during the most turbulent times. Among the many factors, teacher traditions contributed to the survival of Hinduism, even when it lacked political and economic support or suffered from intellectual inertia.

The *gurus* of Hinduism compensated for the lack of centralized organizations. They filled the leadership vacuum, by providing guidance to people and helping them to sustain their faith in the face of suppression and religious persecution. Even today, spiritual masters and teachers play a significant role in Hinduism, reminding people of their obligatory duties, moral responsibilities and the need to live virtuously and work for their liberation. They continue to play an important role in influencing public opinion and government policy towards Hinduism, its beliefs and practices.

Bondage and Liberation of the Self

Much of the speculative philosophy in Hinduism deals with God, life and nature of creation. Scholars in ancient India probed their own experiences and states of consciousness to understand them. They explored their own beingness and consciousness to speculate about reality, truth, God or Brahman, individual souls, their relationship, the nature of creation, aspects (*tattvas*) of Nature, means of liberation and related subjects. The *Upanishads*, the *Puranas*, the *Bhagavadgita* and the *Sutra* literature reflect such earliest attempts on their part to understand the cosmic mysteries that could not be rationally explained or proved otherwise with empirical proof or direct evidence.

Nature and its implications for the soul

The role and significance of Nature in our suffering was another field about which the ancient scholars speculated and came out with a wide range of perspectives and philosophies. They viewed Nature as both an impediment and a facilitator in life, providing the groundwork for our experiences and learning process, and creating awareness necessary to look for truths beyond its confines. In the following discussion, we will examine some of the conclusions and speculations available in Hinduism regarding the mysteries of our creation and existence and the deeper aspects of our personalities and consciousness.

Are we souls? Since ancient times, we have been debating whether there is anything permanent and everlasting in us and whether any meaning and purpose are hidden in life that seems to have arisen from a random process. The *Vedas* say so. They affirm our eternal nature and fundamental oneness with the Universal Self. However, while we may quote the scriptures and refer to them in support of our beliefs and convictions, we cannot answer this question conclusively with our limited knowledge and intellect. The Self cannot be known with the mind and the senses. We cannot know it with ordinary awareness or in wakeful state.

We cannot know it by talking to spiritual masters, studying the scriptures or using our imagination.

All these efforts may help us to cultivate self-awareness and prepare for our liberation, but to achieve Self-realization we have to silence our minds and bodies to the point of extinction. We must live as if we do not exist but only the Self. To the ordinary mind, the Self is ungraspable, incomprehensible and unknowable. Hence, we have so much speculation about its existence or non-existence and its essential nature.

Nature is the biggest impediment on the path to liberation. If we are impure and our consciousness is veiled by ignorance and delusion, we cannot transcend Nature and see the hidden Self behind it. In the context of a living being, Nature means its embodiment or beingness. It consists of the mind, body, and their constituent realities. It is the most visible and tangible part in each being in which a lifetime of experiences accumulate before it disintegrates and returns to the earth.

In our search for liberation, we cannot simply do away with Nature because it is vital for our survival upon earth. In the past, some ascetic sects in ancient India used to encourage their practitioners to commit self-mortification or self-immolation to destroy their bodies and attain freedom from the impurities of Nature. Perhaps they used to do it at the end of a long and arduous practice of self-purification. Even then, it was a crude and painful attempt on their part to end life and release the soul from the bonds of Nature. Extinguishing the body for the sake of liberation is not be a good idea, since one still has to deal with the problem of karma and past life impressions. A more pragmatic and moderate solution would be to transform it and purify it so that it does not interfere with our progress or practice.

Self-realization may not end physical suffering. It gives you the knowledge and wisdom to understand suffering and withstand it. It gives you the ability to remain calm and stable in the midst of adversity and pain. Many people do not care to know what it means because for them living and suffering seem easier than going through the pains of preparing for liberation. Hence, they would not even consider the idea of defying nature for the sake of an abstract experience they cannot comprehend mentally.

Even after you experience the Self, you may not remember all the details of what happened because your mind and wakeful consciousness does not participate in it. It is like trying to know what you were doing or what happened in you when you were in deep sleep. This is the paradox of self-realization. In transcendental states, the mind is absent and in wakeful states, the Self is veiled or hidden. We can break this impasse by silencing our ego consciousness and remaining centered in the inner Self. In this effort, the ego is also a major impediment. It acts as if it is the real Self. Only when it is asleep and subdued, we have a chance to enter into a state of self-absorption, and perhaps remain awake when the mind and body are asleep.

The imagery of creation in the Vedas

From the earliest times, the *Vedas* enjoyed a unique status in Hinduism as the standard of truth. Most schools of Hinduism (*darshanas*), with the exception of a few atheistic ones, regard them as verbal testimony (*shabda pramana*) to validate truths. Whatever the *Vedas* affirm, the Hindu scholars accept it as truth without any skepticism. Following this practice, we refer to the Creation Hymn in the *Rigveda*, which describes the process of creation and the manner in which the worlds and beings were manifested by the Supreme Being. We do not question its validity, since it is affirmed by the Rigveda as truth.

The hymn states that in the beginning there was nothing, neither light nor darkness nor the sun nor the moon, nor the earth, but one undivided nothingness. From this indeterminate nothingness, creation manifested. This state is described in the *Upanishads* and the *Bhagavadgita* as the formless (*amurtam*), unknown (*acintyam*) and Unmanifested (*avyakta*) Brahman. It is also described in some texts as non-existence (*asat*). This was believed to be the original state of Brahman prior to creation. It is also known as His deep sleep state, in which everything is withdrawn and suspended in a subtle state.

If the day is Manifested Brahman, the night is Unmanifested Brahman. The *Puranas* dramatize this condition as the resting phase of Brahman (the Night of God). According to Hindu astronomical calculations, a day of Brahman stretches into trillions of years in earth time, in which numerous *Brahma* days float by and countless *Prajapati Brahmas* manifest from the ocean of pure consciousness and create manifold worlds and beings. Brahman has both wakeful and deep sleep states. He is the space (*akasa*) in the universe. Hence, He is described in the scriptures as both black and blue, representing symbolically the colors of the sky during the night and day respectively.

Triple aspects of Brahman

At the beginning of each cycle of creation, from the Unmanifested Brahman, appear Manifested Brahman, who is then differentiated into the following Triad.

* *Saguna Brahman*, also described as *Purusha* (Person) and *Isvara* (Lord)
* Numerous individuals souls (*jivatmas*)
* Nature (*Prakriti*) also known as the Mother Goddess or *Shakti*

These three are the first manifestations in creation, the triple aspects of That (*tat*), mentioned in the *Upanishads* as the One Absolute Truth. They are also His fundamental aspects. The numerous individual souls and Nature constitute the subtle and gross bodies of the *Saguna Brahman*. In some ways, the three also personify the three functional aspects of the Manifested Brahman, namely creation, preservation and destruction.

Saguna Brahman, the Universal Lord, is the Creator who manifests the worlds through His inviolable will. Resting on the waters of pure consciousness on a bed made of the primal matter, which is depicted symbolically as the multi hooded serpent *Adisesha*, He produces from His navel, *Brahma Prajapati* the Creator of all beings. He is thus Creator of creators.

The individual souls participate in the preservation of life. They sustain life upon earth as preservers of the beings they inhabit, upholding the aspects of Nature while remaining imprisoned inside the bodies. When the souls depart, the beings die. Collectively, they represent subtle body of God. The *Puranas* describe the material universe and the individual souls as the body of *Vishnu*.

The third component of manifestation, Nature, is both creative and destructive. Hence, she is depicted symbolically in the scriptures as both *Parvathi* and *Kali*. When she veils the beings with *maya*, she destroys their freedom. When they attain liberation, she destroys their ignorance and impurities. At the end of creation, it withdraws the *gunas* and the *tattvas* into their subtle states and brings the entire creation to a grinding halt. This function is similar to that of *Siva* as the destroyer.

While the Vedic hymn suggests that three aspects manifested from the same reality, different schools of Hinduism interpret their relationship differently. According to monism, individual souls and Nature are not real but temporary projections or appearances of one eternal truth. The Absolute Brahman alone is real and everything else is a mere illusion arising from the delusion and ignorance of our minds. Some believe that the individual souls and Nature are the dependent realities created by Brahman for the purpose of creation. They are manifested at the beginning of each cycle of creation and withdrawn in the end at the time of the dissolution of the worlds. The difference among them subtle, except in appearance. The third view holds that all the three are eternal and independent realities that take part in creation either under the will of God or on their own. The three entities continue their existence eternally, while creation may appear and disappear in each time cycle. Whatever may be the truth, the three aspects we have mentioned before are the first realities (*tattvas*) to arise from Brahman at the beginning of creation.

The bondage of souls

The independent and eternal souls floating freely in the pure consciousness of Supreme Brahman become dependent and deluded under the influence of Nature. Through modifications and the activities of the *gunas*, they become subject to corporeality and transmigration. The scriptures describe this process as soul's bondage or entanglement with the phenomenal world (*samsara*).

In the embodied state, the souls remain deluded and ignorant subject to the limitations of purity, knowledge, wisdom, time and space. In the *Upanishads*, we find descriptions of how individual souls are ensnared by Nature and how the body is formed around them. For the individual souls caught in the transmigration of life, the body is a major impediment and for the beings, a major source of suffering and bondage. Destruction of the body does not ensure the liberation of a being, because it is not the cause but the consequence of the activities (*prvritti*) of the *gunas*, which tend to suppress and dominate one another. They are chiefly responsible for the actions arising from desires, duality, egoism and attachment and thereby bondage of the individual souls.

In their original condition, the souls have no awareness of otherness, that is, no sense of duality and objectivity. They remain self-absorbed without the distinction of the knower and known, attraction and aversion, and feelings and emotions, and free from experiential memory, accumulated knowledge, perceptions, memory or individuality. When they are bound to Nature, they enter into an alternate and relative reality, which represents a complete reversal of their original, pure, indivisible and absolute state. This union between the soul and body does not change the essential nature of the souls. It just veils their intelligence and brings them into an alternate world of phenomena and objectivity. Hindu scriptures describe this condition as the night for the souls and day for the ignorant and the deluded beings.

Desire-ridden actions arising from the *gunas* bind the embodied souls to the cycle of *karma*. As the beings are drawn repeatedly to the objects of the world, they develop and attraction and aversion to them, which leads to attachment, modifications of the mind, delusion and bondage.

The body is a formation created by the assemblage of various *tattvas* (realities) of Nature, which manifest in creation as the basic building blocks of life and materiality. They bind the soul to the elements and perpetuate its transmigration from one life to another. If Brahman is like the radiant Sun, the souls are like its rays or particles of light. When they become embedded in the flesh and blood of a being and separated from their source, they enter into a state of bondage to Nature and become bound to the cycle of births and deaths. They remain so until they were liberated.

The bondage of the souls is similar to that of floating particles of dust falling on to the ground and entering into plants as nutrients to become food for the beings upon earth. The Vedic people believed that the individual souls, which were like radiant particles of light, became involved with Nature in this manner. According to the *Vedas*, the souls fall upon the earth through rain and enter into the plants through the roots. Through plants, they become food for the beings upon earth, and as part of food, they enter their bodies. Inside the body, each finds its way into male sperm and from there enters the womb through intercourse.

The symbolism of the sun and the moon

The Vedic people used real life analogies to explain life after death. They used the sun and the moon symbolism to explain the two worlds to which the souls went after departing from the body, namely the world of the immortals and the world of the ancestors. Depending upon their *karmas*, those who died went to either the sun where the immortal world was located or the moon, where the ancestral world was located. Those who went to the moon returned by falling down upon earth through rains. From the earth, they entered the beings through food and intercourse and reincarnated again.

To them, the moon did not seem to represent permanence since it waned and waxed, while the sun always shown with the same brilliance and remained full. Its absence during night was not considered a sign of impermanence but a part of the divine order (*rita*) meant to ensure the progression of time and the regularity of the world.

Whoever died during the day or when the sun shone brilliantly in the northern hemisphere during the first six months of the year, went to the sun and became immortals never to return. They went to the sun because they were qualified to be one with it.

Light can join light, but darkness cannot join it. Those who went to the world of the sun were pure beings. Their souls had no traces of darkness around them because they were completely free from impurities. Having ridden all the impurities and regained their pure luminosity, they had no trouble rejoining the Sun, with whom they shared the same light.

However, those who died during the night of the day or the night of the year (winter solstice) went to the moon that waxed and waned, and returned once their *karmas* were exhausted. These beings were not yet free from the impurities. Their consciousness was mixed with darkness like that of the moon. Therefore, they were destined to return to earth and take another birth to continue their bondage and mortal existence. They would continue to repeat this process until they removed all traces of darkness from their consciousness.

This is precisely the story of the souls, which journey from the heights of heaven, in a state of freedom and bliss, with pure consciousness to descend into materiality, ignorance and delusion from where they could escape permanently by going to the sun or temporarily by going to the moon.

The liberation of souls

If the souls become entangled with Nature because of the beings' natural propensity to indulge in desire-ridden actions and their failure to discriminate things, they can also achieve freedom by withdrawing their minds and bodies from the external world and allowing their grossness to wither away through purity and austerities. It logically follows that they can change their state of bondage by reversing or arresting the very processes that lead to it in the first place.

It means one can achieve liberation by distancing oneself from Nature, withdrawing the senses from the sense-objects, suppressing desires and detaching one's mind and body from the bonds formed upon earth with the external world. If creation is an outgoing process, liberation is a withdrawal process. Our scriptures suggest that the embodied souls can reverse their current plight by practicing one or more of the following, not necessarily in the same order.

- Restraining and withdrawing the senses from the sense objects
- Cultivating right knowledge and awareness about the Self through study, recitation of the scriptures and by interacting with liberated souls
- Practicing rules and restraints and controlling life breath to purify the mind and body and prepare it for the rigors of spiritual life
- Practicing concentration and contemplation to stabilize the mind in the contemplation of the Self or God
- Cultivating detachment through renunciation of desires to overcome attachment and suppress the modifications of the mind
- Performing desireless actions without expectations as an offering to God or as selfless service
- Identifying oneself with the inner Self rather than with one's mind and body

- Seeking the guidance of an enlightened master who can show the path
- Cultivating discernment (*buddhi*) to overcome ignorance and delusion and stabilize the mind in the contemplation of the Self
- Cultivating devotion through surrender

Thus, our scriptures describe creation as a temporary process set in motion by God with Himself as the creator and the created. In this vast process, living beings manifest as temporary formations arising from the aggregation of diverse components and elements of Nature around individual souls. What sustain them are the power of Nature and the will of God.

Each living being is a combination of diverse things of Nature and two distinct realities or states of existence, one temporary and the other eternal. The former is subject to various phenomena and modifications while the latter is eternally pure and constant. The two never coalesce, but exist within the same space. An individual self, caught in the whirlpool of life, passes through many cycles of births and deaths before it overcomes it delusion and works for its liberation.

From the heights of immortal heaven, the pure and resplendent souls descend into the depths of Nature and develop the impurities of egoism, attachments and delusion. They go through a long night of darkness and suffering before they see light on the horizon and make an effort to return to their original Abode and their original pristine state of light and bliss.

Aum Tat Sat

Bibliography

Ashby, Phillip H. Modern Trends in Hinduism: Past and Present. Princeton, N.J.: Princeton University Press, 2004.

Badlani, Hiro G. Hinduism: Path of the Ancient Wisdom. Bloomington, IN: iUniverse, 2008.

Baird, Robert D. , ed. Religion in Modern India, New Delhi: Manohar, 1995.

Basham, A.L. The Origins and Development of Classical Hinduism. New York: Oxford University Press, 1991.

Benerji, Sures Chandra. Dharma-Sutras: A Study of Their Origin and Development. Calcutta: Punthi Pastak, 1962.

Bhankdarkar, R.G. Vaisnavism, Saivism and Minor Religious Systems. Delhi: Strassburg, 1913.

Bhaskarananda, Swami. The Essentials of Hinduism: A Comprehensive Overview of the World's Oldest Religion. Seattle, WA. Viveka Press, 2002.

Bloomfield, Maurice. The Religion of the Veda, New York: Putnam, 1908.

Bose, A.C. The Call of the Vedas. Mumbai, India: Bharatiya Vidya Bhavan, 1999.

Bryant, Edwin F. The Quest for the Origins of Vedic Culture: The Indo-Aryan Migration Debate. New York: Oxford University Press, 2001.

Chakravarty, Pulin. The Origin and Development of Sankhya. Kokota: Metropolitan Printing and Publishing House, 1951.

Chaudhuri, Nirad C.Hinduism: A Religion to Live By. New York: Oxford University Press, 1997.

Danielou, Alain. Hindu Polytheism. New York: Pantheon, 1964.

Das, Rasamandala. Hinduism. Milwaukee, WI: World Almananc Library, 2005

Das, Shukavak. Hindu Encounter with Modernity. Los Angeles, CA: Sri Publications, 1999.

Dasgupta, Surender Nath. A History of Indian Philosophy. 5 vols. Rpt. Delhi: Motilal Banarasidass, 1975.

Davar, oze Cowasji. Iran and India through the ages. Mumbai: Asia Pub. House, 1962.

Dawson, John. A Classical Dictioinary of Hindu Mythology, 12th ed. London: Routledge & Kegan Paul, 1972.

De Barry, William Theodore and Stephen Hay, eds. Sources of Indian Tradition. 2 vols. New York: Columbia University Press 1988.

Embree, Ainslee T., ed. The Hindu Tradition, New York: Random House, 1966.

Farquhar, J.N. An Outline of the Religious Literature of India. Delhi: Motilal Banarasidass, 1967.

Feuerstein, Goerg., Subhash Kak & David Frawley. In Search of the Cradle of Civilization: New Light on Ancient India. New Delhi: Motilal Banarasidass, 1999.

Flood, Gavin. An Introduction to Hinduism. New York: Cambridge University Press, 1996.

Fowler, Jeaneane D. Hinduism: Beliefs and Practices. Brighton, Great Britain: Sussex Academic Press, 1997.

Garbe, Richard. The Philosophy of Ancient India. Calcutta: The Open Court Publishing Company, 1897.

Goodall, Dominic, ed. And trans. Hindu Scriptures. Berkeley: University of California Press, 1996.

Griffith, Ralph T.H., Tran. The Hymns of the Rgveda. 2 vols. Rpt. Varanasi, India: Choukhamba Sanskrit Series Office, 1971.

Griswold, Henry DeWitt. Insights into Modern Hinduism, New York: Henry Holt, 1934.

Guenon, Rene. Introduction to the Study of Hindu Doctrines, New Delhi: Munshiram Manoharlal, 1993.

Harvey, Andrew. Teaching of the Hindu Mystics. Boston: Shambala, 2001.

Hemenway, Priya. Hindu Gods: The Spirit of the Divine. San Franscisco: Chronicle Books, 2003.

Hodiwala, S.K. Indo-Iranian Religion with Parallelism in Hindu & Zoroastrian Scriptures, Bombay: 1925

Hopkins, Thomas J., Frederick J. Streng (ed.). The Hindu Religious Tradition (The Religious Tradition of Man). Encion, CA: Wadsworth Publishing, 1971.

Hopkins, Thomas J. The Hindu Religious Tradition. Encino, Calif.: Dickenson Publishing, 1971.

Hubert, Henri and Marcel Mauss. Sacrifice: Its Nature and Function. Translated by W.D. Halls. Chicago: University of Chicago Press, 1964.

Huyler, Steven P. Meeting God: Elements of Hindu Devotion. New Haven, CT: Yale University Press, 1999.

Jagannathan, Shakunthala. Hinduism: An Introduction. Mumbai, India: Vakils, Feffer, and Simons, 1984.

Johnsen, Linda. The Complete Idiot's Guide to Hinduism. Indianapolis, MN: Alpha Books, 2002.

Kane, P.V. A History of Sanskrit Literature. Delhi: Motilal Banarasidass, 1971.

Kinsely, David. Hindu Goddesses. Los Angeles, CA: University of California Press, 1986.

Klostermaier, Klaus K. A Survey of Hinduism. Albany: State University of New York Press, 1994.

-----------. Hindu Writings: A Short Introduction to the Major Sources. Oxford: One World, 2000.

Knipe, David M. Hinduism: Experiments in the Sacred. Prospect Heights, IL: Waveland Press, Inc.1991.

Knott, Kim. Hinduism: A Very Short Introduction. New York: Oxford University Press, 1998, reiss. 2000.

Kosambi. Damodar Dharmanand. Ancient India: A History of Its Culture and Civilization, New York: Pantheon Books, 1965.

Majumdar, R.C., and Pulsakar, A.D., eds. The History and Culture of the Indian People. 11 vols. Bombay: Bharatiya Vidya Bhavan, 1951-77.

Michaels, Axel. Hinduism: Past and Present. Princeton, NJ and Oxford, UK: Princeton University Press, 2004.

Misra, V. N. and Mate, M.S. (eds.). Indian Prehistory. Pune: Deccan College, 1964.

Mittal, Sushil and Thursby, Gene, Eds. The Hindu World. New York & UK: Routledge, 2004.

Mohapatra, Amulya , Bijaya Mohapatra.Hinduism: Analytical Study. New Delhi: K.M.Rai Mittal for Mittal Publications, 1993.

Morgan, Kenneth W. The Religion of the Hindus. New York: Ronald Press, 1953.

Narayana, Vasudha. Hinduism Origins, Beliefs, Practices, Holy Texts, Sacred Places. New York: Oxford University Press, 2004.

Oldenberg, Hermann, and F.Max Muller, tras. The Grhya-Sutras: Rules of the Vedic Domestic Ceremonies. Sacred Books of the East, nos. 29-30. 1886, 1892. Rpt. Delhi: Motilal Banarasidass, 1973.

Powell, Barbara. Windows into the Infinite: A Guide to Hindu Scriptures. Fremont, CA: Asian Humanities Press, 1996

Radhakrishnan, Sarvepalli, Indian Philosophy. 2 vols. New Delhi: Oxford University Press, 1999.

Renou, Louis. Hinduism: The Spirit Of Hinduism . Whitefish, MT: Kessinger Publishing Company, 1961.

Renou, Louis. The Nature of Hinduism. New York: Walker, 1962.

Richard, Glynn. A Sourcebook of Modern Hinduism. London: Curzon, 1985.

Rodrigues, Hilary., Damien Keown & Charles S. Prebish (eds.). Introducing Hinduism. New York: Routledge, 2006.

Rosen, StevenJ. The Reincarnation Controversy: Uncovering the truth in the World Religions. Badger, CA: Torchlight Publishing.

Sankalia, H.D. Pre-history and Proto-history of India and Pakistan. Bombay: University of Bombay, Mumbai, 1963.

Saraswati, Swami Prakashanand. The True History of the Religion of India: A Concise Encyclopedia of Authentic Hinduism. Austin, Tx. : International Society of Divine Love , 2000.

Senker, Cath. Hinduism: Signs, Symbols, and Stories.New York: The Rosen Publishing Group, 2010.

Sharma, Aravind. Classical Hindu Thought: An Introduction. Oxford: Oxford University Press, 2000.

Shattuck, Cybelle. Hinduism. London: Routledge, 1999.

Smith, Bardwell L. Hinduism: New Essays in the History of Religions. Netherlands: E. J. Brill, 1976.

Smith, David. Hinduism and Modernity. Malden, Mass.: Blackwell, 2003.

Smith, Vincent A. The Oxford History of India, 3d. ed. Oxford: Clarendon Press, 1961.

Sugirtharaja, Sharada. Imagining Hinduism: A Post Colonial Perspective. New York: Routledge, 2003.

Teece, Geoff. Hinduism. North Mankato, MN: Smart Apple Media, 1980.

Thapar, Romalia. A History of India vol. 1. Middlesex, England: Penguin Books, 1977.

-----------. Interpreting Early India. New York: Oxford University Press, 1992.

V, Jayaram. Brahman. New Albany: Pure Life Vision LLC, 2010.

V, Jayaram. Tran. The Bhagavadgita Complete Translation. New Albany: Pure Life Vision LLC, 2012.

Vaswani, J.P.Hinduism: What You Would Like to Know About. New Delhi: Sterling Publishers Private Limited, 2003.

Werner, Karel. Popular Dictionary of Hinduism. Chicago: NTC, 1997.

Wheeler, Sir Robert Eric Mortimer. Early India and Pakistan to Ashoka. Rev. ed. New York: Praeger, 1968.

William George M. A Handbook of Hindu Mythology. Santa Barbara, Calif.: ABC-CLIO, 2003.

Zaehner, Robert Charles. Hinduism. New York: Oxford University Press, 1966.

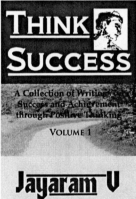

CPSIA information can be obtained at www.ICGtesting.com
Printed in the USA
LVOW081607270613

340557LV00011B/1235/P

9 781935 760115